ANTHONY
MOLLOY

A MEMOIR ON LIFE, GLORY AND DEMONS

WITH FRANK CRAIG

 **HERO**BOOKS

PUBLISHED BY HERO BOOKS
1 WOODVILLE GREEN
LUCAN
CO. DUBLIN
IRELAND

Hero Books is an imprint of Umbrella Publishing
First Published 2022
Copyright © Anthony Molloy and Frank Craig 2022
All rights reserved

ISBN 9781910827574

Cover design and formatting: jessica@viitaladesign.com
Photographs: Inpho and the Molloy family collection

DEDICATION

For Mary Ellen, our angel in Heaven

« CONTENTS »

FOREWORD
PROLOGUE

PART 1

CHAPTER 1 – 'Young people of Ireland, I love you'

CHAPTER 2 – 'Anthony Molloy... the man from the mist'

CHAPTER 3 – 'Say hello to my little friend!
REFLECTIONS

PART 2

CHAPTER 4 – 'A bad day in New York is better than
a good day anywhere else'

CHAPTER 5 – 'You build on failure. You use it as a stepping stone'

CHAPTER 6 – 'Discipline is the soul of an army'
REFLECTIONS

PART 3

CHAPTER 7 – 'Through it all, when there was doubt,
I ate it up and spat it out'

CHAPTER 8 – 'Never apologise and never explain...
it's a sign of weakness'

CHAPTER 9 – 'The trouble with referees is that they know the rules,
but they don't know the game'
REFLECTIONS

PART 4

CHAPTER 10 – 'I'm the best, I can take it more than anybody.
So give me a stage where the Bull can rage'

CHAPTER 11 – 'It's not over till the fat lady sings'

CHAPTER 12 – 'Had we got to grips with Murphy, I'd have been very
interested to see what Dublin's Plan B was or, had they one at all?'

« ACKNOWLEDGEMENTS »

I OFTEN THOUGHT about putting my footballing life and career down on paper and into my own words. I've been approached on numerous occasions. But when Liam Hayes eventually got in touch and we talked about the 30th anniversary of Donegal's famous win in 1992, I finally relented and decided it was indeed now time.

Liam was a fierce competitor on the pitch and was the real driving force behind that amazing Meath side of the late 80s and early 90s. He's a journalist yes, but he's also been inside an All-Ireland winning dressing room. I'd the privilege of coming up against him so often. He was one of my toughest opponents.

So I believed he was the perfect man to help get this project off the ground. He had my trust. And Frank – my own clubman – I wouldn't have wanted to undertake this project with anyone else. To be honest, it would have been impossible. His patience and, sometimes persistence, were key. Every single meeting we had was face to face. And I really appreciated that. He was able to go right back and his research notes were the perfect tool to opening up so many memories that had felt either lost or, at least, buried very deeply at the back of my mind. And it was important that we did go right back to the very beginning. I also wanted this book to sound and read like my own words. And I think we've delivered on that.

Coming from such a rural and simple background, I do believe that everything I managed to achieve on the field – that drive and work ethic – was owed to my upbringing. My own family, we're as close now as we were all those years ago, huddled up together in that little three bedroom house in the mountain. My late father Lanty, and Mother Nora, along with my eleven siblings, all got to see me lift

Sam Maguire. To know that is one of my happiest and most comforting thoughts.

The support and pillars they've all been to me – I remain so grateful to this very day. Uncle Jimmy also, who spent most of his life in New York, had a huge influence on me. He was also a very generous godfather. To have been able to bring the Sam Maguire Cup to his pub, also by the same name, was a magical moment in both our eyes. We cried tears of joy that day.

To all the sides I played on and all the players I soldiered with and even against, thank you. From the very start at my own club CLG Ard an Rátha, and right up through the ranks to the Donegal seniors, every manager or coach I had influenced and impacted me in some way. Again, I owe much of my success to those same people.

The funny thing with acknowledgements is knowing where to start and where to end. I'm not going to name too many names as I'd be worried I'd leave someone out. However, John T Murrin or '40' as he's known to us all, for his friendship and loyalty though the absolute thick and thin of both the good times and the bad, I want to express my absolute gratitude.

Also to Bart and Rosemary Whelan, I want to reserve a special mention. Your door was always open and your house really was like a second home to me throughout the years. Tadhg Lovett is a proud Kerryman but he was a great friend to both myself and the entire Molloy family in America. And when the Kingdom weren't playing, he never had a problem switching his allegiance to the green and gold of Donegal. Finally, Jamesie O'Donnell, I want to say a thank you for everything you have done and still do, not just for the likes of myself, but all Donegal folk in Dublin.

To Macy and Jessica, my best friends, who have brought so much happiness and stability to my life, I cannot put into words the joy you both bring. Every single day is an adventure. And the great thing is there is so much more to come. Your encouragement to take this project on and see it through has been a great comfort. Because it has been a huge undertaking. Going back, trawling through the years, it's hard to believe how fast they fly by. It's been brilliant to look back but it's even more exciting to be looking forward with both of you.

Anthony Molloy
August 2022

◆◆◆◆◆

I WAS ONLY 10-years-old when Anthony Molloy first swung Sam Maguire high into the air. But the memories of that 1992 triumph, along with the homecoming into Ardara as Molloy and 'Martin 'Rambo' Gavigan, alongside Anthony Harkin, carried that big, famous cup into their own home parish, remain so fresh, so vivid.

Three decades later, to have been asked by Liam Hayes to revisit all of that and, as well as so much more; it really has been an honour. Sitting down with the 'Big Guy', trawling through both the good and the bad times, we've pieced together what Anthony has labelled 'his truth'.

Sometimes it flowed, sometimes it didn't. And the task of unlocking so much of that, going back well over 50 years at times, it gave me an even better insight into the man as well as the footballer.

Acknowledgments… I'm sure to leave someone out so I'm not going to deep dive too far here. But I do have to thank both Fiona and Bláithín for their time and patience. They especially went above and beyond.

To my father, John, and mother, Patricia, as well as my three brothers, Christopher, Jonathan and Leonard and sister, Karen, thank you for all your help and support over the years.

Finally, I'd live to say thank you to both Anthony and Liam for this opportunity.

Frank Craig
August 2022

« FOREWORD »

By Brian McEniff
1992
All-Ireland winning manager

ANTHONY MOLLOY, MY leader of men.

The Ardara giant just has this stature, a presence that really stands out. And it did from very early on. He was our captain. You don't pick a leader… you simply observe the pack. Anthony had grown into that leader under Tom Conaghan. And when I came back into the Donegal senior football job in 1990, for a second time around, I saw no reason to veer from that decision.

I observed, and it was plainly obvious that Anthony led this group of men. And they were quite content to follow.

In a similar fashion to how Michael Murphy has held onto the captain's armband for so long with Donegal now, Anthony was in that exact same mould. And as long as I felt he was fit and ready to go, I never saw any reason to move it on simply for the sake of it. Both he and Michael are very different types of players and individuals, but they share something very unique. And it's very hard to describe.

It's a special trait. The personalities, voices and physical presences we had in that dressing-room, down through the years… it was powerful stuff. But Anthony stood out. In the heat of battle, once he crossed that white line, his greatest skill on a training field or in a massive game, was that he kept people honest. He wasn't dirty, but he was a protector. And if he felt one of the boys was getting unfair treatment then he'd take it upon himself to sort that out. He had a brilliant way of dealing with those types. He didn't strike a blow, he just got stuck into him in his own unique way.

And he was also a superb player – much better than he gets credit for. His knee issues are well documented. But I often wonder just how good he'd have been had he not struggled so badly with pain. Months prior to his finest moment, in late 1991, I contacted a knee specialist – a surgeon that had treated some of the very best sports people on this island. We had some scans sent on to his office. We were on a mission and neither Anthony nor I had time for letters. So over the telephone, that same expert's words to me were, 'Anthony has the left knee of a 70-year-old man'.

I VIVIDLY RECALL being down in Sandfield, Ardara, many years prior… in 1980, if I was to hazard a guess. It was an old pitch his local club often used. I remember this strapping, tanned lad approaching me, quite sheepishly in fact.

'Mr McEniff, someone told me to come speak to you. I've serious bother with my knees. And you might know who to go see.'

I was Donegal senior boss at the time and I'd seen enough that day to know I'd be picking him soon enough. Indeed, just three years after that first conversation, Anthony would be lining out for me in an All-Ireland semi-final against Galway.

But that was my first personal introduction to both Anthony and his knees. And it was a situation we'd manage, together, for most of the next decade and a half. Somehow, by the grace of God, we got 1992 out of Anthony. I often wander across the seafront in Bundoran and look across to the lights of west Donegal. I know amongst those scattered, illuminated speckles are so many of my boys.

And I miss them all so much. And I worry about them all in different ways. We created beautiful history together and it's a special moment – a dream that came true for each and every one of us. We were family… we are family. You don't move on in that sense.

You never stop worrying about them.

The fact that Anthony has decided to write this book, his memoir, I know that he's doing very well and I don't have to worry about him quite so much or, at least like I once used to. And he's the best man to write this story. We have a special relationship – one that's had its ups and downs, yes – but we remain very, very close.

We talk quite often on the phone, and he's one of the very few that doesn't need to knock when he calls to the house in person. He's family.

I love Anthony – he's the 'Big Guy' to so many, but he's a good guy also. Something that has always struck me is how much time he takes with the people who still come up to him. He still has that ability to command a room. When he calls to one of the hotels and I observe him walking across the floor, he is still turning heads.

And in 1992 nothing was too much trouble for him. Every single supporter in every single town was accommodated.

Our relationship did strain in 1991, to the point where it looked like the damage might be irreparable. We had a difference of opinion over football. And he briefly retired. But when we thrashed it out, we felt there was still one more run in us… in all of us. I'm a man of faith and I've no doubt my prayers were answered that day, in the MacCumhaill Park car park, when we mended fences. Because I have no doubt we would not have won the All-Ireland without Anthony on board.

And, regardless, the greatest compliment I can pay him is that I don't know if I would have wanted to… without him being a part of it. When he agreed to come back on board, he had only one request. He wanted to lead the boys again. And there wasn't one disgruntled voice in our dressing-room when I agreed to that term.

Anthony was box to box, and he just had this serious level of stamina. He was quite unique in that sense. Despite his knee troubles, he trained like an animal. He'd ice that big left knee, and he'd manage that situation. And somehow, he'd be back through that same door two nights later ready to go again.

I spent a number of years in Canada, and the Canadians had this saying, a term they used to describe courage, strength and defiance in the face of extreme adversity. It often made the sports pages out there. 'Intestinal fortitude'… what a beautiful term. Well, that's what Anthony had.

He dug deeper than anyone had or needed to, to lift Sam Maguire.

You also have to remember just how much pressure was on that group of men he led. They were ravaged in the press. Believe me, it was much more cutting back then, just what they were subjected to. And as captain, Anthony took so much of that personally.

1983's All-Ireland semi-final loss to Galway left a mark on me. And as the years passed, the younger members of that side, kids really at the time, grew into men. And it was perhaps only then that they realised what they might have left behind.

Anthony, Martin McHugh, Joyce McMullin, Charlie Mulgrew and Donal Reid all started that game. Gary Walsh and Matt Gallagher were amongst the substitutes. So we had our baggage, much of it between our own ears, as we chased the ultimate glory. By 1986, in that illusive pursuit, I'd burned myself out. Tom Conaghan came in and, to his credit, he was a disciplinarian – way ahead of his time. And when I did come back into the fray in 1990, I could see he'd left a mark.

That was one of the reasons in 1992, on our homecoming, I brought Tom up to the stage in Donegal Town. PJ McGowan too and his 1987 All-Ireland winning under-21s... that victory gave us an injection of real quality. The final pieces of the jigsaw really. It freshened things up. 1990 and our loss to Meath in the All-Ireland semi-final, just like 1983, was a bitter pill to swallow. But we moved on. 1991 was a difficult season, one where we were swimming against the tide from very early on in.

But 1992, and I've no doubt Anthony will get to it... it was a season where we took a real ownership of our own destiny. Quite simply, the players asked for more. They asked for more from themselves and they asked for more, from us as a management, on the training field. A button was pushed and it yielded spectacular results. Like I said, to have had Anthony at the helm of all of that was extra special.

Molloy was the bond that held it all together. He was never afraid to ask, push a point or relay someone else's grievance. His weakness, if he had one, was that he put others first every single time. But it was also what made him such a fantastic leader.

I'm so happy he's now finally putting himself first. And I genuinely cannot wait to relive the single greatest moment of my life, all over again, but through Anthony's eyes!

« FOREWORD »

Jim McGuinness
2012
All-Ireland winning manager

THE FIRST TIME I ever really 'saw' Anthony Molloy was the summer of 1989. Of course, I'd seen him playing many times, but this was the moment when the full force of his personality really took hold. It was a gorgeous evening and I had been in Donegal Town with my father and my brother. We were heading home with the bay caught in the sunlight on our left as we drove along.

Suddenly, we see this car coming the other way – at a brave rate, it must be said – and it drew my eye. It was a Proton something-or-other, a sports car. And as it came closer to us, I saw the driver was wearing the green and gold jersey of Donegal. It took me a second to recognise him.

It was about a week out from that year's Ulster final and flags were everywhere. I figured out that he was rushing to training at Townawilly.

'That's Anthony Molloy!' I announced to the others.

I was sixteen-years-old and completely starstruck. I wouldn't have believed anyone then, if they told me, that I'd be training alongside him just three years later. I came into the Donegal squad over Christmas of 1991. Anthony was immediately welcoming, and he made me believe that I was there on merit. There were no levels with him.

It was all about Donegal in his eyes. I think that is one of his greatest gifts, that he could make people feel at ease and as if they belonged as soon as he met them.

HE PULLED ME aside before my very first championship match. It was against Antrim in Ballybofey in 1993. Donegal were All-Ireland champions, so the spotlight felt bright. And he just talked to me about how it would feel to be playing in a match of that intensity, for the first 20 minutes.

What is often forgotten about that period now is just how primal the first 15 or 20 minutes of championship games were back then. Players were pent up. The exchanges could be very raw. It was knockout and it was no place for the faint-hearted. It is very different now – the tempo quickly settles into a kind of hypnotic pattern.

So when Anthony Molloy spoke, you listened and he kind of settled me into what lay ahead.

When I think of Anthony in that environment, the Donegal changing room seemed to revolve around his presence. He had an aura. Obviously, his stature and those big shoulders of his played a part but it was his personality as well. He didn't have to dominate the conversation, but he was the main man.

I ended up marking him at training a fair bit – sometimes to make up the numbers. Himself and Brian Murray were the duo in the middle of the park. Barry Cunningham and myself were often pitted against them. It was a brilliant education. He knew his job really well. He knew where he needed to dominate and that was the sky, first and foremost, as well as that connection between the half-back and half-forward line.

He was synonymous with big catches and big hits. But there was a serious level of intelligence to his play as well. That is why he and Martin McHugh had such a strong link. He was always scanning when he got the ball, to see where McHugh was. And he'd chip in with scores himself also.

But his first aim was to slip a pass to the 'Wee Man'.

And when you think of Anthony then, you think of that big old knee strap. To my mind, it was always there. He was either getting the knee strapped, getting the thing cut off or just getting the knee iced afterwards.

And that often made me think, *This is not forever.*

There were periods in those years when we were training very, very hard. He had many tough seasons under his belt by then. And he had that bad knee. It was in terrible shape. But whether he was able for it or not… he ran. It's hard to articulate the depth of impression Anthony made on our county at that time.

He was a superstar. He had that classic, dark Donegal look and he was instantly recognisable. On the bus home after games you'd find him down the back, in the absolute thick of it. And he was a magnet to the other lads.

Every so often, he'd wind up to sing a song and there was a purer silence because big Molloy was singing. You'd always hear Tony Boyle and Donal Reid bellowing, 'Good man, Molloy,' if there was a break in whatever song he was singing. That was because Anthony was centre stage in that moment. And they wanted him at centre stage in that moment ultimately, because they loved him. They loved everything about him.

There was nobody that didn't. It's a rare thing in a group of 30 or so fellas from across the county. But it was true. There wasn't a single person in that group who didn't think the world of him.

There was steel there too. Winning was the most important thing for him. Midfield was a different sort of position in the 1980s and 90s. If you didn't win that sector, you didn't win the game. It was as simple as that. He radiated a sense of command and authority. And because of that, whatever the players thought of him, the public adoration was tenfold. He was the archetype of what a county player should be. And people wanted to speak to him, to know him. He always seemed to have time to stop for people and to chat with them. It seemed like he knew everybody, which added to his mystique in my eyes, a youngster who didn't know anybody.

His face and his speech – *'Sam's for the Hills'* – are symbolic of 1992. That summer reminds me of the Great Northern Hotel in Bundoran. It felt like we were there every other weekend. Those meetings remain vivid. A lot of the time they were held in a room in the leisure centre on muggy evenings after dinner.

I'd scan the room and my eyes would always drift to Anthony. And you could see the focus in him. It was evident in his posture and even in how he listened. Every so often, he spoke. But not always. He could control the group with the opposite of a strong fist... it was with a velvet touch.

That intensity transmitted through the entire squad. He was 30 years old then. That season was so many of the group's 'Last Chance Saloon' and he constantly communicated the message that the opportunity had to be taken.

Our training was off the charts then, but we were very grounded and purposeful. And when Anthony spoke after Brian McEniff, he laid out what had to be done on the field. For him, much of it came down to winning individual battles. His performances in those culminating games – the Ulster final and the All-Ireland semi-final and final were so, so strong. But there was good fun through it all. He could switch into light-hearted mode very easily and that made it possible to enjoy what we were chasing.

TEAMS ARE FUNNY. When that great side broke up, I went from seeing Anthony twice and three times a week to rarely meeting him. He was the kind of fella you wouldn't see for 10 years and then when you bumped into him, nothing had changed. He is this big, strong warm open Donegal man.

Donegal played Armagh back in the championship in early summer of 2022. It was the 30th anniversary of the 1992 season and some of the boys organised an unofficial reunion. I had missed the 25th get-together so I was so excited to see everyone again, in the same room. And what struck me, after those three decades, was that the dynamic was still the same.

The same groups still gravitated towards one another, the same voices. I was still the 'young fella' in the room. And there was a pecking order.

Anthony was our leader and Brian McEniff was our manager.

All of those established roles came naturally into play over the day. It was strange, but it was very beautiful. I realised that day that Anthony Molloy is still my captain.

He always will be.

« PROLOGUE »

'We're putting the band back together'

– Jake Blues, The Blues Brothers

July 28, 1991, Clones.

'TO HELL WITH this shite, I'm out of here... I'm done! You coming?'

Donegal are trailing Down by eight points in the Ulster final with little over five minutes to go. I'm stuck on the bench, where I've been for most of the season... and I've had enough.

I've had enough of Brian McEniff... enough of watching this crap and enough of putting my body on the line for Donegal. Martin Shovlin... Ulster Footballer of the Year in 1990... is also inexplicably sitting on the bench beside me for this massive game.

When I ask him if he's also seen enough at this stage, he agrees and we both head for the dressing-room. We didn't need to shower. And no doubt, by the time the others trudged back in through the same door, myself and Shov were already down the street, in Clones, at the Roost Bar.

This wasn't the way I envisaged going out with Donegal. I genuinely believed, after 1990, that we'd at least be back in an All-Ireland semi-final. And my intention was to throw the kitchen sink at it one last time. But man plans and God laughs...

MY KNEE BEGAN to play up just as we were getting back down to business, on the training field, in late 1990. It forced me to have another scope, a cartilage procedure – but it was a minor surgery that went well. Despite that, and despite me being up with the pace soon enough back on the training field, it felt pretty obvious that I was being edged towards the periphery of things.

Was it an intentional move by Brian? I don't know.

Something just wasn't adding up. In a league campaign where wins were achieved over the likes of Dublin, Kerry and Cork at home, it was hard to kick up too much of a fuss… and that made the thing all the more frustrating.

I was stewing… angry as hell, but I could say damn all.

I was also privately seething that 'trial by TV,' a new thing in 1990, had cost me an All Star when the best of the best for the season were announced in early December of that same year. A video replay of our Ulster Championship win over Cavan, back in the summer, helped retrospectively earn me a red card for my part in a melee during what was a heated contest.

Joyce McMullin was included in the All-Star XV, deservedly. But myself and Declan Bonner, who'd had a brilliant campaign as well, but also suffered a sending off in the same fixture, couldn't even be nominated because of a stupid rule that prohibited anyone dismissed on the field of play from receiving a nomination.

McEniff was selected as an All Star boss for the trip to Toronto, while Shovlin and Martin 'Rambo' Gavigan would also end up on the plane as All Star replacements. It was just a very sour ending for me to what had been one of my best seasons. I was more determined than ever to prove my doubters – of which McEniff it seemed was, suddenly, now one – wrong.

AS THE LEAGUE got going once again in early 1991, I was making appearances off the bench, with the likes of John 'Bán' Gallagher, Gavigan, Michael Gallagher and Barry Cunningham all taking turns to partner Brian Murray around the middle of the field. From the outside looking in, some probably assumed the other lads were just keeping the captain's spot warm. But I knew the score.

And so too did the others, as the armband started to get passed around from arm to arm, week after week. It was a f***ing joke.

Not once was I given the opportunity, from the very start, to stake a claim. I was an unused substitute as we suffered a narrow league semi-final defeat to

Kildare in April of '91 and that did trouble us. Not so much the fact that we wanted to win the thing, it just grated at what was an already fragile enough confidence in relation to our record at Croke Park in big games. It made for dismal reading.

We should have had our eyes completely trained on holding onto our Ulster Championship. But I could see standards slipping. I could see old habits, the ones that the previous manager Tom Conaghan had so forcefully rooted out, being allowed to creep back in. The lads that were training were going through the motions and the 'injured' others were simply taking the easy way out.

The group needed leadership.

But how could I lay down the law from the sideline?

If things weren't bad enough, ex-Mayo star Padraig Brogan was the new head barman in the Great Northern Hotel, in Bundoran, which Brian owned, of course. He was also the new Donegal midfielder as well, it seemed, as McEniff named him to start, right away, alongside Murray in a McKenna Cup game against Monaghan that April.

Our new signing also floated over two points in that seven-point win. Brogan had lashed in a quite brilliant goal for his native Mayo back in the 1985 All-Ireland semi-final loss to Dublin and it was one of those scores that stands the test of time… 'til this day, on YouTube.

But he was a funny sort of a fish – that's how one teammate who roomed with him described him. And after that bright enough beginning in a Donegal jersey, it was all downhill for Brogan. The lads simply couldn't warm to him. After a number of weeks… close to a month even training with us, he still didn't know our names.

It was if he didn't care to even learn them. And he barely broke sweat in training. He walked through every single drill. In a Q&A style interview in the *Donegal Democrat*, McEniff was pressed on why he'd chosen Brogan ahead of myself, against Kildare, in Croke Park, when he ran his bench in the second-half.

'Because Padraig had scored three points in the previous outing. I had hoped that his previous Croke Park experience would help the side and, the fact is, Anthony had not been at training — he was moving house — on Tuesday night and maybe I wasn't all that happy with that.'

1991 was proving to be an absolute shambles and the parachuting of Brogan into the mix typified just how ridiculous it had all become. After being edged out by Meath the season before, we were supposed to be harbouring real designs on getting back to an All-Ireland semi-final. And we knew that meant coming through the provincial door with the Anglo Celt under our arm once again. But the Ulster title hadn't been retained in 14 seasons, with Derry the last side to go back-to-back in 1976.

In between our first round opener against Cavan in Ballybofey, there was a McKenna Cup final against Tyrone still to contend with. This was my chance. I was finally given the opportunity to start a game and I did reasonably well. And up I went, as captain, to pick up the cup.

But come our Ulster Championship opener against the Breffni men, at MacCumhaill Park, I was back picking splinters out of my arse, on the bench, with Donal Reid leading the boys out.

Literally, I spent the entire first-half pulling small shreds of wood that were straying out of the old subs bench, out of my backside. I was still paying enough attention though to notice that Stephen King had an absolute stranglehold on midfield, as we exited at the break lucky to be level at 1-4 to 0-7. I was called into action, but not right away and not from the restart. No, for some reason I was left until the 45th minute.

Strange… senseless, in fact.

But in I came, sprinting to prove a point, and to a massive applause from the home supporters. Through gritted teeth, I made a silent promise to myself, *I'll show him*. And by the end of a 2-14 to 0-12 championship victory, I'd 1-1 to my name.

I'll show him… well, I HAD showed him. And with three weeks to go until our provincial semi-final with Fermanagh, I'd no doubts I'd passed McEniff's test… whatever that test was, I wasn't sure.

But I had surely just played my way back into his starting plans.

AGAIN, MAKING ANY kind of logical assumptions in 1991 was setting yourself up for a fall. And the midfield pair chosen for the Fermanagh game was Murray and Michael Gallagher. I would be sprung eventually, but long after the game was won… 1-18 to 0-13, there was no reason for anyone to be shouting for my inclusion too loudly. But the quality of opposition was masking just how much of a mess some of us privately believed we were in.

It was obvious from our in-house jostles in the lead-in to our Ulster final clash with Down that I wasn't going to be making my return to the starting line-up in Clones. Bizarrely, a week out, Charlie Mulgrew was told he'd be captaining the side. So at that stage, even with two final training sessions to catch the eye or stake a claim, I knew I'd be for the dugout.

Unsurprisingly, Down did a real number on us.

By half-time, at 1-9 to 0-5, the game was already over. Noel Hegarty and Brogan were sprung in the first-half, at a time when the thing was still there to be rescued. A third change… James McHugh for captain Mulgrew, only came about on 50 minutes. The truth is, had I been asked to come in at any stage after half-time, I was prepared to tell Brian where to stick his slip. And it wasn't a sunny location.

And maybe that thought crossed Brian's mind as well, as both Shov and I were left twiddling our thumbs. In the end… well, our end on that day at least, we made our point by washing our hands of it all long before the final whistle.

The capitulation at midfield caused problems for both our half-backs and half-forwards. And our failure to contest that area was, perhaps, the worst aspect of this pathetic performance. Even if Down go onto win the All-Ireland this performance will still rank as pathetic.

This was how the *Democrat* summed up our showing in their following edition. But it gave me no satisfaction to read that paragraph. And the same scribe would go on to write a number of Donegal footballing obituaries in the piece.

August's county board meeting was heated and McEniff's judgement – on a number of fronts regarding his team selection for Down – was severely questioned. A blow-by-blow account was carried in great detail in the local papers. There was a black mood in the air and there was a mood too for change, it seemed. But with one year left to go on a term of three, it was eventually decided that Brian would get the chance to see out his final season at the helm in 1992.

Any lingering doubts I had about hanging my boots up evaporated that instant. I was done with both Donegal and Brian. All I expected was a bit of loyalty, but I didn't get it. I don't mean loyalty at the expense of picking me over someone that was better or fitter than me at the time. I just wanted the chance, from the off, in the lead in to that Ulster final, which we were always going to get to, to prove I was still *the man* around the middle.

I didn't get that and I took it very personally.

But it wasn't personal, Brian wasn't that type. He just felt and believed I wasn't good enough anymore and that's what hurt. Sitting at the kitchen table, helping go through invitations that August for my upcoming wedding, I quietly slipped Brian and his wife Cautie's away and into my back pocket. Cautie is a real lady and a woman I've often poured my heart out to, when no one else would listen. It was wrong.

But later that evening as I lit the range, in it went. It was petty but I was bitter. I would eventually high-tail it off to America, hold my own against some of the best midfielders money could buy, and come home refreshed and, being honest, not so bitter.

IT WAS OCTOBER now, and the Ardara minors had made it all the way to the county final where Ballyshannon's Aodh Ruadh provided the opposition. In what was a very exciting tussle, with future Donegal greats Damien Diver and Brian Roper going head-to-head, it was my own club that just about got over the line by a few points.

At a certain stage I could see that Brian was also present in Ballybofey. I could see him positioning himself in and around my vicinity during the presentation. Every now and then he'd shuffle a step or two sideways, edging further towards me.

To hell with this, I thought, I wasn't going to stand about as others must have noticed and it was a situation that had the potential to become awkward. As soon as the Ardara captain Adrian Cunningham had been presented with the cup I slowly back-peddled and managed to finally dip my head down the tunnel towards the car.

As I'm about to open the door, I hear Brian softly call, 'Anthony!'

I turn around and back myself up against my own vehicle, arms folded. I'm pretty sure he's looking to attempt to mend a bridge here, but only that. I can't believe it when he says, 'I need you back in, I got it wrong!'

Right away, he's taken a sledge hammer to the huge wedge of ice that had been separating us. I wasn't looking to get back or go back, I was happy enough with my decision. But I appreciated that he was willing to admit he was wrong. I'd completely cut off connections with him. He knew I was so angry. But he showed balls in coming to me like that. I felt I'd been wronged, plain and simple.

But the more he talked, the more of what he said made so much sense. Any other year, I wouldn't have swallowed it. But the conversation kept going back to Down and what they'd just achieved. The more he talked, the more I listened. And the more I listened, the more he reeled me right back in all over again.

But I needed to take back some ownership of the situation, some pride even. And I had only one request when he asked me one final time if I was in or out?

I took a deep breath and out it came... 'I'll come back Brian, but I have to be captain.'

It had been taken off me wrongly. He smiled back and said, 'No problem!' Brian explained that he was in the middle of ringing around and, to a man, everyone he wanted was now back on board for this one last shot.

THAT WAS THAT.

He'd gotten his way, like he so often did, but I'd had the last *real* word and I was coming back on my own terms. I'd nothing to lose – I certainly didn't have any cartilage left to lose in my troublesome left knee. It was bone on bone at this stage, and the reality of that was dawning on me, after the blood had finally died down on the car drive back home.

1992?

It was in the lap of the gods, but I was prepared to see where that took us...

The Sam Maguire Cup (above) became a constant companion in my life after September 1992, and the requests for appearances at home and abroad, in addition to all the media attention (below, appearances on RTE, with Mike Murphy and Bibi Baskin), soon left me a shell of myself.

PART ONE »

« CHAPTER 1 »

'Anthony Molloy... the man from the mist'

– Mícheál Ó Muircheartaigh

HOME IS LEAMGOWRA. It's a small and often misty townland nestled high above the famous Glengesh Pass just outside the town of Ardara. To the uninitiated and, at the wrong time of year, it might seem drizzly, desolate or, even bleak. 'The back of beyond,' is how I often recall it being described by people that didn't know any better.

But believe me, hand to God, I owe everything to my upbringing there and those simple surroundings.

May 28, 1962 was when I entered this world. I was baby number seven at the time. My parents Lanty and Nora would welcome five more children after that, to bring the total number of Molloy siblings to 12.

Mary, the eldest and first born, was followed by Connie, Ita, Frank, Margaret, Lanty, myself, Liam, Terrence, Catherine, Columba… and, finally, Paul… the baby of the house. Ours was a family of 14… eight boys, four girls and mammy and daddy. My father was a small farmer. It was a simple life, a very simple existence when you stand it up next to today's way of going.

We were very much self-sufficient. All that was really bought back then were bags of flour. Bread was baked, and the empty bags dusted down and pressed out. You had your individual and collective responsibilities, serious ones at that. In a way, and it was the same for every household then, it was a strict upbringing.

I don't mean strict in a draconian sense. But you had to tend to your chores and tasks. We all depended on one another in that way. It was also a traditional Catholic upbringing, very reflective of its time. The rosary was said every single night. You had to be there….and you didn't dare miss Mass on a Sunday.

That was our life. But we were very happy. Some of my happiest days were enjoyed growing up at home. If ignorance was bliss, then we were some of the happiest and carefree children in the world. We didn't have electricity – we didn't have power until 1975. I was only 12 years of age at the time, but almost a teenager. All we really had was the gas light tilley and the gas cooker. When you look at the young people of today, all that they have… and all that they expect to have. It was still such a very different world for us back then.

I often think of my mother and what she put herself through to feed, wash and clothe all 12 of us. She truly was an amazing woman. She never complained. People were resilient, simply because they knew no different or better. Even something as simple now as a nappy… we were wrapped in those same dusted down and pressed flour bags. That's what was used. Nothing was wasted.

They were then washed in the stream after and used again. It wasn't anything unique or out of the ordinary. That's just how it was in the mountain or, as they said… 'The back of beyond.' You made the most of what you had.

We would have kept a few hundred sheep at the time. We also had six or seven cows roaming about. Those cows were milked, and that was usually done before school. We'd often go to school smelling of manure. But it didn't matter. We didn't stand out and it wasn't out of the ordinary. In fact, our teacher Kathleen Campbell, another woman I remember so well… she kept cows also. And she would have carried out the very same task herself before coming to the classroom.

CROVE NATIONAL SCHOOL was three-and-a half-miles from home. We'd walk to and from there and sometimes, on the rare occasion, my father would take us. At school, the likes of Sean and Paddy Gavigan quickly became close friends. Seamus and Noel Carr, again two excellent footballers and uncles of Republic of Ireland and Everton captain Seamie Coleman, also went to Crove NS at the time, so we all quickly buddied up.

That was our initial clique. Indeed, over the years, that tiny one-room building would go on to produce seven senior county footballers. Home was in the parish of Ardara, but just about. And Crove NS, just a few miles in the road, was in the parish of Kilcar. Again, just about. Glencolmcille hugged both boundaries so there were a number of claims made on any young aspiring footballer inside that very complicated intersection.

But early on, none of that registered with me. The significance of that geography, from a footballing perspective, certainly didn't. My new friends, the lads I'd initially kick my first football around with, would all go on to represent the likes of Naomh Columba of Glencolmcille and Kilcar.

But the famous 'S' bend, down towards Ardara, a long, winding and at the wrong time of year treacherous passage of road, was the route I and my brothers would eventually take.

Connie, the eldest boy in the house, was a fine footballer. He was a big, powerful teenager and more than ready to play adult football by the time he was approaching his 17th birthday. But again, a decision would have to be made. Frank also had that physical presence on the field and you could see from very early on that he had the potential to be a real force. Lanty was a little smaller, but he was the skilful one. Connie will still say, to this day, that Lanty was the best player in our house. Paul as well, had real natural talent. But both he and Terrence would leave the football behind them as they exited their teens.

I vividly remember a car landing at the house to take Connie into training at Naomh Columba. It would have been early 1974. They had made their move... Glen were laying claim to our Connie. To be truthful, they were laying claim to the other seven boys in the house as well. If Connie had set that precedent, then there is no doubt the rest of us would have followed.

Fr James McDyer and Paddy 'Beag' Gillespie, they were huge Glen men and their intention was to get the eight Molloy boys into Páirc na nGael. Connie's head was turned slightly and he did play one game for Naomh Columba. However, the following week Joe Larry Gallagher Snr, the Ardara vice-chairman at the time, arrived at the house in an even bigger car... a sparkling white Ford Zephyr.

And off the courted Connie went again, sitting in the front seat all smiles, down towards Pearse Memorial Park.

There was no obvious footballing pedigree in our house. My father didn't play and his interest was only generated as a result of our involvement thereafter. But eight boys... sure that was more than half a football team! And if either Naomh Columba or Ardara could mould even one or two of us into players, sure it was worth the shot. But those best laid Glen plans were well and truly scuppered by Joe Larry and that impressive white Zephyr!

Still, there is no doubt my grá and passion for gaelic football was founded and forged in those rugged hills and valleys. Battle lines were drawn in the muck and sometimes even moved, to make sure the various townlands could field 15 in what would become fierce local contests. In those unofficial clashes, organised amongst ourselves, you were going to war with your friends and neighbours. It was often vicious and bloody.

IT WAS THE early 70s now, and I was approaching my 10th birthday. But we were already having some of the tightest and toughest games I would ever be involved in. I just didn't realise it at the time. The families there, they were all so steeped in rich footballing heritage. So it was no coincidence we were being brought up with little else but football to occupy the small bit of spare time we all had.

We had absolutely nothing else in the mountain but football. Our chores were the bog, dipping and clipping sheep, winning the hay and milking cows. We found it so hard to get a bit of grass or field to play a wee game on. Whatever grass was there, was precious. The aul fella wouldn't allow us into the fields. But we always managed to find somewhere. We used to wait so hard until the hay was cut at the end of the year.

We thought we were in Croke Park!

All those fields were along the river. So when things got heated, men sometimes found themselves going for an unintended dip. In the evening we'd be out on the street… we broke more windows and slates! My mother and especially my father, would go mad. Eventually, as we progressed through our teenage years, it moved on to even more serious games involving outside townlands from even further afield.

They were sometimes nasty affairs that often got completely out of hand. And by the time it got to the stage of provincial finals, All-Ireland semis and finals on the television, the blood was well and truly up. There were now gangs of 15 coming up from the likes of Maghera and Laconnell, areas much nearer to Ardara town. They were up to beat the s***e out of the 'mountain culchies'. That's what they called us.

And we took those intentions and name-calling personally. They thought they were the big city boys, equivalent to … I don't even know what they thought we were. But it wasn't good. However, more often than not, they were sent rolling back down the hill with their noses bloodied and their tails between their legs.

These were full-on contests with no referee. We were a sort of an amalgamation at that stage but the townies were ignorant to that fact. Our team was now taking in further afield areas like Meenashask and Largnahara. We'd also borrow the likes of Sean Gavigan from Crove. Sean was a county minor. He was like an All Star and he took no prisoners.

But the townies, for all their cuteness and smartarseness, didn't have the best grasp on mountain geography. After all, it was pretty complicated even for the natives. So local rivalries our end were put aside those rare days, and it was great. Still, those truces were usually short lived. And when Leamagowra came up against Crove and Sean a few weeks later, those previous bridges built were blown to smithereens once more.

Connie, on one of those occasions, was looking to prove himself. He hit Sean with an almighty shoulder near the river's edge and landed him into a deep pool. It was a huge scalp for our fella. But knowing the townies would be up the road again soon enough, we begrudgingly pulled Sean out. Sean, to this day though, remains a great friend of mine and a great friend of our house. Even when I eventually would come up against Naomh Columba for Ardara, those initial concerns of personal ties possibly being damaged or worse, severed for good, never materialised.

What happened on the pitch stayed on the pitch. The way it should do. And the Molloy boys playing for Ardara was never really any kind of issue. It was a small thing but something deep down, I will always be grateful for. Like I said, there was absolutely no other pastime in the area but football.

You'd a ball in your hand, or else you were playing cards at night. There were one or two TVs in the wider area and if you were allowed to make the trek in the road, it felt like a really big deal. You knew it was a special occasion.

JOHN 'PAT GALLAGHER and Con O'Donnell were the lucky men in possession of those magic boxes. That's where we all would gather to watch the big events, like the All-Ireland and FA Cup finals. You wouldn't have got into those houses come throw-in or tip-off. When we got brave and familiar enough with both men, we also became regular visitors on a Saturday night to take in the shenanigans of Benny Hill.

Young fellas came from all around. They literally came up over the mountain, from the Maghera side and beyond. Dad, like I said, wouldn't have had a great interest in football. He certainly didn't during those early days when it threatened to get in the way of our responsibilities around the house. We used to have to steal away as there was always work to be done. It often caused rows.

The compromise, the middle ground to end those types of arguments, was that our chores were now being carried out in the morning before school. That allowed us to get away in the evening. It didn't cost us a thought either to spend a full Saturday and half a Sunday bent over in the bog to free up some spare time in the middle of the week.

There was no such thing as under-10s and 12s back then. Your first taste of proper competitive action came at under-14. It was a competition called the Schoolboys Championship. My very first game for Ardara was at that grade back in 1976. My initial interactions with those boys, my new club teammates, had come from my first two years in Glenties Comprehensive School.

So there was at least some familiarity at that stage. But before that, there was little or no contact with most of those lads… bar, of course, those fierce townland games. School, up until that point, had been Crove, and Mass was attended in Meenaneary. All in the road. All my neighbours and national school friends would eventually progress on to Carrick Vocational School. But the trend of heading down to Glenties, both the old McDevitt Institute and later the new Comprehensive School, had already been set by Connie and my older sister Mary. Our under-14 bosses were Tom O'Donnell and Frankie Brennan. In those early days, it was like a treat to get down the mountain and into the hustle and bustle of Ardara.

We'd seldom go down the road. Glenties was really the start of it and at that age, entering my teens, I made some great new friends. But at the same time, I never lost my original ones. And that still means a lot to me.

'The Comp' as it would become known, drew its numbers from the likes of Glenties, Ardara, Fintown, and some of the Rosses. There hadn't been that much of a footballing tradition at the school. But in that group of First Years in 1974, there were some *serious* footballers. In our five years there we won under-15, under-17 and under-19 championships.

In that first year with the Ardara under-14s, we had managed to lift the county title, beating a fancied St Eunan's by 7-5 to 4-5 in the final. It was a convincing scoreline but we got off to a terrible start. Inside the first quarter, we'd fallen 2-4 to 1-0 behind. But by half-time we'd pulled it back to just two points thanks to a goal from the classy Gerard 'Bán' McNelis, and follow-up points by both Patrick McLoone and myself. We owned the second-half and our superior fitness… yes fitness, meant we ran out comfortable 12-point winners.

I was awarded the 'Man of the Match'. Gerard probably should have received it but he was sent off with five minutes to go. He'd clashed with a guy called Jimmy Kennedy, who'd been hanging out of him the entire match. Once Gerard knew we were over the line, he sought a little retribution of his own. Gerard 'Bán', though, was an exceptional player. He had everything. He was two-footed, athletic and could hit frees. He just had a natural flair.

I still have that wee trophy to this day.

In amongst all the big shiny stuff that would come later, there it sits and still stands out. I was by no means the star of the show at that time. Gerard undoubtedly was. He'd have been ahead of me as a footballer back then, no doubt. But that win, and that small bit of individual recognition, it definitely stirred something inside of me. A young Martin Gavigan, at 11 years of age but already with a thick cut to him, played wing back that day and more than held his own. I remember thinking he'd be one to keep an eye on.

That winning under-14 side, the lads that helped me secure my first really significant medal, lined out as follows: John Boyle; Paddy Watters, Paddy Brennan, Vincent Cassidy; Martin Gavigan, Patrick Moore, Joseph Shovlin; Gerard McNelis (2-3), Anthony Molloy (1-1); John McGill, Paul Brennan (1-0), Conal Breslin; Ted Breslin (1-1), Patrick McLoone (2-0), Sean Hannigan.

IT MIGHT SEEM like a strange thing to say in this day and age, or it might not, but as I've said, we were a ferociously fit under-14 side. We had to cycle everywhere back then. If you didn't have a bike… you walked. And sometimes, it was easier to walk as many of the bikes had punctures, with the forks or rims hitting the sides of the wheel bars. At 14, I was already working part time in Errigal Fish Factory and, in the summer, that progressed to full-time.

Connie 'Beag' Cunningham was my supervisor. He was football mad and he always facilitated me. Aodh O'Donnell was another that was high up there and he always allowed me to stray away that little bit earlier. I used to do 12-hour shifts. the factory was flying.

I would cycle to work at seven in the morning and, come eight in the evening, cycle back home. I'd get paid by cheque for my first 40 hours and the rest... I'd get in cash.

They were great times. You'd contribute some of your earnings to the house, of course. But the rest was yours to do as you pleased. My mother and father, to be fair to them, were very good and fair in that sense. I'd earned it so it was only right, they felt, that some of it was mine to purchase the necessaries. For myself, that had to be a set of wheels.

I started off on a motorbike. I'd a Yamaha 100. I eventually moved onto cars. Myself and my brother Lanty, there was only a year and a half between us, went everywhere together.

Martin Boyle, who was a little further in the road in Owenteskna, also ran about with us. He'd come as far as our house and we'd thumb or walk to the discos and dances. But, without fail, we'd always end up walking home in the bright of morning. But we were in our element, we were carefree.

That same group of under-14s failed to set the world alight at under-16. But both Gerard's, and my own stock, continued to rise. In 1978, we were picked to be part of a Donegal under-16 select that was to travel to Croke Park and take on our Dublin counterparts. The game would precede that year's NFL Division 1 final between the legendary Kerry and Dublin sides of that era.

Jackie McDermott, from Ballyshannon, was the man in charge, and it was a seriously talented group of footballers. In front of 30,000 supporters, many decked in the green and gold of Kerry, we annihilated our hosts on a scoreline of 6-8 to 1-5. It was an unbelievable experience. The Kerry ones cheered us on as if we were their own. With all that familiar colour, it felt like they were there *for us*. Gerard was superb, helping himself to 1-3 and I felt I'd more than held my own around the middle.

We were treated like kings and, later on that evening, the Donegal Association presented the team with lovely inscribed medals to mark the occasion. It really struck me how the Donegal people who had made lives for themselves in the big city, were so keen to look after their own.

My first involvement with a Donegal XV lined out as follows: John McGlinchey (Naomh Conaill); Sean Bonner (Na Rossa), Seamus Meehan (Four Masters), John Doogan (Kilcar); Brian Tuohy (Aodh Ruadh), Tommy McDermott (Aodh Ruadh), Gerry McHugh (Na Rossa); Paul Carr (St Eunan's), Anthony Molloy (Ardara); Sylvester Maguire (0-1, Aodh Ruadh), Gerard McNelis (1-3, Ardara), John Farren (0-1, Urris); Cathal Campbell (St Naul's), Martin Williamson (2-2, Aodh Ruadh), Vincent Furey (3-1, Naomh Conaill).

By the time our under-14s had progressed to under-21 level in 1980, tired stories of our famous victory over St Eunan's were less frequently told. We'd failed to back that talent up at under-16 and minor level. And we knew that this was the last chance for many of that same group to land another underage title. Accounting for St Mary's of Convoy in the first round of the championship, we disposed of Bundoran in the quarter-finals. Killybegs were swept aside in the last four to set up a final meeting with Kilcar.

The game, like so many deciders of that time, was played in Fintra. And it was a nasty, spiteful contest. The crowd was huge... they'd come from all around. Kilcar were the senior champions that year and had a number of those same players in their under-21 ranks.

The most dangerous was, of course, a certain Martin McHugh.

Martin was an unbelievable footballer who deserves to be mentioned in the same breath as many of the greats. And there was no doubt, if we were to stop Kilcar adding another county title to the senior one already residing in Towney, then we'd have to put the shackles on McHugh. Limit Martin's influence as best we could, and we'd beat Kilcar. Those were our orders and that was our team talk beforehand from our manager Seamus Gallagher.

Thuggery was one of the sub-headings included in the following Thursday's *Donegal Democrat* match report. And then it read, *There were a number of what are euphemistically referred to as 'off the ball' incidents, with one particularly blatant piece of thuggery, when an Ardara player was grounded by a deliberate and pre-meditated punch to the stomach, provoking a minor invasion by irate Ardara officials and supporters. The game was held up for a number of minutes as referee Thomas McBrearty insisted on the removal of all unauthorised persons from the enclosure. That was only* *achieved to a certain extent and there was again a big crowd on the pitch when Kilcar player Michael McFadden was injured, entirely accidentally it should be noted. Lest it be taken from any of the above that all the villains were on the Kilcar side, it should be made clear that both sides had their hatchet men.*

And maybe the *Democrat* was right. However, the main headline that very same Thursday, the only one that really mattered, heralded a win for the underdog.

Molloy inspires Ardara to victory

When bouts of football did break out in between the fisticuffs, we'd managed to get ourselves in at half-time 1-4 to 0-3 in front. Kevin McGill grabbed a crucial goal after Kilcar had made the better start. I nabbed a point and Gerard 'Bán' added another three from frees. We lifted matters again early in the second period with Gerard stretching our lead out to six. McHugh, leading what at times seemed like an almost single-handed fightback, did net late on. But it only served to add a little more gloss to the scoreboard. We'd dominated. I felt I'd dominated… and we won the game by 1-9 to 1-4.

The side that helped secure my second underage county title that day was: John Kennedy; Frankie Cassidy, Francis Gallagher, Conal Haughey; Donnie McCole, Lanty Molloy, Leo Watters; Anthony Molloy, Gerard McNelis (0-6); John McGill, Francis Connolly, Kevin McGill (1-0); Paul Brennan (0-2), James Gallagher, Eamon Watters. Subs: Sean McGuinness (0-1), John Boyle, Paul Brennan, Paddy Breslin, Stephen Sweeney, Hugh Gavigan, Matthew Shovlin and John Kennedy.

I was only 18 at the time, with a few years still left at that grade. We'd get back to the under-21 final again in 1982 but were well beaten, 2-10 to 0-5, by a seriously strong Aodh Ruadh/Ballyshannon outfit. Still, most of us were back on board again less than 12 months later. And in 1983, my final year at that grade, we'd gain sweet revenge. In the lead-up, all I could think about was the previous year's hammering.

I'd whipped myself into a bit of a frenzy. Our opponents, with 10 county under-21 panellists to our one… me, were even bigger favourites this time around.

That fact wasn't lost on our management team of Kieran Keeney and Conal Aidan Gildea. They told us we'd been disrespected in terms of our limited county representation at that same grade. This decider was again fixed for the close confides of the old Fintra pitch, just outside of Killybegs.

And that suited me just fine. Aodh Ruadh held a 1-2 to 0-3 advantage at half-time. But, much different to the previous year's hammering, we were hanging in there. A huge second-half saw us surge two clear near the end through Eamon Cunningham and John McGill. But two late frees from my future Donegal midfield partner Brian Murray snatched a 1-6 to 1-6 draw for the current holders and forced a replay.

The replay was quickly fixed once again for Fintra, just a week later. But Aodh Ruadh, the same men that sauntered onto the pitch first time out, laughing and joking, now suddenly had a problem with the venue. Those objections though fell on deaf ears. But again, it was something for Kieran and Conal Aidan to use in the lead-up.

An even bigger crowd showed up this time out, with interested spectators coming from all over to see who would edge this second tussle. They'd turned up from Glen, Kilcar, Killybegs and further afield. The following week's edition of the *Democrat* would note that £900 had been lifted at the gate.

Once again, it was a niggly and nervous affair.

Niall Campbell departed the action early on bloodied and needing stitches. But we didn't fall into that physical trap and a huge first 30 minutes rewarded us with a 1-4 to 0-1 half-time lead. With the likes of Gerard 'Bán', Paul Brennan, John McGill and Eamon Cunningham on the mark, and a 16-year-old Luke Gavigan out-jumping future All-Ireland winning 'keeper Gary Walsh to flick home a goal, this game was now very much ours to lose.

We'd only add two more points in the second-half, but we still managed to keep Ballyshannon at a comfortable enough arm's length. A late goal did pull them back to within a point but time was up, and they knew it. That 1-6 to 1-5 under-21 win, besides 1992, is the other one that will always stand out for me. It was really satisfying.

No video of the contest exists and, in a way, it's even more special because of that. To have those memories and tales, with a few exaggerations added over the years, always makes it so enjoyable to reflect back upon any time we do get the rare chance to all meet up. Unsurprisingly, the club was contacted that Monday morning by a sheepish Donegal under-21 boss Jackie McDermott – coincidently an Aodh Ruadh clubman – and four additional Ardara players... Gerard 'Bán', Paul Brennan, John McGill and Martin Gavigan were hastily added to his panel.

The winning Ardara side that day was made up of: John McConnell; Thomas Maguire, Martin Gavigan, Jimmy Caffrey; Ted Breslin, Paul Brennan (0-1), Niall Campbell; Anthony Molloy, Eamon Cunningham (0-2); John Kennedy (0-1), John McGill (0-1), Patrick Gallagher; Luke Gavigan (1-0), Gerard McNelis (0-1), Jimmy Brennan. Subs: Paddy J. Cassidy, Peter Breslin, Jackie Gallagher and Pat McGill.

BY THE TIME I'd progressed onto the Ardara senior squad in 1979, things were getting a little awkward. And by that, I mean coming up against my friends from near home representing Naomh Columba. A new competition, the Senior Shield, had been set up in 1978 with the aim of providing clubs with extra games in the winter months.

The competition really caught the imagination and ran through to March of 1979. We'd managed to qualify for the final. And providing the opposition would be my old friends at Naomh Columba. They were now a seriously impressive outfit at that level and were aiming for a clean sweep of trophies. They were already county champions and had also picked up both the league and All-Ireland Comortas Peile na Gaeltachta titles of 1978.

Fintra was once again the setting. At 16 years old, and having only just come into the reckoning, I was named amongst the substitutes. Still, this was a big deal for me and I made sure, from there on in, that I'd always have the right socks and togs to go with our club jersey colours. It was something I couldn't stand, seeing a stray pair of shorts or a blue or red sock interrupting that flow of green and gold.

Times were different back then and the onus was on you to purchase your own. All the club handed you out of the kit bag was a jersey; sometimes still stinking from the previous week's endeavour. But, for my first big senior final, I made sure I was at least looking the part.

With a serious breeze at our backs, we only managed to take a two-point lead in with us at half-time, 0-5 to 0-3. For those present, the momentum was expected to shift rapidly once Glen had the stiff Atlantic breeze in their sails. But a Conal Aidan Gildea goal immediately after the restart shook Naomh Columba and their usual composure deserted them as we instantly jumped five clear.

Glen did reduce arrears back to a single goal approaching the final 10 minutes, just as I was entering the fray. I'd barely taken up the unfamiliar station of corner-forward when the opposition's goalie, Michael Donovan, misdirected his kickout straight into my arms.

I couldn't believe it.

It felt like I'd an eternity to size up the opportunity. Glen, with the breeze and the need to find at least a goal themselves, had pushed up in anticipation of a long dispatch. But poor Michael took a little bit of ground and ball at the same time. I managed to compose myself and easily fired home that gift of a goal.

A 2-7 to 0-7 win over the current county champions, many of them my closest friends, made that first senior medal all the more special. PMPA Insurance were the competition's official sponsors and they'd commissioned a beautiful trophy in the shape of a Celtic Cross.

We were told it was valued at £500. We celebrated that success as if it were a county title. It meant that much to the club. But I made sure I'd composed myself once again, by the following Tuesday, as I made my way back into Errigal Fish Factory where so many of the Naomh Columba players also worked. Of course, the talk was only just beginning to settle in the canteen by the Thursday, when the *Democrat*, hitting the shelves once again, stirred conversation once more.

Glen's 'Triple Crown' attempt foiled, read the match report headline.

The winning Ardara team, welcomed back to the parish as heroes, was: Patsy Harkin; Frankie O'Donnell, Eamon McNelis, Patsy Gildea; Noel Watters (0-1), Kieran Keeney (0-1), Martin Sweeney; Anthony Harkin, Josie Gallagher (0-3); Conal A. Gildea (1-0), Connie Molloy (0-1), Seamus Gallagher; Frank McGee, John Boyle, Lanty Molloy (0-1). Subs: Anthony Molloy (1-0), Eddie McLoone, John Herron, John M. O'Donnell and Gerard McNelis.

With a marker of sorts laid, we immediately targeted that year's senior championship title. Our last Dr Maguire win had come way back in 1928.

It had been far too long. The potential and ability we all felt... knew even, was there. And our complete focus immediately shifted to ending that baron 51-year spell.

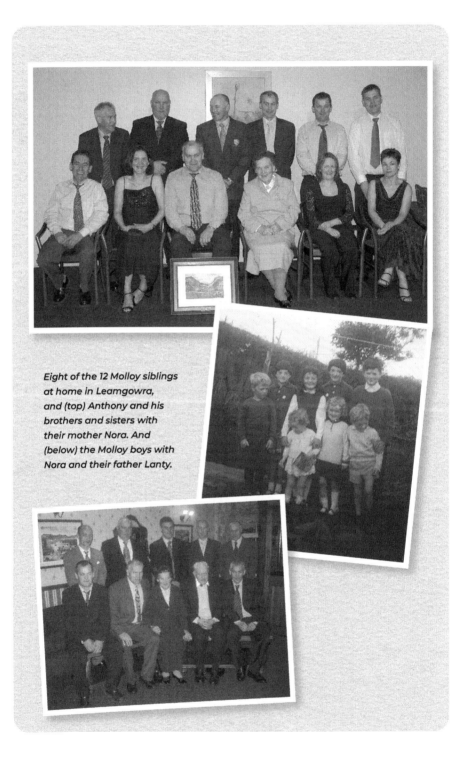

Eight of the 12 Molloy siblings at home in Leamgowra, and (top) Anthony and his brothers and sisters with their mother Nora. And (below) the Molloy boys with Nora and their father Lanty.

« CHAPTER 2 »

'Young people of Ireland, I love you'
– Pope John Paul II

I WAS STILL only 17 years of age as we entered the new decade… the 1980s. Pope John Paul II had visited Ireland to close out the 70s. I was still saying the rosary. And the magnitude of that Papal trip… it felt hugely significant at the time.

There probably was this innocent sense that we were all about to experience a change in direction. It felt exciting. I was running around now, enjoying myself. Football was high on the agenda but, truth be told, not at the very top of it. From a county perspective, I was still a little oblivious to the significance of all that… representing Donegal, I mean.

I had been called into the Donegal under-21 side by then manager Gerry Griffin. But our season ended as soon as it had begun with Down, the reigning Ulster and All-Ireland champions, stuffing us 7-10 to 1-5 in Ballybofey. I was a second-half substitute, coming on in place of Martin Shovlin. It was an instantly forgettable experience.

That was late April. Come June, it was minor time and I'd much more interest in that. My brothers Connie and Lanty had both played at that grade. This was my second and final year so I wanted to leave an impression.

In the first round, we were pitted against Antrim in a contest fixed for Irvinestown. The Donegal seniors' Ulster SFC quarter-final clash with Tyrone was the main event. For some reason Antrim were favourites that day but we made light enough work of them, winning 1-9 to 0-6.

Jackie McDermott, our manager, was a wily one. And he'd his homework done. And the likes of Paul Carr, Sean Bonner, Brian Tuohy and Vincent Furey were particularly impressive for us. Coincidently, the senior side were hammered 1-17 to 0-8 by Tyrone. So we now carried the county's remaining hopes for that year. Our six-point win meant that a semi-final showdown with Derry loomed. In what was a strange game, a contest we dominated for large spells, we still somehow found ourselves on the wrong end of a 0-11 to 0-6 loss.

Donegal contribute to their own downfall, screamed the headline in that week's *Democrat.* For the second game in-a-row, I'd been left at full-forward and, truth be told, it hadn't been a happy hunting ground.

It obviously wasn't, as in the same newspaper report the writer queried: *The big problem for Donegal was up front and one wonders why, yet again, Anthony Molloy was left at full-forward. It was obvious from very early on that the big Ardara lad was not happy there.*

1979 WAS A YEAR that we targeted in Ardara.

Following on from our Senior Shield win the previous March, hopes were high going into that season's senior championship. In what was a titanic tussle with St Eunan's, a home win and an away loss forced the first round encounter to a play-off.

The game was fixed for MacCumhaill Park. And a seven-point win, 1-9 to 0-5, buoyed belief that this could indeed finally be our year once again. In the quarter-finals, Ardara overcame Rosses Rovers, a serious amalgamation at the time of Dungloe, Na Rossa and Naomh Muire.

MacCumhaills would provide the opposition in the last four. With the likes of Martin Griffin, Brendan Dunleavy and PJ McGowan in their ranks, they would of course be favourites. But we thoroughly believed we had their number. Fr Tierney Park in Ballyshannon would play host to that semi-final. However, once again, we'd find ourselves edged out, this time by just two points, on a difference of 1-9 to 1-7, and we'd only ourselves to blame as we missed at least a half dozen scoreable chances. In the final, MacCumhaills were squeezed out by a single point by eventual winners Bundoran. I don't know if that meant anything, but it at least suggested we weren't far away.

To break up the winter months of late 1979 and early '80, the Senior Shield once again took centre stage. We'd topped our section and beat Robert Emmetts in the semi-finals. In the final, our old rivals MacCumhaills, from the previous season's county final, awaited, so we certainly didn't need any motivation. Fintra, that happiest of hunting grounds, would stage the decider.

Given the time of year… March, it was an unsurprisingly unforgivable day and snow and water had to both be cleared off the pitch. The contest was hardly memorable as a result. Crucially though, in the end the poor scoreline of 1-4 to 0-5 was in our favour. And that was all that mattered.

We felt we'd laid a marker. The signs remained good come May as we took the Donegal Comórtas Peile title thanks to a 0-10 to 1-6 victory over another big gun, Gaoth Dobhair. In the first round of the championship, we again fended off the challenge of Gaoth Dobhair over both legs. We'd edged the first game 0-7 to 1-3. And we'd three to spare away from home, in Magheragallon, on a scoreline of 2-4 to 0-7. However, towards the end of that game I'd felt and heard a strange pop in my knee as I landed awkwardly.

THERE WAS NO immediate pain.

And I was able to see out the last remaining moments of the match. But as I cooled down afterwards, it began to swell and some soreness crept in. But I brushed it off.

I was working and living at the time in Dublin.

Connie was an engineer there and had got me a job with John Sisk and Sons Ltd. They were a huge outfit. So a few of us had to quickly jump in a car. No one was too concerned about my knee. 'It's probably just a bit of fluid', was something that would frequently be uttered by someone who really didn't have a clue.

You were very much on your own back then with that kind of thing.

Throw some ice on it, and hope for the best. I was 18 and working with the biggest construction company in the country. The problem was that I'd an inter-firms game with the work crew the very next night, Monday. I was mad keen to play. It was a final.

And looking to steal away a few hours here and there for both club and county football, I couldn't be then missing a game of this size for my employer. Inter-firms was serious business back then and it wouldn't be the last time it got me in real bother.

I managed to see out close to most of the first-half but, near the midpoint, there was an even louder 'POP'… and the pain this time was excruciating. There was none of the knee jargon or expert talk that everyone throws about, now.

I genuinely didn't know what was wrong.

But that day… Monday July 6, 1981, would signal the start of it for me, knee trouble that would forever more threaten to derail and even end my footballing career. Ardara had been pitted against Naomh Columba in the last eight of the championship back in Donegal. The Glen men would have been the fancied side regardless. But my absence, the great hope, meant that the local papers were now tipping Naomh Columba for a comfortable enough win.

However, a brilliant Ardara performance would see them blitz the pre-game favourites by 2-7 to 0-7. Me? I was sitting on the sideline watching the entire thing transpire. I still didn't know the exact extent of the damage to my knee. We were going into the month of August and I wouldn't go under the knife until early December. Ardara would eventually qualify for the 1981 county final, disposing of the reigning champions Kilcar in the semi-finals, 1-5 to 0-5. It was a massive statement and result.

But my role, again, was a watching brief.

With the swelling going down and a decent enough degree of movement back in the left knee, Charlie Mooney, our manager and a really good guy, afforded me a token appearance right at the end of the decider. At that stage we were 1-7 to 0-6 up on Four Masters or, as they'd say, home and hosed.

It should have been the happiest day of my life. It was what the team dreamt of… our parish craved it. They genuinely prayed and lit candles for it.

The moment that myself and my brothers Connie, Frank and Lanty had discussed so often, awake in our bed late at night, was now upon us.

Grown men were crying. Thankfully, everyone was crying.

I was too. And that sense of euphoria all around me masked the real emotion behind my own tears. A large part of me was simply devastated.

The win was celebrated for weeks in the town. And it seemed like sort of a chore to have to turn out against Ballinderry in the Ulster Club Championship come late November. We were easily swept aside by the Derrymen, 2-9 to 0-5. And that Christmas period was again a chance to celebrate or, in my case, drown a little more of my own sorrow.

Don't get me wrong, I was delighted for everyone else.

I just felt I hadn't contributed and that the medal I would be handed at that year's Dinner Dance hadn't been earned. That walk, through the packed dining room, was a difficult experience. The claps for me, in my own mind, sounded a little slower and a little less louder. They felt like ones of pity.

The knee issue would also curtail my involvement with the Donegal under-21s that season. I'd started both wins over Cavan and Down, but missed the Ulster final loss to Monaghan. It only served to compound my misery.

Monaghan's midfield mastery defeats Donegal was the headline above that week's *Democrat* report. And those words were cutting. I somehow interpreted them as my absence being the deciding factor.

I eventually got the knee looked at, in Jervis Street Hospital in Dublin a few weeks before Christmas. Thankfully, it was, the surgeon said, 'just cartilage'. There was no x-ray or MRI. But the doctors there were able to tell by some physical tests that no really serious damage, like the cruciate ligament, had been done. The arthroscopic procedure, or scope, was a relatively new thing in Ireland. Connie had cartilage removed before and he'd the scars to prove it. But once the swelling had subsided, two little neat holes and a shaven leg was the only real evidence left on me.

I VIVIDLY REMEMBER coming round from the anaesthetic and being surrounded by complete strangers. There was up to a dozen people ringed around the bed.

Was I dead?

It took me a few seconds to remember exactly where I was. Because this was a new and modern procedure, a crowd of student doctors had stood in on much of it and they were obviously being debriefed on that process, just as I was wakening up.

I was given a set of crutches but, truth be told, after a day or two they weren't really needed. The doctor in Dublin had assured me that with the right rehab, a term and process that I also knew very little about, I would be back flying in a matters of a few months. With the club championship celebrations still in full swing and with it being Christmas, I vaguely followed the programme of exercises given to me on a few A4 sheets of paper. But it was half-hearted.

It was January 1982 and, as usual, I was wintering well. That was nothing out of the ordinary back then. But a combination of my knee issue, a fortnight of Christmas dinners with all the excess trimmings of so much self-pity… well, it meant that I'd a wee bit more weight packed on around the midriff by the time I decided to start addressing the issue.

Off I went down to Pearse Memorial Park, close to six weeks after my procedure, attempting a light jog around the muddy winter field. There were no lights, not even street ones along the road. It was pitch dark.

It was a routine that would become all too familiar to me over the subsequent years. I'd fall, I'd go into holes and a lot of the time the knee simply buckled as it just wasn't ready to stand up to that kind of load.

Still, at the beginning of 1982, time was still on my side, or so I imagined. In my own mind, I'd decided I'd be passing up on the county under-21s that year. I still had one more year left after that. I'd maybe look at all of that once again closer to the time. Delusions of grandeur, they were.

But the plan was to ease myself back into shape in time for the serious business of the club season. But one thing, or person I didn't factor into all of that planning, was Tom Conaghan.

Fate, to me, is a real thing.

In life, it smiles your way once or, if you're really lucky, sometimes twice.

I do believe that I have been steered a particular direction on a number of occasions so far in my lifetime. And there is no doubt fate, or just the single-mindedness and sheer bloody perseverance of Tom, helped drag me back into an environment that I was about to walk away from.

My brother Frank was already in the States by that stage, and Connie and Lanty were in the midst of planning their own escape. Every fortnight, Frank would call the landline and regale us all with tales of fortune, adventure and near misses. There was also football. And the scene he was describing sounded so far removed from what was going on at home.

Gaelic Park, sunshine, barbecues… beer and girls!

My ear had been bent and my head turned. But a forceful knock at the door one evening would nip any thoughts of making a break for it firmly in the bud. Bart Whelan, the then county secretary and also current Ardara chairman, was at the door. Behind him stood his good friend and new Donegal under-21 manager Tom Conaghan.

I knew what was coming.

I listened, I nodded… and said I'd think about it. But I was just being mannerly.

GAELIC PARK, SKYSCRAPERS and the adventures of New York City were still waiting for me. By that time, I was halfway through a three-year stint in Portlaoise with the end goal to qualify as a linesman for the ESB. It would be a good, steady-paying job at home and there was also that scope allowed to give football serious commitment.

But there was *real* money to be made in America and the notion was still in the back of my head to leave the studies behind, even defer, for a year or two spent in the Big Apple. Maybe there would be some resistance from my parents. Even then, it was still an option later that year… in the summer, possibly.

I was 20 years of age now. And the truth is I really didn't know what I wanted. But I still had no intentions of dragging myself out onto the winter training fields for a side at a grade we just didn't do well in. My woes and worries at that stage were trivial ones.

But on March 24, like a lightning bolt, word came through that my good friend and club teammate Kevin McGill had died in Holland. Kevin had only just arrived there. He'd been working in Dublin and was another one of the lads making that weekly trek along with the rest of us. Kevin was a brilliant fella.

He was full of fun and mischief. He was a damn good footballer as well. He was central to our underage success and was part of the senior squad that had finally landed the Dr Maguire Cup the previous season.

He was also a free spirit. And he'd headed off in search of fun and adventure. But his passing dampened my own enthusiasm about flying the nest. There was hesitation there now and, suddenly, home and the familiarity that it represented didn't seem as tedious as it had just a few weeks previously.

Was I ready for that responsibility, being away from so many of my family and friends?

The calls from Tom were still coming and the curly finger from Bart was persistent any time he'd see me jogging around the club pitch. But I thought all that badgering was over when come April, the Donegal under-21s took to the field in their first round Ulster Championship clash with Cavan in Breffni Park without me. The fact that they saw off the challenge of Cavan, 1-10 to 1-7, would definitely mean I would now finally be left to my own devices?

But come May, in the Ulster semi-final at home in Ballybofey, the side almost threw their season away against Down. Glued to the radio at home, I listened tentatively as the lads worked themselves into a two-point lead going into the final 10 minutes, before a goal and a point from Mickey Linden nearing the end pushed the Mourne side two clear.

However, Martin McHugh, with what the radio commentator described as a 50 metre free, boomed them back to within one. And unsurprisingly again, in added time, it was Martin saving the day with another placed ball effort right on the stroke of full-time.

The final and frantic moments of that live broadcast thrilled me.

I was jumping about the kitchen catching and kicking every ball. But when the adrenalin drained back, I realised that this side was now moving on without me. I was much too proud to pick up the phone, call Tom or even apologise. Amazingly, and against all conventional thought, wisdom and probably opinion, Tom landed on our street the very next day.

I'd made my bed, but Tom, wasn't going to let me lie in it. He would have shipped some criticism for it but there he was, once again, offering me a way back.

'I'm not asking you to make a commitment.' he said. 'Just come to training on Tuesday night, get a feel for the group, the set-up… and see what you think?'

I said I would.

And inside, there was this sense of relief and gratefulness.

Tom had gone above and beyond for me, and I'd never forget that. The fact that the replay wouldn't take place until the start of July, a six-week gap, probably influenced Tom's mindset. My own clubmate Donnie McCole was also on the squad, so off the pair of us went that following Tuesday night to training.

And come the replay with Down in Newry, I was named to start in the middle of the field. It was an against the grain type of move by Tom to take me back, and there is no doubt some were waiting and wanting it to fail. But a hard-fought 0-9 to 1-4 win pushed us into the final.

Again, we were made wait.

September 5 in Omagh, we'd battle Derry for the right to be crowned Ulster champions. Derry, with the likes of Eugene Murphy, Damien Barton and Dermot McNicholl in their midst, were a powerful outfit. McNicholl was a beast of a man and he was a seriously impressive footballer. Indeed, it was no surprise a few years later when Australian Rules clubs came calling for him.

But there was no doubt about it, when the dust settled we were the deserving 0-10 to 1-5 winners. A poor early concession of a goal was put to bed quickly and we soon set about making amends. Tom's punishing midweek regime of three training sessions meant we were in serious shape. And I do believe we simply overran the Derry.

Martin kicked seven of our winning tally, but the impact of Matt Gallagher and Sean Bonner in taking out McNicholl was also crucial. The likes of Charlie Mulgrew, Joyce McMullen, Paul Carr and Donal Reid also enhanced their growing reputations on the day.

WE'D BE PITTED against Laois in our All-Ireland semi-final.

The game was fixed for Pearse Park in Longford. There was no such thing as an overnight stay back then so off we went that morning. The skies were already opened from very early on that day. And by the time we reached the ground, both the weather and the conditions could only be described as atrocious. People often reference Clones and our senior loss to Derry in 1993, but what greeted us that day in Longford was much worse. Unsurprisingly, it was far from a spectacle.

There were massive puddles all over the pitch at throw-in and by the time we reached the midpoint the entire surface had been ploughed into an arena of black mud. Points were hard earned but, at the break, we had our noses in front, 0-3 to 0-2, thanks to two McHugh frees and a Tommy McDermott point. It was more of the same in the second-half. Balls were landing flat in pools of water. Men were falling over as they looked to change direction and claim the floating O'Neill's. Laois would square matters and move in front by the midpoint of the second-half. But back we battled and through a massive McHugh '45', we tied things up once again.

Donal Reid, who had come in off the bench, revelled in the conditions. And it was he who would prove to be the hero with the game's winning effort... 0-5 to 0-4 isn't a scoreline you'd associate with an All-Ireland semi-final win, but it was what got us over the line in 1982. Afterwards in the dressing-room, there was some commotion as Eunan McIntyre and Tommy, who had both shifted heavy knocks, had to receive medical attention. Eunan, especially, was in a bad way. He had taken a severe blow to the head putting his entire body on the line to halt a late Laois burst. Concussion was the word used to describe their conditions. Again, back then, it meant very little. All these years later, given the conditions that day, I'm shocked there wasn't a really serious injury.

The final against Roscommon was marked down for Sunday, October 29, in Carrick-on-Shannon. On the way to the venue Tom or one of his backroom team of Donal Monaghan, Michael Lafferty and Eamon Harvey would stand at various times and give us some words of wisdom. But none of it really registered as most of the whispers and talk on the bus concerned Tom's decision to drop Ballintra's Pauric Gallagher from the starting team.

Pauric was a brother of Matt's, our 1992 All-Ireland winning full-back, and he was a fantastic lad. More importantly, he was a superb footballer. But his crime was that he'd supposedly turned out in a game of soccer the week previously for Finn Harps.

Now, by today's standards, that punishment fits the crime. But back then, this appeared ruthless... cut-throat even. But this was the direction Tom was determined to steer Donegal football in, and if there was resistance or a reluctance to bend to his will, he'd happily drag us to that point.

There was no doubt here that he was laying his first real marker. He was a serious disciplinarian. We were training three times a week in Tawnawilly, just outside Donegal Town. If you were one minute late, you were turned on your heels.

Reid arrived once, just a few minutes past what Tom had instructed. The gate had now been closed and Tom warned him, from the other side of the pitch, to not dare jump it. 'Be here the next night... but be on time!' was the short and sharp instruction.

Tom was tough but it was something he had to summon. There was a really warm side to him as well and being a taskmaster was something he had to, at times, force. There was always a way back with Tom. But the pride that would often need to be swallowed in those situations would always have to be eaten by the player.

They were sickening training sessions under Tom that pushed you to your absolute limit. Eamon Harvey, who had an impressive athletics background, manned the whistle. But the levels we would eventually reach would propel us all the way to an All-Ireland final. Pauric would tragically die in a road traffic accident in Boston in 1989; his contribution to that year's All-Ireland win was crucial. In the end, he only missed the first eight minutes of the final, as he was more or less instantly sprung in the place of the injured Sean Bonner. Sean had carried a back problem into the game and it gave up on him instantly. Pauric though, was now a man possessed, and he almost rattled the net with his first touch, but the ball just went the wrong side of the crossbar.

That intervention squared matters up at two apiece, after Martin had kicked an opening free. Pauric almost found the net again soon after but the Roscommon goalkeeper just about denied him. By half-time, the sides couldn't be separated at 0-5 each, with Reid and three McHugh points accounting for the reminder of that opening tally. Playing with the breeze in the second-half, we were able to peg Roscommon in.

In fact, they would not score again for the remainder of the game. Martin would eventually bring his haul to five, while Reid helped move us onto seven. Fittingly, and deservingly, the last meaningful word in the match would go to Pauric.

Pauric had taken his medicine.

And when he got his chance, he proved his point. I can still see him now, wheeling away, face beaming and fist clenched. There was still a quarter of an hour to go but he seemed to know that we'd done enough. There had been no real build up to the final.

Carrick-on-Shannon wasn't Croke Park, so the scale of what we'd just achieved was probably lost on many of us in the moments that followed the final whistle. But looking at the faces of the majority of the 12,000 supporters after, and hearing the tremble in Tom's usually unwavering voice behind the dressing-room door as he thanked us for our efforts, it instantly registered like a wave crashing down upon me.

'You are the first Donegal side in any grade of inter-county football to win an All-Ireland football title. Remember now... this moment.

'But more importantly, remember what you sacrificed to get here!

'That is the basic requisite from here on in. We've set ourself standards on and off the pitch. And we'll carry them to the f***ing ends of the earth from this point on!'

Tom was already looking down the line and, in that moment, there wasn't a single doubt in my mind that he would – sooner rather than later – be leading us all at senior level.

We didn't know it at the time, but 1982 was a crucial building block, perhaps the cornerstone, for what would eventually come down the line 10 years later.

What we'd achieved quickly caught the imagination of the Donegal supporters and it was no surprise that Brian McEniff would flood 10 of us onto the senior squad in the weeks that followed.

And, as we started to find our feet in those ranks, there was a real buzz at the beginning of 1983. We'd never won an All-Ireland of any description. So we'd created our own little piece of history. It was a very welcoming senior dressing-room but even if it hadn't been, we would still have walked in there with our heads high and chests out.

If we were good enough at under-21 level, why wouldn't we be good enough at senior.

'The Comp' winning team (below, with Anthony on the left in the back row) in 1978, and two years later Anthony is still taking up the same position on the Donegal minors.

« CHAPTER 3 »

'Say hello to my little friend!'

– Tony Montana, Scarface

POUND FOR POUND, Martin McHugh was as good and often better than most players I've ever played with or against on a football field. He'd already two seasons under his belt at senior level when the other under-21 contingent of myself, Donal Reid, Tommy McDermott, Joyce McMullin, Charlie Mulgrew, Brian Tuohy, Matt Gallagher, Seamus Meehan, Eunan McIntyre and Paul Carr walked in the door.

Just a week after our under-21 All-Ireland heroics, the seniors' 1982/83 National Football League Division 3 campaign got under way with a less than glamorous trip to Louth. At just 21, there was already a seriously intense side to Martin when it came to football. I see it in his son Ryan now when he runs out for Donegal. He has that exact same steely look in his eyes. It's cold. And it was something I believe rubbed off on many of the rest of us under-21s, initially anyway, as we prepared to make the step up to senior county football.

Myself and Martin were good friends by now, but he was already a leader in that dressing-room… he was to the new clique anyway. He was now making Ulster Railway Cup sides and getting the better of many of the country's best players, lads with All-Ireland medals in their back pockets. There was no inferiority complex with Martin. He was good and he knew he was good.

We needed to get onto that way of thinking. It wasn't arrogance, it was confidence. And right away he was coaxing us all along and telling us that enough was enough and that, 'This crap of playing in Division 3 has to end. We are better than this'.

Truth is, we weren't.

Or at least we weren't for the majority of that terrible league campaign. We opened with a 1-11 to 2-4 defeat to Louth. I didn't get a run out that day but I knew there would have to be a reshuffle the following week when Monaghan came to Ballyshannon. I was named on the bench once again. Just like the week before, we were very slow out of the blocks and fortunate enough to be going in just 1-4 to 0-3 behind, with Martin accounting for our complete tally at the break.

The *Democrat's* take on that first half hour was, *Midfield was a disaster area for Donegal in the first-half with the partnership of Pat McCrea and Brendan Dunleavy not hitting it off at all.*

I was sprung for the second-half in place of Pat and immediately settled. I was up against Dermot McBride. His claim to fame was that he was the son of Big Tom and the Mainliners. But I was the one hitting the right notes in the second-half and, by the end, we'd managed to wrestle the result back our way to win out on a difference of 1-7 to 1-5, with my own club mate Kieran Keeney hammering in the decisive goal.

Kieran is now a friend but he very much felt like a big brother and mentor back then. And he really looked out for me in those early years. He was a quality player and his goal, along with McHugh's five points, made the ultimate difference that afternoon.

Next up with another away trek, this time to Laois. On a miserable day in Portarlington, I was handed my first senior Donegal start in the middle of the field. In the end, it took a late leveller from Michael Carr to nab a share of the spoils at 0-7 each. Still, I felt we'd been the better side and had we taken our many chances, we'd have won the game.

The Thursday match report in the *Democrat* noted, *So, despite a great display from Anthony Molloy in the middle of the field, who gave our half forward-line of attack chances galore, our full forward-line was relatively idle.*

Our last outing before the Christmas break saw us go to Longford on December 3. With Martin hitting 1-4 and Reid also finding the net, we grabbed our second league win, 2-7 to 1-9. It meant we split up for the festive break sitting second in the table on five points from our four outings and, just one shy of leaders Louth.

Unsurprisingly, we came back after an almighty Christmas blow out and, from our remaining three games, we took just two points. We'd lost the little bit of momentum we'd built up in the league and many of us returned to training in horrendous shape. McEniff and his management team of Pauric McShea, PJ McGowan, Austin Coughlin and team doctor Jim McDaid had no choice but to run us. That first week's effort at training was an embarrassment, but at least it was shared amongst ourselves. No one else outside the group had seen it. But what we couldn't hide from was the humiliation of a 0-8 to 0-7 loss to Clare, in Ennis, when we did return to action in February of 1983.

It was a result that wobbled us. A week later Wexford would come to Ballyshannon and earn a deserving 1-8 to 1-2 victory. My one mention in the scathing *Democrat* report was that I had been *ineffective throughout*. Criticism, even if it was tame enough, was something new to me. And it hurt. The promotion dreams we'd had before Christmas had now turned to very real concerns of relegation to Division 4.

I OFTEN TALK to former players, the likes of the Kerry legends. I have no doubts now looking back that ability-wise, we had the capacity to be meeting the likes of them and Dublin on an annual basis. But we just didn't take the thing seriously enough.

They'd have their fun, they'd admit that. But once it was parked, they went at the task like animals. They were doing four nights a week without the ball. And there we were struggling to get everyone to buy into two. And that was the big difference between those years in the 80s and when things finally did come together in 1992. There is no point saying otherwise, there was a complete lack of discipline.

And we were all guilty of it.

AHEAD OF THE final round of league games, Longford had already been relegated. Fermanagh were second from bottom on four points with ourselves just above them, on five. That effectively meant that our meeting with the Erne men in Ballyshannon was a relegation decider. Lose and we were down. Thankfully, we finally showed up when it was needed most and in a pulsating game, we ran out comfortable and deserving 3-12 to 2-9 winners.

The humour was good and it was a noisy dressing-room after. We wondered and debated where we should go? Donegal Town would be hopping but Bundoran was only in the road. But when McEniff called for hush, we were left in no uncertain doubt that our efforts, on the whole, just weren't good enough. But it was our attitude which really stank.

'Lads, we're smiling, we're laughing and that's okay. You've just beaten Fermanagh to stay out of Division 4. So well done. Congratulations.

'We've three months now until we're out in Ulster… a championship we've only ever won twice. The last of those came eight years ago… I've both medals at home.

We haven't passed the first round since 1979. It's time for you boys to knuckle down now and win one for yourselves.

'Are ye prepared to do that?'

There was no roaring, shouting or cursing from Brian, that was very rarely his style. But his words were cute and almost taunting. Avoiding Division 4, downing Fermanagh… was that really the height of our ambitions? But it felt like a slate had been wiped clean from that point on. There would be no great celebrating staying in Division 3 and we quickly moved things on in training. And a win over Armagh, following a replay, would qualify us for the McKenna Cup semi-final. I'd also scored my first point for Donegal in that opening drawn encounter in Lurgan.

Some bad blood accompanied the lead-in to the replay as a row had erupted following that draw, where Armagh insisted that extra-time should be played. The referee didn't agree or, he didn't initially anyway. We'd already headed for the dressing-rooms and with most of our lads showered the match official, a Cavan man called Michael Greenan, eventually knocked on the dressing-room door.

In his hand was now a copy of the official guide and, as he pointed out sheepishly to both McEniff and a completely naked, wet and vexed pair of Michael Lafferty and Martin Griffin, Armagh were, in fact, right.

'Too little, too late!' was the gist of McEniff's response.

Armagh were still on the field but we continued to dry ourselves off before eventually departing the ground. With a large crowd present and with the rule book proved to be on their side, it was surprising to say the least when the Ulster Council ruled in our favour. Armagh had just topped Division 1 of the league, undefeated, and were the reigning Ulster champions. We'd also been drawn to play them in the first round of the Ulster Championship in Ballybofey.

Did we really need to be pissing them off and making them angry before all of that? Needless to say, there was a nice wee edge to the replay and we'd plenty to reference ourselves and get wound up about at training in the lead-up. Men were, not angry… but pumped you could say by the time the Orchard County rolled into MacCumhaill Park the following weekend.

Armagh had also made it all the way to the previous season's All-Ireland semi-final before being downed by eventual winners Kerry. But they'd just gone through Division 1 without losing a single game. This was a dress-rehearsal ahead of the serious business of June's encounter.

There was already bad blood and both teams would have intentions of laying markers. But in the end, we stood firm and won through to the last four by way of a 1-6 to 1-4 victory. It was another small sign that progress was being made.

In the semi-final against Monaghan, we delivered a storming first-half performance. And even without the injured Martin, we exited at the break in Ballyshannon seven in front. We still had our noses ahead by four going into the last three minutes of the game. But somehow, we caved completely. First, Dermot Mulligan's sideline effort into the area seemed to catch in the wind and squeeze in between the bottom of the crossbar and the tips of Noel McCole's fingers. Niall McKenna then squared matters seconds out from the end of normal time. And, to hammer the final miserable nail in our McKenna Cup aspirations, Ray McCarron clipped a winner.

Somehow, having been 2-4 to 0-3 clear at one stage, we eventually lost by 1-9 to 2-5. McEniff, normally so clear and articulate in his summing up of games, went ballistic. By the time he'd calmed down, he explained that we needed the extra game time that the final against Down would have presented. Instead, he barked, *'We'll just have to find that edge on the training field!'*

And that didn't sound good.

BRIAN MCENIFF WAS an instantly impressive individual.

He spoke softly, but firmly, and was quick to the point. Being a businessman and, because of that, a people's man, he just had a way of cutting through the bullshit. He'd spent some time living in Canada and because of that had a sort of worldly suaveness that was very easy to warm to. I still, to this day, haven't come across anyone who could deliver a team talk, off the cuff, like him.

He had an unnatural sense and knowledge of other teams, and he knew every single player on them. This was long before you had the televised and online coverage we have now. Being a hotelier, he had access to all the local papers in the country and that was how he sourced so much of that information. I recently watched a documentary on the legendary Manchester United manager Sir Alex Ferguson. When asked how he assessed players, even in his final years when there were iPads all around him, he said he still relied mostly on his own instinct and gut feeling. He'd see other managers scribbling away on pieces of notepaper during the game or with a headset on. But Ferguson… he said he never took his eyes off the action.

And Brian was like that. He had an organic feel for matters and that included the individual as well as the collective. And he cared about us as well. He was a father-like figure to all of us.

On too many occasions he went above and beyond for his players and, in a way, his greatest strength was also probably one of his few weaknesses. At times, when we were taking the piss, there just wasn't enough tough love. But is it right to even label that as any kind of weakness? He sourced jobs for so many players over the decades and no doubt helped out in so many other ways that no one will ever hear about.

Imagine putting a price, in real money, on what he's given to Donegal?

It would be an eye-watering sum.

He was one of the biggest hoteliers in Ireland at the time, but you would still receive three or four calls a day from Brian. He might have looked to talk to you at seven in the morning or even close to midnight. Time was never a concern of his. His days were 24 hours. He woke in the morning with football on his mind and he went to bed the exact same way. How he managed to run a dozen or so hotels in between, I'll never know.

Even after all these years, he'll still check in to see that we're all okay. In January of 2021, his name flashes up on my phone… *The bossman.*

I answer and he tells me that he intends to call all the lads, to check in on us. And by 'us' he means the entire 'Class of 1992'. The Covid pandemic is rampant but he tells me he's sick to the back teeth of the restrictions and the isolation.

I don't know how many of the others he actually did ring in the days and weeks that followed. But one number he definitely didn't call was located in

Bavin, Kilcar. Martin McHugh and Brian had a well-documented fallout and there has been no relationship there now for over 20 years. Both men, I'm sure, have their own take on who or what caused the bad feeling.

Martin wanted the Donegal job in 1994 after Brian left. He didn't get it and maybe feels Brian had a part to play in PJ McGowan eventually succeeding him.

It's a sorry mess and it's something that makes me very sad. It's always there, in the background, whenever we do meet up... like the 25th anniversary reunion when we were presented to the Croke Park crowd back in 2017. I'm close to both men but it's something I stay out of.

I just hope there is a reconciliation of sorts there, somewhere down the line, and before it's too late. Because back at the very beginning of that now fragmented relationship, there was an amazing synergy between the pair. It was a joy to witness. And there is no doubt that Brian adored Martin as a footballer. He was and always will be his favourite. He was the axis that McEniff knew he'd have to build his team around. Watch the 1992 final back. At the final whistle, McHugh is the one Brian instantly looks for. And he holds him up in his arms like a child when he eventually does find him.

REGROUPING AHEAD OF what would be a nine-week lead-in to our 1983 Ulster opener with Armagh, we openly talked and discussed our aims and ambitions. Were they genuine? That was the question Brian and his management team kept posing to us. Do you really, *really* believe you're good enough?

In between, Brian, Martin and Michael Lafferty helped Ulster to the Railway Cup with a 2-10 to 2-4 win over Munster. When they came back in, there was a lot of talk, particularly from Brian, about just how good most of those lads *weren't*.

Brian was telling every single one of us that we were better than our Railway Cup counterpart in our position. I remember Matt Gallagher eventually asking Brian if that was really true then why, as manager, didn't he select a few more of us?!

Brian joked that he just couldn't be seen as being bias and, because of that, '*We were the country's best-kept secret!*'

But we were building a good camaraderie now and we were settling in well with the more experienced campaigners. Training was hard but there was a sense of satisfaction after. In between, we got the defence of our Ulster and indeed

All-Ireland under-21 crown up and running with a 2-8 to 1-4 win over Antrim in Ballybofey. I'd also pick up the under-21 club title with Ardara. So at least we were spared the extra running at the weekend with the county squad. Our clash with Aodh Ruadh had, of course, gone to a replay. And that meant we'd miss another weekend's slog, which was a bonus of sorts given what we were already being subjected to midweek.

But Brian was happy for the younger lads to play football – it was of more benefit. With Armagh and our huge Ulster Championship opener now looming, the doubt or concern in the lead-in was Martin. His hip had been giving him bother. There was even a rumour going that a specialist had advised him to quit the game altogether. But that was just paper gossip. However, it was a niggly issue that, like my knee, would have to be managed as the years went on. And of course Martin would have multiple surgeries on it in later years.

People might forget now, because of the way he transitioned and looked after that hip, but Martin was an exceptional placed ball kicker. He was the very best I'd ever seen in Donegal. He was knocking over balls from 50 and 60 yards as an under-21. He would spend hours upon hours at Kilcar's ground in Towney… booming them off the ground. And once he'd find his absolute range, he'd edge it back just another few yards… mark it, and rest up for the next night.

And he'd batter away again until he'd clear the crossbar from the new gap, and so on… and so on. We'll get to it, but his effort against Cavan in the drawn Ulster clash in 1992 is the best pressure kick I've ever witnessed on a field.

Sunday, June 13… and a massive crowd has descended upon Ballybofey for what is an eagerly anticipated encounter with Armagh. Donegal, or at least Donegal without its new under-21 blood, had somehow let the same opposition squirm off the hook in the corresponding fixture the year before.

It wouldn't happen today, not even a National League game could stir it, but there was also an edge to matters because of what had transpired in the McKenna Cup. Every game, every yard conceded back then counted for something down the line. Could you imagine, in 2022, Declan Bonner or Kieran McGeeney referencing a McKenna Cup game in their opening Ulster Championship team talk to get their players going? Football has certainly changed but, in my opinion, not for the better.

Martin's hip was still giving him bother and that morning he received a painkilling injection to ease the discomfort. We got off to an absolute flier, as Charlie Mulgrew fired in a goal. And by half-time we led 1-5 to 0-4 with Martin (four) and Mulgrew having grabbed our points tally. Credit to Noel McCole as well. He'd managed to save a softly awarded penalty, when he guessed right to deny John Corvan.

It was a big moment in the game, perhaps a turning point. Joyce widened the gap soon after the restart, before Martin put six between the teams with a routine free. However, in doing so, he immediately went to ground in agony, holding his hip, and it was a worrying sight to see him being stretchered off. Still, even in his considerable absence, we didn't buckle and saw out the remainder in relatively comfortable fashion.

Armagh seemed to run out of ideas and, at the same time, throw in the towel. Kieran, Michael Lafferty and Padraig Carr would add final points as we won comfortably on a scoreline of 1-10 to 0-7.

Our semi-final clash with Monaghan was fixed for Irvinestown. We should have beaten them in that previous McKenna Cup clash in Ballyshannon. We'd thrown the game away. That was our solid reference point. We felt we were a better side.

But we were dealt a real blow in the lead-up as it became obvious that Martin wasn't going to be fit enough to start. The right noises and sounds were made in the papers by Brian but we knew if we were going to make our first Ulster final in four years, we'd have to do it the hard way and without our play-maker and best player.

Monaghan's early intent was obvious – they wanted to rough us up. And it was a ploy that played right into our hands. We concentrated on settling and by getting an early upper hand, we were allowed to then set the pace. We played the game on our terms and even with a terrible refereeing performance to contend with, we didn't buckle.

And by the time Joyce cracked in a fabulous 20th minute goal, we had taken a real control of matters. I managed to get on the scoresheet as well and we exited with a commanding 1-9 to 0-5 lead at half-time. Now, we'd been here before against this lot. But seething from some of the unsavoury injustices that had occurred in that first half hour, we made a promise, to a man, that there was no way we were going to throw this one away. Again, off the ball incidents were going unpunished, with Cavan whistler Jim McCorry struggling to keep up with the play. Whatever control he might have had was now completely gone. We were still six clear heading into the last quarter of an hour.

And that was the stage that Monaghan's frustrations blew over.

With the referee's back to the play, one of their players struck Charlie Mulgrew across the face with a cowardly blow that would fracture Charlie's jaw. It was an act that would deny Charlie his spot in the Ulster final starting team. His replacement Frank Rushe wasn't on the field that long when he too took a blow to the head. Eugene McSharry was the culprit on this occasion. And at last, the referee decided he had to take some action as he brandished a red card.

All Monghan's hope, I felt, was now departing with the walking of McSharry. But the sending off seemed to spur something in them and they managed to drag themselves back to within three with seven minutes still to go, thanks, in large, to a Hugo Clerkin goal. We were nervy now and on the ropes. Thankfully, we steadied ourselves and a point from Kieran finished off the Monaghan muscle men. But even at the final whistle, their petulance didn't end. I laughed loudly as their goalkeeper took his frustrations out on both the umpire and his flag, which he hopped off the goal frame... splitting it in two! But there was no doubt he overstepped the mark when he pushed the same umpire into the side netting of the goal.

The Donegal contingent in the 12,000 strong crowd were in fine form. We were back in an Ulster final with provincial aristocrats Cavan lying in wait. We were gunning for a third title at this level as Cavan chased number 38.

THERE MIGHT HAVE been an historic gap in terms of success but, come July 24 at Clones, we firmly believed we were going to topple Cavan. Maybe it was stage fright or nerves, but we couldn't have made a worse start to matters in that final. Inside the first five minutes Cavan had raced into a 1-2 to 0-1 lead, with lethal full-forward Derek McDonnell netting their goal. Martin, back in the fold, had kicked our opening score in between that early blitz.

Slowly but surely, we began to settle and it was Martin once more, from a deep free, that cut matters back to three. Joyce added another before a third effort from McHugh left the minimum of margins in it at the quarter hour mark. What we didn't need or couldn't afford, was to rely on Martin to dig us out of trouble all on his own and I was relieved to see Reid bomb up from defence and kick us level.

Points were traded at either end of the field but on 29 minutes, a massive moment arrived when Eugene Kiernan pulled down Kieran inside the square. Seamus Bonner made no mistake from the spot to fire us two clear. By the time we reached the midpoint, we were still in front, but only just on a difference of 1-8 to 1-7.

With McDonnell continuing to cause real bother, his early second-half brace meant the lead changed hands once more. Michael Carr managed to tie it again before McHugh, and Joyce once again, put us two in the clear. Martin would nail a seventh and final point, but it would prove to be his last act. I've mentioned the similarities I see in Martin and his son Ryan. And just like Ryan today, Martin shipped more abuse, so reckless at times, than most players. But as he was helped to his feet following another vicious chop down, it was obvious that it wasn't his hip that was the issue.

There was a different kind of concern on the Donegal mentors' faces, including Dr Jim McDaid. It would transpire that Martin had suffered a collapsed lung. It was a distraction in more ways than one, seeing him depart in that traumatic manner.

And, as we looked to find a degree of composure once more, Cavan substitute Stephen King kicked a point with his first touch to leave two in it once again. Michael Carr, deservingly named Man of the Match, responded following a superb fetch and run. And while Cavan would again bring themselves within two, a late penalty, wisely clipped over the bar by Seamus, earned Donegal what was only a third ever Ulster title.

It was a huge win and the magnitude of the occasion, the crowd, what it meant to Brian and the older lads… you got swept up in all of that.

It was quickly back down to earth though for the under-21s, as we'd a chance to make it a provincial double in our own final against Derry. For whatever reason, maybe it was the euphoria of looking forward to an All-Ireland semi-final, we were abysmal in that decider and were hammered 3-13 to 1-3.

WE SOON GOT back down to preparing for our All-Ireland semi clash with Galway. We were a fortnight out now from that encounter at Croke Park. But on the Monday after the Ulster Under-21 final, I was down to play an inter-firms match with an ESB amalgamation against our Kerry counterparts.

Our side was sourced from workers in the Sligo, Mayo and Donegal divisions of the company. Willie Joe Padden was my midfield partner at the time. Again, people will question my wisdom in taking part but football wasn't paying the bills. I wasn't long in the job and there is no doubt my profile as a footballer had helped with that. So there was pressure and some influence put on me to play.

And of course, the ultimate risk had the ultimate consequence, as I again hurt that same previously troubled knee. Reporting back to Brian, who'd warned me of the obvious chance I was taking, wasn't an easy task. But Brian felt there was enough time, 13 days to be precise, to get the swelling down. I did, and with the aid of some serious support strapping and pain killers, I was named in the team to start.

I knew I was in no fit state to be playing a game of that importance. Again, nothing was reported in the papers in the lead-up, which was strange. No leak had made its way to them. But the sight of the big white bandage on my knee prior to throw-in left my opposite number Richie Lee in no doubt how to play me. And as much as it boosted him sizing me up hobbling about before the throw-in, I could also feel any lingering thoughts that I might get through this fall to pieces.

Players like Noel McCole, Michael Carr, Michael Lafferty, Kieran Keeney and Letterkenny native Paul McGettigan, who was based in Merlin Park and played for Galway in the 1978 Connacht final, all had experience in Croke Park from the 1970s. And they were intent on not letting this late chance to reach an All-Ireland final slip. The game itself was poor fare. We went in 1-6 to 0-6 in front at half-time with Keeney, having gobbled up a rebound after Michael Carr's shot came back down off the upright, hitting the net.

One of the biggest cheers that day came at the break, when news of Eamonn Coghlan's gold medal at the 1,500metres at the World Championships in Helsinki flashed on the Nally Stand scoreboard. Deep in the bowels of Croke Park, the old stadium shook like it was going to come down on top of us.

Going into the final eight minutes, we still led by a point, when Galway were awarded a '50', as it was still known back then.

Stephen Joyce placed the ball and went about his routine purposefully. But he would scuff his effort and Val Daly, Galway's half-forward, somehow grasped possession at the second attempt after a fumble. Shooting for a point, Daly's hooked strike was as unclean as they come, but it flew past Noel and into our net. And try as we might, we just couldn't get back on level terms.

When referee Weeshie Fogarty blew for time, we just slumped to our knees. We'd let a serious opportunity to reach a first ever All-Ireland final slip, as Galway edged us out by 1-12 to 1-11.

OF COURSE IT hurt. But there and then, the magnitude of what had just slipped between our fingers was lost on many of the younger lads like myself. But back in the dressing-room, it soon became apparent. There was just this sense of utter devastation on the faces of the older campaigners.

And Brian was shattered.

Genuinely, those lads were in mourning. That is the only way to describe their pain. That quietness, and anyone who's ever been in a losing dressing-room where so much was at stake just minutes prior, will know exactly what I'm talking about. There are just no words. Nothing can pull you back to that moment... the split second where you sensed danger but didn't, or just couldn't, divert it.

Eventually, someone breaks the silence and stillness, and slips into the showers. And that is the unwritten cue which allows everyone else to finally go about their business of cleaning up and packing up.

And eventually, off we slip in small fragmented groups into the city.

Amazingly, and a little bizarrely, the Galway boss Mattie McDonagh got in touch with Brian a few days after. They were now preparing for the All-Ireland final against Dublin, but wanted a challenge. It would have been a difficult enough sell to most of the players but it was dressed up and presented to us as a deserving end of season blow out. Still, when we were back on that pitch, something instinctive clicked and, in our own warped way, we looked to make amends for what had happened previously.

We won by seven points. And it felt great.

Or at least it did for a few fleeting hours as we toasted our revenge after.

But the stark reality would slowly sink in. We were drinking pints, celebrating a challenge win, as Galway went back about their business in preparation for an All-Ireland final. I had completed my final year at Portlaoise the previous June and I was now a fully qualified ESB lines technician.

As we broke for summer, I vividly remember Dublin's Kieran Duff, who was on the course with me, saying, 'I'll see you in September'. Kieran would uphold his end of the bargain with Dublin's '12 Apostles', dubbed so as they'd have three men sent off, and still managed to dig out a two-point win in the final.

It was a serious opportunity passed up upon, but it wasn't something that registered or haunted me at that point.

All that would come much later down the line!

The Donegal team which was beaten by Galway in the 1983 All-Ireland semi-final (Anthony is third from right in the back row), and manager Brian McEniff leaves the field in Croke Park in disappointment.

REFLECTIONS

'Tough times don't last, tough people do'
– Robert Schuller

I'M SITTING ON the edge of my bed.

It's dark, but the little bit of early morning light that is beginning to creep in the window suddenly hits the Sam Maguire and... there it is once again. It's mid-February of 1993 and I've long since had enough.

Physically, I'm exhausted and mentally... I'm completely spent.

But soon enough, it'll be time to go again. Someone somewhere, later that evening, will want the presence of the Sam Maguire and the Donegal captain Anthony Molloy.

We're a duo now... and where ones goes the other must follow.

And the truth is, it's become like a ball and chain around my ankle. I'm sick looking at that damn cup at the bottom of the bed...

THE GREATEST THING I've ever done in my lifetime is lift Sam Maguire, after Donegal's first ever All-Ireland title, high into the Croke Park air. That moment back in 1992, the one immortalised on so many walls throughout the world, that is me. Or, it was me.

New York, London, Sydney... even a bar in Kerry of all places... every now and then, it crops up in the most unlikely of locations. But I can look at it now and smile. I can let my mind wander back and remember that exact moment.

It still has the power to warm me.

But there was a period when it all just became overwhelming. Not so much the actual feat of what we achieved... that always has and will be special. But the manic workload and responsibility that came with the historic win was simply crazy... inhumane.

AND I DON'T blame anyone else.

At the time, I just didn't have the confidence or courage to say 'NO... not tonight!'

And our All-Ireland triumph came very late. Within the space of two seasons after, I was done with Donegal and, three years after that, I was finally forced into full retirement because of my knees. It was one extreme to the other and, I suppose, life did take a sort of tailspin.

It was a negative period in my life.

It did eventually pass, but some demons had to be exorcised along the way. I don't dwell on the hardships and losses suffered as a result. The truth is, I was a young man thrust into a limelight the likes of which the county of Donegal had never seen before and – even with 2012's glorious follow-up – hasn't seen the like of since.

The recklessness indulged in and even entertained... modern life and sport just doesn't allow for that kind of excess now. It was a much different era and we were a much different generation.

I'D JUST TURNED 30 that summer of 1992.

But I'd still a lot of learning to do... life learning for want of a better phrase. And looking back, especially after our All-Ireland win, I should have learned much quicker.

I was everyone's friend.

And I thought I had a lot of friends.

But I found out different and I found out the hard way.

You see, there is a big difference between a friend and an acquaintance. I've come to understand, and I'm around a long time, that besides family, I can count on one hand the actual real friends I have that... if I needed them this moment, they'd be there at the door.

I'm not unique in feeling that way.

That's life.

I just didn't get it back then.

I THOUGHT I had thousands of friends in September 1992.

I didn't want to let anyone down. Believe it or not, that was my mindset. At the end of the day these people were just paper friends.

There is no doubt about it… I drank a lot.

But everyone did. But because I was captain, I was in the limelight. I had to go to every opening, every sponsorship do. In the end I just couldn't escape it.

Did I let things go a bit too far?

Of course I did. But it was something that was very hard to pull a hand-break on once it got going. Anyone that was there will tell you the scenes in this county after 1992 were mental.

That's the only way to describe it… absolutely mental.

The county lost the plot. It was one big party.

The ESB gave me six months leave – they thought they were doing me a favour. I was travelling the schools by day, and I enjoyed that. But it was the social markings at night, those were the ones I eventually grew to despise.

I see photos now on social media, or someone tags me in something… and it'll often be a blur.

And it wasn't because of drink or anything like that.

It was just so hectic that you kind of emotionally just checked out at a certain stage. The first four or five weeks were great… special even. But the novelty eventually wore off.

I was meeting the same people coming around.

ONE NIGHT, LONG after the buzz was gone, myself and Martin McHugh had to go down to the Limelight nightclub in Glenties. The new season had already started and we both weren't long off a plane following a whistle-stop tour of the east coast of America.

But we were still being wheeled out on the local circuit.

Of course, there were pints… there had to be to make it bearable.

We didn't get out of there until 6am.

And a few hours later that morning, we were on a bus to bloody Carlow.

That same night, I had to go onto Wexford with the cup. There were four or five stops lined up there for us and I eventually got back up the road and into bed... back home in Killybegs, just as the sun was coming up.

That damn cup ...

MCENIFF SHOULD HAVE given a few of us the early part of the league off in late 1992/93 as it was just crazy. We were in Division 2 and the truth is a few of us just weren't needed in most of those games.

He should have thrown some of the younger lads in.

A good few of us ended up injured by the time the real business started later in 1993. I was crocked, 'Rambo' was sidelined, and so too was Reid. It was Division 2. We ended up winning all seven games, before losing the final to Dublin.

It was a gauntlet of 10 outings that many of us simply didn't need.

We would reach the Ulster final once again and, on that infamous Clones quagmire, our bitter rivalry with Derry resumed. They gained their revenge and I'd more than an inkling that sour day we had also just relinquished our All-Ireland title to the very same opposition. I was still out injured.

Tony Boyle missed the whole of '93 with a shoulder injury. The entire spine of our team was missing. Noel Hegarty was sent off in the semi-final, 'Rambo' also didn't feature. And everyone remembers the deluge... the weather. The game should never have been played. But the Ulster Council put serious pressure on the referee to play it... it had to go ahead. Even after a minor broke his leg in the curtain-raiser, it wasn't called off.

A lot of the old Derry guard will say that regardless of the weather, they were still going to beat us that year. But the truth is they beat half a Donegal team. Even at that, we only lost by two points.

I WAS STILL doing the rounds at that stage... locally, nationally... and even internationally. It was ludicrous stuff.

Only for Columba Diver, one of a number of mine and Sam's drivers at the time, I'd never have entertained the thought of trying to get home. Columba, Michael and Sean Watters, Gerard Slowey and especially Stephen McCahill were the men that carted us about.

Stephen did the logistics on all of it.

Without him, I'd have never got through it.

It wasn't all doom and gloom. And the odd time, in between that madness, there were some real laugh out loud moments. Gerard, who is sadly no longer with us, was a character. One of the stops that time in Carlow was at an Ideal Homes Exhibition.

McHugh by now, wisely, had bailed on the touring circuit. But he'd been marked down for this job and so many Carlow folk were intent on getting their photo taken with the great 'Wee Man'.

Gerard, a wee man in his own right, but so full of wit and divilment, was never going to pass up on such an opportunity.

So Gerard suddenly begins announcing himself as Martin and standing in the pictures. And I'm sure, to this day, there are more than a few photos of 'McHugh' and Sam hung on the walls in Carlow!

My big problem at that time was that I felt I was letting people down if I didn't show up for these things. I was accommodating to a fault and to the detriment of my own health and well-being. It took me a long time to figure out I was pleasing everyone, but myself.

Because believe me, the fun went out of it all soon enough.

I grew sick of looking at the Sam Maguire, at the bottom of the bed and, in the end, I couldn't wait to hand the bloody thing back. Come June of 1993, I was never as glad to part company with it.

But I was so far down the track now… it was hard to pull the nose back up.

I DETEST THE word 'alcoholic', but I did develop an unhealthy relationship with drink for a period. I'm thankful to say I sought the required help and I managed to put that period behind me.

But what I have found is that if you get the reputation of an early riser, then you can lie to dinner time. And there is no truer saying. I got that name back then, deservedly, and it's never truly left me.

There was a massive drink culture surrounding football in the 1980s and 90s. We'd go to training and run ourselves into the ground. The training was severe and cruel. But on the way home groups of us would still stop for pints.

After county and club games the sessions went on until morning.

That was the madness of it all. Everything revolved around drink. It was just the times that were in it. Manchester United players back then, even in professional football... it was the big thing.

Paul McGrath, Brian Robson, Norman Whiteside... they would have fitted right into the GAA scene.

Towards the end, it was getting the better of me. I wasn't my own man any more. But I looked for help and I got it. I don't mind saying that and I don't feel one bit embarrassed or ashamed.

I went to AA and it was the best thing I ever did.

I found out so much about myself.

AA and the meetings... they weren't all about drinking and being down in the dumps. Much of it centred on talking about living and that's where a lot of the issues and troubles in your life become clearer and the reasons for them more obvious.

I know absolutely nothing about drugs because, thankfully, I never took them. But I can go out now and take a pint or leave it. The problem most people have is realising there is a wee issue there and addressing it.

IN 1992, I DIDN'T need a brandy to make a speech in front of 70,000 people.

And while the crowds aren't as big today, I still don't need a drink now to step up and address an individual or a room. There was a time in between where I was worried or concerned that something I might say could upset someone.

Today, I don't give one damn what anyone else thinks.

I had to learn to look after No 1. And not in a selfish way, but in a productive way that gets me through the day and allows me to look myself in the mirror. Speak your truth... be honest and try to be fair.

But don't worry what other people think.

The truth is, it took me a long time to get to that place.

BUT THERE IS no doubt, there were mistakes made along the way.

Drink and being away every single night of the week, for the best part of a year, no doubt cost me many things. It certainly contributed to the breakdown of many relationships at the time, including my marriage.

Success can come at a price.

You live and learn and that process never stops. To be at that point, at the end of it all, handing the cup back, there was just space to breathe. You were still able to talk about it and look back, but at least the madness had stopped. But another problem for me, something that maybe fanned my demons, was that my career was more or less now behind me.

I couldn't throw myself back into the football because my knees were completely shot.

I was on the home straight, holding on when I wasn't fit to do it anymore. I was gone from Donegal in 1994 and, by '95, I was retired completely. And that contributed to some of the lows I was feeling.

I didn't even have an aul' club game to fall back on.

Less than three years after reaching the pinnacle in my sport, I was on the scrapheap. I look at Martin Shovlin now, at 61 years of age, still togging out for his club's junior team. It's amazing. But the worst thing I thought I could do at that time, even at just 33, was to hang around a team and chat shite.

So I chose not to.

So there probably was a loneliness there.

Your complete identity came from being a footballer. In 1994, on a wet, miserable day, I was taken off against Tyrone in Breffni as we exited the Ulster Championship. And I knew that was it.

I threw my gloves into the crowd and disappeared down the tunnel.

When you retire, no matter how you got to that point, there is a massive vacuum to be filled. And for GAA players it's a very complicated experience. Talking with others since, I wasn't alone in going through that process.

At the end of the day, we are still amateur players. But in what other amateur sport do you get to play in front of 70,000 spectators? And so many cross channel Premier League players struggle with that same sudden change.

Even with all their millions in the bank, they struggle to replace that void and change of routine. In life terms, early- to mid-30s, you're in your prime. But in a sporting sense, you're on the way to the glue factory. And so many good GAA men have found that transition impossible to make.

I count myself as one of the lucky ones. But there are others, that when they didn't have that routine, their training schedule and so on... they simply crumbled. For most, I do believe it's simply the camaraderie of it all.

But for others, it's that thrill of running out onto the field in big championship games. I missed both of those things.

RETIREMENT IS AN interesting thing, or at least the process of what you go through in your own head is anyway. There are a heap of different ways you can go. You can walk about the pubs talking about how great you were… the glory days. And you'll get plenty of people slapping you on the back and saying the same thing.

But you'll only be out the door and those same people will be laughing at you or calling you a bum. I know it. So much of that transition and that struggle simply isn't spoken about. All of a sudden, you find yourself at home on a Tuesday, Thursday or Friday evening and you've nowhere to go. And the discipline, that knowing there is a big game on Sunday brings, that is suddenly gone.

I threw myself into management right away. I took over the county minors in 1995. And it bridged a gap of sorts. I really enjoyed it. We had a great run and could possibly have won an All-Ireland. But we came a cropper to Laois in the semi-finals. It was a great learning curve, seeing things from that side of the fence.

I'm content now and, funnily enough, politics, and being a county councillor, and a Supervisor with Údarás na Gaeltachta, it's not a nine to five job. But I don't mind the late calls because again, I have something to focus on, to keep busy with. Even throughout the pandemic, there were countless calls and Zoom meetings to get through each week. And golf… golf has been brilliant, a real saviour. I took it up, like so many do, and I love it.

Again, I might be away at eight in the morning on a Saturday or a Sunday and it's something that I want to be fresh for. It's competitive and it means I'll head onto bed at a reasonable time the night before. It brings routine. It's a fantastic social outlet.

I often came back in after playing a round at Portnoo and I could have 20 missed calls on my phone. But they aren't missed calls because I'm still in bed nursing a hangover or that I'm hiding under the duvet. I leave it behind that one time of the week. That's my schedule on a Saturday. Because if I'd nothing to do on a Saturday, I'd still be wide awake at seven in the morning.

You can only watch one Premier League game before you get bored. And I can't watch TV all day anyway. I'm just not that person. So what do you do? I have to get out of the house. And for me, without routine and some structure in my week, out of the house would be over the town. And again, that's not because of a want for alcohol.

And I'm not lonely. I just feel restless and bored.

And the devil makes work for idle hands.

SOMETHING THAT I have struggled with in the past is seasonal depression. And I don't use that word lightly or carelessly. I dread the days and nights closing in because it plays havoc with my routine. Because of the shortened periods of daylight, I can't get out on my bike. I won't cycle at night because I'm petrified I'll get knocked down.

I had one or two moments like that and, the truth is, it's just not the same in the dark. I love looking around me, taking in the scenery and even stopping along the way for chats. November is a difficult month and it takes me a wee while to get a handle on things. But I do always get a handle on things.

In some way, I'll still struggle somewhat until the thing starts to change and brighten up once more around March time.

It's November 2021 now as we speak. And the process of putting this book together has really only taken off. And fair play to Frank and the patience he's shown all summer trying to pin me down. But I've intentionally thrown myself into things at a greater pace these past few weeks. I'm enjoying it.

I've also taken up a new task. I'm refreshing my Irish. My Irish is at a good standard but it used to be even better. So I'm reading and reading. I've a few new text books 'as Gaeilge' and I also have my trusty Foclóir for the times I might come on a word I struggle with. And I can easily get lost in that enjoyable task for two to three hours.

As the world continues to change at a serious pace there are so many new words to learn! If I didn't have simple structure like that I might decide to wander over the town to see what's going on. And the funny thing is, there is never anything really going on, especially at this time of year.

The GAA, to be fair to them, and especially the GPA, they have both really pulled their socks up with these types of struggles and there is help and assistance there now. And it's very discreet, which is a good thing. But again, for a particular generation, that wasn't always the case.

I'D SOMETHING LIKE eight surgeries, over all, on my knees. In the end, they were in horrendous shape. Dr Austin O'Kennedy, our team doctor with Donegal back then will say, to this day, that they were as bad as he's seen.

In the end, in 2008, it was time to have the left one replaced. All of those previous operations were funded by my own insurance and the county board also helped out when I was playing. I was an asset to them at one stage. This time out, I was given the choice of attending the Mater Private or to wait for a year. And the cost of this operation at the Mater, one of the best facilities for that kind of thing, was over €20,000.

I was well and truly on the scrapheap now with my own county board. So they didn't care. There was no interest there. I was in severe pain and riddled with arthritis.

I believed I'd the best personal premium cover at the time so I went ahead with the private appointment. But it turned out that only three-quarters of the bill was actually covered and there was a surplus of around seven or eight grand.

I began receiving solicitors' letters from the hospital. And they soon began to pile up. It caused me great stress and anxiety. I'd given my life to the GAA, and as it turned out, I'd also given my knees. But in my late-40s, I could barely walk. I eventually turned to Dessie Farrell and the GPA. And to be fair, that was the last I heard about it.

The GPA is there for everyone to use, and in so many capacities. And while I haven't used it, I hear counselling and help for different addictions or even struggles like retirement are all in place now as well. It's often kept under wraps but so many players have gone off the deep end... but because of this help now, many have been pulled back from that dangerous brink.

The great thing about the modern game, and even society in general, is that people are talking much more. There isn't that embarrassment or even shame now of hiding hurt. Young people today, they have a much better grasp on all of that. And that's brilliant. But my generation, they still need that little nudge or push to go and find the help and assistance that is out there.

I WAS LUCKY to have got 1992.

My knees at that stage, they were bone on bone. I, at least, have something to show for my efforts and pain. Austin O'Kennedy... I owe a lot of people but I owe the 'Doc' especially. He had a medical side but he also had a sporting empathy and he patched me up, at times no doubt against his better professional judgement. I was advised on more than one occasion to retire. But I'm so grateful I hung on in there.

I probably was angry or a little lost at the time, when I did eventually stop playing. But today, it's only good memories and a real appreciation of what I have and what I did. So many Donegal players before and after have nothing.

I look at Mayo and their almost eternal suffering. Just think of all the Mayo players that have moved on but no doubt must still sit and reflect on so many near misses and disappointments. I'm at a good place.

When I look back it's with fond memories and when I look around me or dare to look ahead, I hope for or anticipate mostly good things.

Again, you can never look too far ahead.

You just don't know when the rug will be pulled out from under you. 'Man plans and God laughs...' I don't know who said that, but it's so true. All anyone can really do is take it one day at a time and try to enjoy it.

That's my intention also.

PART TWO »

« CHAPTER 4 »

*'A bad day in New York is better than a
good day anywhere else'*

– Unknown

FROM THE VERY first moment I set foot on American soil, I fell in love with it. To a young and wide-eyed country lad, it instantly gripped me.

The truth is, even from afar, it always had a real lure. I loved watching old westerns growing up, but by the early-80s, my attention turned to gritty action flicks with skyscrapers, fast cars, beautiful women, adventure and danger lurking around every corner, with Tubbs and Crockett sorting a lot of it out on a weekly basis.

America just seemed like the place to be.

Of course, so many people's reality was that they were simply left with little or no choice but to leave. Our country was on its knees in terms of employment at the time and America was 'The Land of Opportunity'.

IT HAD TAKEN me a little longer than I expected, but in late September of 1983, less than a week after Ardara had been beaten by St Eunan's in that year's county final, I first stepped off the plane and into John F Kennedy Airport. I'd already made it further than I had ever imagined… certainly much further than it looked like I was going to make it just 24 hours earlier.

Word had only been sent to me on the Thursday morning that I was being called upon by the Donegal club in New York. And they needed me togged and ready to go on the Saturday. There was no time to waste. I was as green as the hills outside my bedroom window. But I felt my experiences of living and working in Dublin would stand to me in the 'City That Never Sleeps'. So I wasn't too nervous leaving Donegal Town that morning on the bus. I'd a suitcase, my passport and some dollars that were sent over to me by Liam, Connie, Frank and Lanty, who were now all well settled Stateside.

First, I had to make a quick dash to Portlaoise to pick up some of my remaining belongings that I'd left behind. My 'going out' clothes so to speak, the gear that had served me so well in the dance halls down there would have to be taken with me if I was to make an impression on the other side of the Atlantic. I can laugh now, looking back, at the innocence of the provisions I was making for my big trip.

I needed somewhere to stay on the Thursday night before I departed on the Friday afternoon. I also needed to be careful with my money. And there was only one man to call when you were in a jam in Dublin City... Jamesie O'Donnell, a brother of Donegal's most famous crooner Daniel, who was already a well set up businessman in the capital in the early 80s. Over the years, he's owned some of the most popular bars in Dublin and he's been a real friend to so many Donegal folk that now call it home.

Jamesie is very proud of his family's musical heritage and his sister Margo is also a household name in country music. But Jamesie is a much different character to both his sister and brother. He's a serious GAA man and loves the craic. I bunked down on Jamesie's couch that night and, in the morning, he had a huge cooked breakfast ready for me. I showered and dressed but as I reappeared in his kitchen doorway, he wasn't impressed.

'What in under God are you wearing?'

I'd on what I thought were a good pair of jeans and a battered enough looking pair of runners, I suppose, and a jumper I'd gotten for Christmas. Jamesie, to his credit, took me down the street and purchased me a brand new outfit. 'Smart trousers, shirt and shoes,' he told the shop assistant.

It probably cost close to one hundred old Irish pounds and that was a hell of a lot of money at the time. Jamesie then drove me to the airport and – almost by the hand – led me to the last possible area he'd permission to pass through.

And then, I was on my own.

I had a few pints to settle the nerves and, soon enough, I was on a plane for the very first time. I watched a film or two, ate whatever I could and had another few drinks. I was in my element. Eventually, we touched down on the far side. Connie was there to meet me and, all of a sudden, as those big airport doors opened, it was as if the dial on life had suddenly been cranked up to an unsafe level. That's the only way I can describe it. For a moment, it was overwhelming. It was a jungle that I stepped out into. Manners go out the window and you have to push for absolutely everything.

You literally have to push for space, and we had to push for a taxi. At times, you have to push your luck or you'll simply get trampled on or left behind.

Connie laughed and told me to get used to it… 'There's more where that just came from'. The big brother had obviously left his manners well and truly behind him at this stage as well, as he'd one of those big yellow taxis stopped dead in front of him in no time. Expletives were exchanged with one or two disgruntled individuals flagging the same ride but, it seems, Connie had also broadened his vocabulary since I'd last seem him!

We eventually made our way in towards the city, me looking out the window in awe. I was suddenly seeing the pace of everything from a much more placid vantage point, slowly finding my bearings. And I learned pretty quickly, from my airport experience, that this was just the way it was there. Connie was living in the Bronx at the time and there was a bit of a welcoming party with so many familiar faces from home gathered at the Forge Bar, Fordham Road, just down the street. There was food, music and just this seriously exciting vibe to it all. Foamy headed draft beer was being served in huge frosted glasses they kept in the fridge and, to a young and impressionable 21-year-old, this was the big time.

It was late or early even, depending on how you want to look at it, when we eventually made our way back down to the apartment. On the way, we were able to lean in small windows and order pizza and Chinese food… from the street, with portions that would feed a small army. So much of it was still on the table and floor when the sun started to rise around 6.30 that same morning.

I probably had two or three hours sleep. But I needed to shake myself.

It was September and temperatures in the mid-70s Fahrenheit were, I was told, on the milder side of what they're used to at the height of summer.

I showered and attempted to eat a big pan of eggs and toast that Connie had rustled up. To be fair, I came around pretty quickly and it was tiredness more than anything that was weighing me down as we finally made our way over towards the famous Gaelic Park. I'd heard so much about the venue… now I was finally going to see it for myself.

TO SAY I was disappointed and initially underwhelmed by this almost mythical ground would have been an understatement. It could have best been described as ramshackle. Our dressing-room had no windows and the lights didn't work.

There was a one-tap shower at the very back of it, if you were brave enough to go find it. It just felt like a massive let down, a lie even. Slowly but surely though, as the stands started to fill up, it's real magic and aura finally became apparent. It was now an arena.

And the noise, colour, people and smells were what lifted it. It camouflaged its many imperfections as opponents Sligo rolled in through the big old gates. I was told it was a Junior Championship game that lay ahead of me.

I'd just played in an All-Ireland Senior Championship semi-final… I felt… *I'm already big stuff.* And thinking this might be a little beneath me. But there is a pecking order in New York and as well as the brought in talent from home or, should I say, 'bought in', there are also a number of permanent fixtures that just don't get moved on or to the side all that easily. That's just the way it was in New York.

Connie was quick to tell me that there was no real distinction made between the two sides in America. 'It's not like home… they are senior and junior in name only'. Mickey Niblock – a Derry football legend – was named in the middle of the field for Sligo. Mickey was not just a man whose name had been written into Oak Leaf footballing folklore, he was also a household name on both the American GAA and soccer scenes. He was in his late-thirties, at least, at this stage, maybe even early forties.

But he took me to the absolute cleaners that day.

He landed me on the drum of my back straight from throw-in and I never really recovered. I spent most of the remainder of the match coughing up blood. To be fair to Mickey, there wasn't any dirt involved. I don't think he was that kind of player. Or maybe it was just the fact that on that particular day, he didn't have to stoop to that level.

I would, in the years that followed, find out that the rules of gaelic football weren't applied with any real authority in America. It was an often thuggish and lawless battleground where just about anything went. But Mickey just seemed to take pity on me that afternoon. The humidity meant I spent the entire game gasping for air.

'Keep up pup!' was all that Mickey would really ask of me.

We lost the game and I was back home the following week. But I'd gotten a taste for it. Next time, I promised myself, I wouldn't be as green on or off the park.

It would be the guts of three years before I finally made my return to America. This time out, I sourced work through Connie, who was a carpenter, and had decided to give it three months. Tom Conaghan had just stepped up to replace Brian McEniff as Donegal boss back home and he'd made it clear to me before I left that I was a big part of his plans. But this was something I'd waited for.

As fleeting as it was, I'd loved everything about my first experience of New York, bar the football. I was older now and somewhat wiser. I was definitely a better player. But things had ramped up a level or two there as well with some serious acquisitions made ahead of that summer.

The Donegal manager in New York, Donal Gallagher, nicknamed 'The Veteran', had done well for himself in America and wanted to put the team back on the footballing map that side of the pond. He was an accountant by trade but also owned what must have been a very profitable business in the Catskills called 'Guaranteed Irish'. They stocked everything from home and it never cooled. All the essentials from the Emerald Isle could be purchased there. He was a shrewd individual. Originally from Killybegs, Donal emigrated to the US back in the 1960s. But in 1985, he spread an ambitious net far and wide and managed to haul together some of the best players in Ireland. They won the championship that year, edging past Sligo after a replay.

But Donal didn't rest on his laurels and the following summer, 1986, some more of the worst 'carpenters' America must surely have even seen, including myself, were flown out in a bid to go back-to-back in the New York Championship. And that boldness paid off as we steamrolled towards the title, downing a pretty impressive Cavan by 3-10 to 1-3 in the final. That Cavan team possessed 13 county players at the time, with three All-Ireland winners in the form of Kerry's Ger Power, Gerry Carroll of Offaly and Meath's Bernard Flynn. But on that day, we simply blew them away.

Besides the Donegal 1992 All-Ireland winning team, this was the best group I ever had the pleasure to be part of. It was dripping with pure class.

The side that annihilated Cavan that day was: Kevin Nolan (Kildare); Dennis Kilbridge (Kildare), PJ Buckley (Dublin), Cathal Campbell (Donegal); Eunan McIntyre (Donegal), Eugene McNulty (Down), Lanty Molloy (Donegal); Anthony Molloy (Donegal), Pauric Dunne (Offaly); Dave Synnott (Dublin), Larry Tompkins (Cork), Kevin Madden (Carlow); Anthony Collins (Cork), Pat O'Toole (Wicklow), Martin Connolly (Cork).

Over the next few seasons as we came and went, the likes of Jack O'Shea, Ross Carr, Pat Spillane, Aidan Wiseman of Louth, Ciaran Power from Waterford and Martin McHugh would all be added to the late-80s mix as Donegal dominated in the Big Apple. And lads that you wouldn't have heard of at home, or at least seldom came across… players like Wiseman and Power, they were often the best players on the team.

The Donegal club gave those fellas the chance to prove and show just how good they were. And as for Tompkins… Larry will tell you openly that there would have been no switch from Kildare to Cork had it not been for Donegal in New York.

LARRY, KILDARE CAPTAIN at the time, came out in 1985 as part of that year's All Star tour and ended up staying on. Work was scarce at home, but Donal soon sorted all of that. On the promise that a return flight would be there for him, Larry did go home to play for Kildare in the Leinster Championship that same year, but after losing to Meath in the semi-final, the Kildare County Board reneged on an earlier arrangement.

But Donal once again stepped up to the plate and Larry would make New York his permanent home for a few years. During that time he became huge friends with Castlehaven and Cork pair Anthony Collins and Martin Connolly. When the boys eventually decided to return home to play with their club they somehow managed to convince Larry to come too.

That's all it really was at the time.

But the rest, as they say, is history.

In fact, if the Donegal County Board had any real foresight at the time, Larry could even have ended up turning out in the green and gold of Tír Chonaill. It was mentioned, and Donal had that kind of influence. But it was something that our gang at home didn't even think of pursuing.

Larry was a physical specimen. And as well as being a ferocious trainer, I'd often spot him heading around the block – gear bag on shoulder – to the local gym. He was lifting weights at the time... this was 1986! Don't forget, the Donegal senior football panel, and only when Jim McGuinness came in, didn't start proper strength and conditioning programmes until 2010. Tompkins was so far ahead of his time.

What he must have learned and picked up in those gyms was probably priceless. I went one day. It was an intimidating mix with all types of individuals going through various routines. And every single one of them looked really angry. It was a gritty setting. There was a strange but almost hypnotic rhythm as in the Cuban corner, a boxing gang skipped and took turns on the speed bag. I didn't stick it out. I was more of a laps man... around a park, and that just wasn't going to change. Besides, New York was there to be discovered and I needed my spare time to do that.

'The Veteran' had an apartment down on 234 Street on Broadway. It was kept exclusively for lads coming out. The likes of Tompkins, O'Shea and Spillane all stayed there. There could be as many as 10 big strapping men in there at any one time in this compact two-bedroom apartment. The lads didn't mind that though because it was free. The heat was that bad, all you really needed was a sheet on the mattress. But it wasn't just footballers Donal looked out for, he looked after plenty of others from home too, folk who either fell by the wayside or were just down on their luck.

And Gaelic Park was a huge part of that.

I've no doubt Gaelic Park saved people. It saved unemployed people surely, who knew that they'd find some kind of work if they showed up there and mixed. Someone always knew someone looking for extra help. But more importantly I feel, it helped save lonely and lost people. No one was ever left on the street. You hear so much about the great success stories of the Irish in America. Believe me, there were just as many tragic and sad tales back then too, but nowhere near as many as there would have been had it not been for the likes of the GAA, Gaelic Park... and men like Donal Gallagher.

Away from home, like we all were, you genuinely needed the help of others to get by, to survive. And that bonds people in a very special way. I made some serious friends in New York because of all that. There was this real camaraderie and joy to it all. Work was so much different to what you'd experienced at home. The talk at lunch or break centred on things like unions, blue and white collar, medicare… so much of it all passed over my head at the time.

No one really kept tabs on you either or what you were doing. The numbers on site, on any given day, were astronomical. You took your gear bag in the morning and straight after finishing up time, you headed for Van Cortlandt Park. We were run into the ground there. The bars would be hopping as we walked home with music blaring outside of them. Ladies of the night stood nearby and all kinds of shady looking characters lurked in the shadows. You had to have your wits about you every single second.

It was an eye opener on so many levels. But I quickly fell into the swing of things. I found New York so easy to navigate around. It was actually easier to get around than Dublin was or still is. You jumped on the subway and A went to B… B went to C, and so on. The only man I ever remember getting lost or going missing was Spillane!

There were no mobile phones at that time and just as a search party was about to be sent out for the Kerryman, he thankfully turned up. Pat was just off the plane at the time and as a sort of 'get to know the lads' type of gesture, we took him to a place called the Celtic House on Broadway. The place was owned by two more really influential movers in New York football circles, Mike Cassidy (RIP) and Danny Doohan (RIP). It turned into an almighty session and as we moved on through the night somehow Pat got left by the wayside. He wasn't best pleased about his ordeal, but he eventually thawed by the time we met up again for training.

Pat was one of those that often just flew in for the weekend, played a game and flew back home on the Monday. But he was another one that was great craic and full of mischief. And again, when else would I have had the chance to get to know him had it not been for Donegal in New York? From 1983 right up until '93, I travelled over. New York is so big, but for the Irish at that time so small also. We went to the same three or four bars, ate in the same places and had our own little beaten patch of it that we rarely strayed from.

I'M SURE A lot of those lads were rewarded with more than just work for coming out and playing in America. I know they were. At the height of the madness, serious money was both generated and spent by the New York clubs. You might have close to 2,000 people at a dinner dance back then.

Gaelic Park just couldn't facilitate that. So it was usually pushed out to some sort of catering hall on the fringes of the city. And something about those places always seemed off. I was told many years later that those halls were often mob owned and run. But they were well run and probably represented the best value for money at that time. Some of the top fly in/fly out stars, usually the Kerry ones, would be put up in Times Square, both they and their partners. They would have the best tickets for the top Broadway shows and would have had reservations in the best restaurants nearby. And I'm sure they'd get some kind of envelope on the Sunday evening, before they'd be sent on their way once more.

But the truth is, and I've no reason to lie about it, all I ever received to go to New York was the price of my flight. Even in 1992, as the All-Ireland winning captain, that didn't change. My Uncle Jimmy McGonagle paid for that early on. Like so many, Jimmy was also forced to emigrate in the 1960s.

Jimmy, along with my brother Lanty, opened the famous Sam Maguire's in Riverdale in the 80s and, just a few short years after, they were very proud men to see their own nephew and brother walk through the front door with the real thing. Jimmy served as club president there on a number of occasions and was one of the Donegal club's real cornerstones. Sadly, Jimmy passed away in November of 2012. He was 72 years old. But shortly before he died, he got his hands on Sam one final time when Jim McGuinness brought the cup over, just a few weeks after Donegal had rescaled the All-Ireland mountain.

I'd win a second New York Championship in 1992, just three weeks after our All-Ireland triumph. As well as myself, Declan Bonner, Tommy Ryan and Tony Boyle all made that season's trip. We'd account for Connemara Gaels in a very close decider, 0-10 to 1-6. The game itself had to be played at Rockland County, about 40 minutes north of the city, as Gaelic Park was having some much-needed redevelopment work done. Tony, Tommy and Declan accounted for eight of our 10 points. And Paddy Hegarty, a brother of Noel's, who would go on to play senior football for Donegal, came off the bench to kick the winning point.

That side lined out as follows: Andy McGovern (Donegal); Michael Moynihan (Kerry), Vincent Hatton (Wicklow), Niall Cahalane (Cork); Eddie Fitzsimons

(Antrim), Michael Brosnan (Kerry), Jim Donoghue (Wexford); Anthony Molloy (Donegal), John 'Cookie' Meehan (Donegal); Declan Bonner (Donegal), Tony Boyle (Donegal), Murt Fleming (Wexford); Declan McNicholl (Derry), Tommy Ryan (Carlow), Leslie McGettigan Donegal). Sub used: Paddy Hegarty.

Of course we celebrated the win with an almighty party. We were scheduled to fly back into Belfast on the Monday night. We'd only got back going the week previously at home, with Donegal against Kildare in the National League. McEniff and the boys had gone to London with Sam the same weekend we went west and they had also arranged a few games in Ruislip.

But the American quartet were under strict orders to be back home in time for training that Tuesday ahead of a second league outing away to Carlow.

Our flight out of Kennedy Airport didn't depart until seven that evening so naturally enough we were all back in Sam Maguire's early on the Monday. Our Monday, shenanigans were nothing out of the ordinary. And I'd done it countless times in the past. But I'd always make those flight doors, sometimes by the skin of my teeth, and soon enough be settling back into my seat heading back across the water.

This time out, the craic was seriously good. We were All-Ireland champions and we were really enjoying ourselves and all the extra attention and rounds. With time getting short, the four of us Donegal players squeezed into a taxi bus with our bags... which had been sitting upstairs in Sam Maguire's all day. Traffic was particularly heavy and our driver was really struggling to make his way through it.

We eventually made it to the airport and arrived at the gate. It looked like we were just going to make it. Flustered and a little merry, someone, not me, said something that wasn't well received by the lady at the desk. And whatever chance we might have had of getting aboard that plane was suddenly gone. Rearrangements had to quickly be made and we finally got home on the Thursday with a very angry Donegal boss to contend with.

Believe it or not, myself and McHugh were back on a plane in early December with Sam Maguire strapped between us as part of a whistlestop tour of the east coast. It was a trip arranged by Donal Gallagher, at very short notice, and we visited four cities in six days... Boston, New York, Philadelphia and Chicago were all hit.

It was absolutely mental. Before we departed, we looked to get a hold of Sam but it was already booked for elsewhere. There was absolutely no point in landing in America without the cup. Michael Gillespie was a Kilcar club man and a former Donegal GAA chairman. He was also a high up figure in the GAA at this stage.

MCHUGH GOT IN contact with him and he pulled a few strings around Croke Park and somehow managed to smuggle the old or original Sam Maguire out of Jones' Road for us to take with us! The night before we flew out, I'd to take the cup up in Faughanvale in Derry. Later that same evening, we'd to be at a function in Meath. With Columba Diver driving, we landed in Derry at 7pm. We were due in Meath at 11, but we only got away from Derry at that time.

There was severe frost, but we finally arrived in Navan at 1.30 in the morning. We managed to get a few hours' sleep… then it was off to the airport to catch a flight to Boston. Now, myself and McHugh had talked about maximising our earning ability when in America. But Boston, the first night anyway, caught us on the hop.

It was bedlam. We must have stood for over a thousand photos.

The photographer was getting on our nerves. With a huge flash attached to his camera, he kept repeating, 'Watch the lens… no blinking'. I was that blinded… I was constantly blinking. I'd love to see some of those photos today.

The next night, there was another function but this time we were ready. We were getting 10 dollars a photograph… and 20 for signed balls! And a batch of t-shirts that Donal had organised also arrived. From Boston it was onto Chicago, then Philly before finally hitting New York.

It was an extremely stressful six days. But bar the first night, it was also an extremely profitable six days. We were flush. On our second last night, in the Big Apple, the cup suddenly went missing. We'd taken a break signing and standing for photographs in Sam Maguire's pub and when we got back to the table the thing was gone.

Sam has a bit of a habit of getting lost in New York. I believe Kerry also misplaced it in 1980, while the Dubs were also parted from her on their visit in 2018.

Thankfully, after an eight-hour absence, the search party was called off when Sam eventually reappeared. I never really got to the bottom of what had exactly happened. But our 'inside' man at HQ, Michael Gillespie, wouldn't have been best pleased had we got back home without the original Sam Maguire!

THIRTY YEARS DOWN the line, so much has changed in regards to gaelic football and that whole American adventure. The likes of what we experienced, at that time of life, just won't be seen again. The stealth and leeway that existed for players, you just don't have that any more. The world is a much smaller place. And things have got to such a serious level at both club and county here at home, that America just isn't on anyone's radar now.

It certainly isn't for the cream of the crop.

I go back as often as I can. I have so many family and friends still there, including four brothers... Connie, Frank, Columba and Lanty. Connie is managing the Donegal team there, while Frank, 'The Chief', remains a huge presence around Gaelic Park. And Columba is still the main ticket seller at the venue. Over there, it's lovely to bump into people, unexpectedly, and just reminisce and look back at some of the shenanigans we got up to. The lure of going over and that wee buzz I still get is just as strong as it ever was the first time out, even without the football.

Again, I believe that is because of the 24/7 nature of the city. I don't waste a minute. I don't get bored. Whether it's four in the morning or four in the afternoon, I can take a little wander and just pass the time. Believe it or not, so much of that time isn't spent in the pub. I can stop for a coffee, some food or just drift along the streets and avenues for a walk. I do wonder how things might have panned out had I decided early on, like so many of my family, to throw my lot in with America and had looked to make a life there. There would have been no All-Ireland for me, of that I'm certain.

What kind of life would I have made for myself there?

But the truth is, and I can say this without any doubt in my mind, lifting Donegal's first All-Ireland title and the joy it brought to an entire county, is the single greatest thing I've ever done.

And while I bounce around a few 'What ifs' I still come to the same conclusion that sticking it out at home was the right decision. I believe the reason that America remains so special to me is that I continue to dip in and out.

Life's hardships don't get left behind simply because you up sticks and go somewhere else. The significant ones will still find you.

Anthony's education as a footballer began early with the Ardara senior team in 1978 (top), and continued with the Donegal club in New York, where he won his first NY Championship in 1986 (bottom). And two men who would teach him so much about life and the game were Larry Tompkins and Donal Gallagher (photographed in 2020) in New York where Anthony enjoyed a 10-year 'career' with the Donegal team in the Big Apple.

« CHAPTER 5 »

'You build on failure. You use it as a stepping stone'
– Johnny Cash

WE REGROUPED TOWARDS the end of 1983 intent on drawing a line under the past. We'd raised the bar and we were determined to hit the ground running. The usual noise… yes, but we were firmly targeting promotion from Division 3. Ardara had made it all the way back to a county final but in a poor game, and St Eunan's would defeat us 0-8 to 0-3.

There was a gap in the calendar, and I saw it as a chance to finally experience America and New York City.

But we were right back down to business with Donegal in October. And from our five pre-Christmas outings, we won four and lost just one. Wicklow, Laois and Clare were all accounted for at home. In two away trips, we downed Westmeath but lost out to old foes Monaghan, the only blip on our record. Still, we were joint top of the pile and firm words were had on December 4, after toppling Clare in Ballybofey, that we couldn't afford to let our guard down again and make the same mistakes we'd made over the previous Christmas.

'Enjoy yourselves, but don't tear the f***ing arse out of it!' said Pauric McShea as we departed MacCumhaill Park.

I don't know about the rest of the lads but I did enjoy myself and, to be honest, there were quite a few nights that I did 'tear the f***ing arse out of it'. But I felt that Pauric's words were more for the ears of a few of the longer toothed members of the squad. There were men there now well into their thirties and they just couldn't get away with the same craic we were getting away with or, that they used to get away with.

The acid test, post-Christmas, the game where we'd find out exactly where we were at was against Antrim… Casement Park on February 5, 1984. I'd had another knee scope in early January and had to make do with a late appearance in off the bench. And, suffering a 1-6 to 0-8 loss, it was pretty obvious that I wasn't the only one that overindulged in the 'off' period. It was a dire showing. And it meant that our promotion chances hinged completely on our final game away to Carlow. With the stakes high, we blew them away by 2-11 to 0-3. Still, we initially felt that would only secure a promotion play-off clash with Wicklow, our nearest rivals in the table for second spot. However, they could only draw with Westmeath, so it would be ourselves joining Monaghan in making the jump to Division 2.

We'd another encouraging enough McKenna Cup campaign with wins over Armagh and Antrim taking us into the final. The McKenna Cup was still big enough stuff back then, well big enough to coax two of my good friends John 'Baker' Boyle and John T. Murrin to drive up the road to the famous old Antrim venue for the semi-final.

NOW, WE'RE TALKING about 1984 here, and Belfast.

But the two boys were undeterred. Most of the lads were straight out of there after they'd showered. But I'd decided I'd get a lift back down with 'Baker' and John T.

I could take a few cans with me without fear of reprimand or judgement. They'd be much quicker and we'd be back in the safe sanctuary of Donegal Town before the rest were even halfway home. But of course, the two lads were already in the bar by the time I'd got cleaned up. What was there to do, only join them.

I'd kicked three points in a pulsating 1-10 to 2-6 win and I was on a bit of a high. I deserved a few pints, or so I felt. Some Antrim lads, the likes of Mickey Darragh and Kevin Gough had coaxed them in as they'd waited outside the dressing-room doors. So I land in as well. We'd a great few hours and the conversations grew deeper as time went on. I loved my football but it was still very much a pastime to me at that stage of my life. But the GAA, and playing gaelic football, meant the world to those Antrim men.

It actually meant *everything*. The laughing and joking about the previous 60 minutes soon subsided and I vividly remember leaning in and just listening.

Donegal, of course, hugs Derry, Tyrone and Fermanagh, but for the large majority of us back then, ignorance was still very much bliss in relation to the Troubles and the harrowing events taking place in the 'Six Counties'. But it was a very palpable and potent ingredient, which I often felt we were battling with and against, any time we crossed the border. It had to have been a factor for those sides. I've made plenty of friends over the years, lads who played for the various counties there.

And playing football was a big part of what kept them going in those dark years.

We'll never know what those boys went through. Going to and from training, the same buckos in their armoured wagons would stop them two, sometimes three times on the one night. They'd be put out of the car again and their gear emptied out of the boot and onto the ground by the same individuals. By in large, we never really experienced the Troubles in Donegal. And thanks be to God we didn't. But there are some horrific stories of what went on there at the time. And for the GAA community in the North, it was pure intimidation. But it must surely have driven those teams on.

But, it was a brilliant few hours spent with the Antrim boys and it gave a young and innocent enough me a little more sense and understanding of the conflict there and what their identity as GAA people meant to them. It was powerful stuff and it was a badge that had to be worn proudly and, as the lads explained, sometimes defiantly.

THE MCKENNA CUP final against Tyrone was fixed for May 12 in Irvinestown. In a poor game, they held the slight upper-hand at the break, 0-4 to 0-3. However, with the likes of Plunkett Donaghy, Damien O'Hagan and Eugene McKenna in particular to the fore, we were eventually beaten 3-7 to 1-4. We'd the guts of a month to prepare for the trip to the Athletic Grounds to take on Armagh.

It was a difficult start to the defence of our Ulster crown but one we felt we were good enough to get over. We were provincial champions and there certainly wasn't any fear of going up there. In fact, I couldn't wait. My trip to Belfast and the conversations we had after meant I was now intrigued by what was going on in Armagh as well. We upped the ante as usual in the weeks in between, but approaching the game, Martin was struggling with a hamstring complaint.

Still, on the Thursday night before going our separate ways, there was hope, or at least there seemed to be, that Martin would make it. Anyway, Sunday arrived and we were scheduled to meet up in Donegal Town. Arriving at the hotel I was surprised to see Gerry Curran of Aodh Ruadh in the vicinity. He must have been there to wish the other Ballyshannon men luck… or so I thought. Gerry was an excellent placed-ball kicker, deadly in fact for his club. But he hadn't been a part of the county squad all season. But with huge concerns still there over Martin's fitness, McEniff had drafted in a replacement.

On the morning of the game!

It certainly raised eyebrows, but we didn't really have time to digest or even discuss it as we departed for the Athletic Grounds. A decision had now been made on Martin. But it was a young Brian Murray that was given the nod to come in at wing half-forward, with Reid moving over to the centre. Still, Murray picked up a knock less than a quarter of an hour in and Gerry Curran, without a single county training session under his belt, was sprung!

We were trailing at that stage, marginally, at 0-2 to 0-1. But a penalty was awarded to us, after a ball I'd sent into the area was held onto for far too long by Armagh 'keeper Brian McAlinden. Seamus Bonner was usually so accurate from the spot but he scuffed his shot and it was easily stopped. The atmosphere at the ground had already turned at this stage and referee John Gough was under real pressure… the ugly type.

We surged ahead thanks to a couple of Sylvester Maguire efforts and a brace of points from Gerry Curran… yes Gerry! Like I said, they were spitting venom now from the terraces but Gerry's first two acts following his introduction was to saunter up to the ball and batter over a pair of almighty frees.

Things looked good approaching half-time as we led by four. But some slacking off in the final moments afforded John Coven and Brian Hughes opportunities to split the gap in two. And it was a lapse that would prove costly. Soon after things got going again, Gerard Houlihan goaled for the hosts and Coven clipped a pair of points. From two up, we'd suddenly found ourselves three down.

Two remained the gap, but going into the last quarter we were dealt a serious blow when Tommy McDermott was given his marching orders. The deficit was stretched to four by Armagh and, in between, we also lost Noel in goals with a young Gary Walsh coming on in his place. Armagh themselves then went down to 14 when Colin Harney was also flashed a red card.

With the playing field levelled once again, who was the man stepping up to kick three more serious frees… only Gerry. This was 'Roy of the Rovers' stuff from the Aodh Ruadh man and we were back to within one point of Armagh. We threw everything at those dying moments but we just couldn't force one more score to tie matters. Despite the fact that they'd just won, some eejit in the crowd hit the referee with a golf ball as he made his way off. It was a sour end to a hostile afternoon.

It was a cruel way to relinquish our Ulster title. But it is a game that will always stick in my mind for the simple reason that Gerry Curran appeared out of nowhere to kick five points in a 1-10 to 0-12 loss. Part of me felt a little relief at the end, even if it was just for Gerry. Imagine the backlash both Brian and probably he would have got, had that risk not paid off? It was a massive gamble. They'd have been castigated. Again, it's another example of just how much things have changed. Imagine a similar risk or stunt being undertaken in this day and age, by a top manager, the very day of a huge opening Ulster Championship game? But the truth is that both Brian and Gerry had done their bit. The shortfall, well the rest of us would have to take responsibility for that.

●

I QUICKLY GOT back at things with Ardara.

We'd qualified for our fourth county final in five seasons. It was the GAA's centenary year so the 1984 decider had even more meaning attached to it than usual. It would be extra special to lift the Dr Maguire Cup that year.

Along the way, we'd defeated Red Hughs and Killybegs to set up a semi-final with MacCumhaills. Connie and Lanty had flown home especially for the game and went straight into the team. And even though we were up against a side that had the likes of county stars Brendan Dunleavy, Martin Griffin and Michael Lafferty in it, we delivered one of the best club performances I've ever been involved in to dish out a 1-15 to 0-1 hammering. If our semi-final efforts were Trojan, our attempts to take home another county title in the decider were the exact opposite.

We were simply abysmal. We'd got off to a great start against Four Masters with Kieran Keeney goaling and young Patrick Gallagher hitting a point. But even though they would go a man down in the second-half when Seamus Meehan was sent off, the Donegal Town men would eventually win out by 0-9 to 1-2.

With the new NFL season approaching, and with Donegal up to Division 2, McEniff called a sort of get-together to thrash out plans for the new season. A few challenge games at various club pitch openings were also arranged. Our league campaign was due to begin in mid-October with an away trip to Roscommon at Dr Hyde Park. Against a good Rossies outfit, a side that would eventually secure promotion to Division 1 with a second place finish, we were so unfortunate not to get out of there with a win.

We'd made all the usual promises, as a group, beforehand. But this was Division 2, the gateway to the big time, and it felt different on the way out onto the field. We were 0-4 to 0-2 up at half-time and things looked good. We were two clear going into the last seconds of the game. Dermot Earley tapped over a close range free to half that, but there had been no major stoppages in the game and we expected the whistle to go.

On matters went, and the home side were awarded a free wide on the right and from a huge distance. Earley worked the 'give and go' with full-forward Eamon McManus but it was a laboured and low return which allowed a number of our defenders to close the man in possession down. With nowhere to go, Earley theatrically threw himself to the ground. It was an embarrassing piece of play acting that I was about to afford myself a chuckle to.

But to my utter amazement and shock, the referee bought it. Earley's 'performance' had won him a free much closer to goal and it meant that they tied the game up with the very last kick. We were absolutely fuming. But it was a lesson. The teams weren't just better in the second tier in a footballing capacity, they were also much cuter.

For some reason, we weren't scheduled to take on Mayo, our next opponents, until November 11. That was a full month away. What we needed and, even though we didn't realise it at the time... what our season needed, was an immediate follow up.

With the best part of four weeks to stew, the call once again came from the States. Donegal in New York were in the junior and senior finals and they needed some heavier artillery. So for the second year in-a-row, I decided to spend a few weeks in America living it up and playing a bit of football. A number of others like Martin, Joyce, Brendan Dunleavy and our captain Michael Lafferty also took bites out of the Big Apple in the four weeks in between. But in our absence and behind closed doors, an almighty storm was brewing back home.

The Donegal County Board hadn't been happy with this practice for a while and they felt it was finally time to make an example of someone or some people. But what they came up with was comical.

It was completely farcical.

Michael was stripped of the captaincy and the county executive, in their wisdom, also decided to deny the entire panel their travelling expenses between the start of November and Christmas. The correspondence delivered to the squad also added that, *Players will not be served their customary steak dinners after their twice weekly training sessions. All members of the panel must give the county board a written commitment of full loyalty to the team before the next match against Mayo in Ballybofey. Anyone who does not give that commitment will not be considered for the Mayo game.*

The county board chairman at the time, Michael Gillespie, said that the sanctions had the full support of Brian and his management team. I found that surprising as both Brian and Pauric McShea had probably set the original trend years before, that of going over to America to play. Anyway, the best place to clear the air and dismiss the hearsay and rumours, was behind the dressing-room door. And that's what we did. It was a storm all right but, in the end, one in a teacup.

We, the players, realised we had the ultimate leverage in these circumstances. And it was agreed to threaten to not field against Mayo if the board didn't back down. And at a subsequent and quick one-hour meeting between all three parties... the board, the team management and the players, the board yielded in their stance.

And the Saturday night before the Mayo game it was agreed that no further public comment, on the record at least, would be made by anyone on the matter and to simply move on.

And move on we did. In front of a sizeable crowd, no doubt intrigued by all the previous week's drama, we hammered Mayo, 1-13 to 1-5. Martin Shovlin had been introduced to senior football and played a blinder. The energy and directness of the Dunkineely man was simply astounding. We'd a number of lads like Reid and Joyce that came from an athletics background and were super fit. But Shovlin came in and was immediately on another level. From that point on, and right up until the moment he called it a day, Shovlin would run the very best of them into the ground.

In our final two away games before Christmas, we'd lose to both Offaly and Monaghan. I'd been used against Monaghan in a more advanced role at centre half-forward and I didn't like it. I didn't see the sense of it as I thought I'd held my own in the previous games at centrefield. We were now in real relegation bother.

As if things couldn't get any more difficult, the visitors to Ballybofey the following weekend, our last outing of the year, were Dublin. The Dubs had been beaten in the 1985 All-Ireland final by Kerry. For what felt like the umpteenth time, we thrashed things out between ourselves and again made one of those collective promises that we were going to prove our doubters wrong against the Dubs.

AND, ON AN emotionally charged afternoon, where we no doubt emptied ourselves, it looked like we were on the verge of giving a two-fingered salute to our many detractors. Despite Martin being denied from the spot by a brilliant John O'Leary save, we still managed to battle our way to a 1-4 to 0-6 lead coming up to the 60-minute mark. We'd felt aggrieved about the awarding of the penalty as Martin had already prodded the ball into the net before the whistle was blown. And the strike should have stood.

Regardless, Shovlin had been amazing up until that point and had already been awarded the official 'Man of the Match' as we approached full-time. But our Achilles heel, those all too frequent late lapses in concentration, was once again allowed to rear its head. And right at the very end, Barney Rock popped up to punch home a decisive goal. Dublin hadn't led the entire game and it had looked like an obvious square ball call. But it wasn't given.

So there Dublin were, inside a matter of a minute or two, celebrating the win. And like only Dublin could and ever did, they rubbed it in.

Above anyone else, they were the one team that always seemed to take great satisfaction in stealing wins. I don't know if there was an arrogance attached to some of it, but it stung. And it wouldn't be the first time they'd shove something like this, a real smash and grab, in our faces.

Well, they did for a number of seconds, but a baying and angry mob was already over the wire and making its way onto the field. And as quick as a flash, the gloating city boys were making a break for the sanctuary of the dressing-rooms. One man not prepared to yield or cower was Dublin midfielder Brian Mullins.

He seemed to have eyes in both the back and sides of his head, as he fended off invaders left, right and centre. He wasn't throwing any digs or jabs, he just simply tossed whatever obstacle was in his way, out of it.

Truth be told, it was quite impressive.

Someone who didn't have quite the same batting skills as Mullins was the match official. Brian, McEniff that is, was first on the scene to let him know exactly what he thought but a couple of yahoos quickly arrived by his side and things threatened to get out of hand. It was alleged that the referee was pushed, dragged or interfered with in some form or manner. Brian would eventually have to answer to the dreaded Games Administration Committee at Croke Park. They were the GAA's disciplinary body at the time and to this day, regardless of the guise, name or abbreviation they operate under, anyone that has sat in their company at Croke Park will tell you it's a very surreal and strange experience.

Their deliberations, interpretations and indeed verdicts are often puzzling and delivered with a real arrogance. You need to have your homework done, that is without question. But you also have to show a sort of subservient humility if you are to gain any sort of leverage on the possible outcome. From talking to lads that have gone to headquarters in recent years, to have their cases heard, that hasn't changed one bit.

Still, Brian was and still is cuter than most.

And with the aid of some video evidence... yes video evidence back in 1984, he not only showed that he didn't interfere with the match official, but it was, in fact, McEniff that actually intervened and pulled away the overzealous supporter that had managed to get a hold of the back of the referee's jersey.

Furthermore, the allegation that the incident or interaction between the pair had lasted five minutes was quickly eliminated as Brian, stopwatch in hand apparently, was able to clock his verbal interaction with the ref at a precise 52 seconds! Brian was a shrewd operator and much too cute for the crusty lawmakers at Croke Park.

Again, Christmas came and went and, thanks to Austin Coughlan's excruciating sessions on Inver Beach, so too did all the festive guts that we carried into the new year once more. Under car lights, we were back at it in mid-January. And we felt in good enough shape once again come the resumption of the National League on February 3.

Luckily, we were handed what felt like a soft enough reintroduction to competitive action with an away tie against Louth. But at St Brigid's Park in Dundalk, we'd suffer an embarrassing 0-10 to 0-8 loss. It was a performance described in the *Democrat* as our worst in 14 years and a, *'showing that has the potential to put our All-Ireland aspirations back by at least five years'*. I'd love to know what formula or metric the journalist used to come up with that conclusion.

But what was certain was that we were now in real danger of dropping back down to the third tier along with either the Wee County or Offaly. But the one thing about us, the most frustrating element to it all, was that we were just so damn unpredictable. And just a week later, against promotion-chasing Wexford, who had beaten Dublin the week previously, we delivered our best showing of the season to date to run out comfortable 1-12 to 0-6 winners. It meant that we'd forced a relegation play-off encounter with Louth, to be held in Clones. In what was an instantly forgettable and scrappy game, we edged matters by 2-7 to 0-5. We'd secured another year in Division 2 and that was important. But while the *Democrat* seemed to have some sort of idea, for the rest of us it was difficult to gauge exactly where we were at.

The Open Draw Cup – a sort of follow-up to the 1984 Centenary Cup – provided some distraction. We scored wins over the likes of Laois, Wicklow, Waterford and Fermanagh to set up a semi-final meeting with Cork at Croke Park. The Rebels would edge us out there by 0-10 to 1-6. It was nice to get a run out at headquarters but the truth is, we just didn't play well and the fact Cork were missing some of their better players meant we brought some underlying concerns away from Croker that afternoon.

We did manage to get our McKenna Cup campaign off to reasonable enough start with a five-point win over Derry, but the remainder of the competition was put on the long finger as our preliminary round Ulster Championship opener with Down came into focus. In front of 7,500 supporters, we delivered a serious performance.

Martin was majestic and kicked 1-7. We'd started really well and worked ourselves into 1-4 to 0-2 lead by the 20th minute. But a disastrous end to the first period meant they somehow went in at the break 2-4 to 1-4 up.

I'D STARTED THE game at wing half-forward once again, and it was the kind of thing that was really starting to bug me. I wanted to be in the middle… I was a bloody midfielder. It was thrashed out at the break that our late problems in the half had come from the middle sector.

And a decision was made to switch both myself and Michael Lafferty.

Big Griffin, who was also playing around the middle, gave me a wink and a nod going back out. And when Martin Griffin winked and nodded at you, it usually meant only one thing. It was time to bang some heads. We tore into the Down pairing of Liam Austin and Adrian McAulfield and we bossed that previous problem.

And from that point on, we were back in our earlier groove. *'Midfield had been a problem area for Donegal but the move of Molloy to there in the second-half rectified all of that,'* read the following Thursday's *Democrat*.

Anyway, a 2-12 to 2-8 win over the pre-game favourites meant we progressed on to meet Monaghan, in Castleblaney, in the first round. But, in what the local paper would label a *'shameful defeat'* a disastrous effort resulted in a 10-point drubbing. The truth is we allowed Monaghan, who would go on to win Ulster, to bully us. They pushed us around and because of that it was a *shameful* defeat, in more ways than one.

Speaking after, McEniff told the press it was a, *'Pathetic display'*.

He added that, *'If the problem is myself, I'll go. No one will have to tell me to go. I'll go myself. But I have to find out for myself what the issues are'*.

Unsurprisingly, Brian and his management team were now coming under real fire. But with the uncompleted McKenna Cup still to be played for, there would be no knee-jerk departure there. The pitchforks were well and truly out for Brian and he was already on record as saying he was considering his position. But our outstanding semi-final clash with Down was an immediate opportunity to shake things up a bit. Charlie Mulgrew was back in the fold having previously gone to America while serving a suspension, while the likes of Gary Walsh, who'd already made his championship debut at this stage, Martin Carlin, Declan Bonner and Manus Boyle all came into the fold.

Amazingly, an experimental Donegal team would put the Mournemen to the sword convincingly, 0-14 to 0-5. And the bounce from that encouraging win prompted Brian to announce he was staying on. And the naysayers were further silenced when the side, makeshift in the extreme, delivered Donegal its first McKenna Cup title in over a decade. Many of the established lads, including myself, were absent as our clubs were involved in the championship. So it definitely meant there were nerves and an uneasiness ahead of the 1986 season. But that had to be a good thing.

There may have, and understandably so, been a hesitancy by Brian to put some of the older brigade out to pasture. But the task of edging a few towards the door was now being forced upon him. And who would ever have imagined that a delayed McKenna Cup campaign, where he'd been forced to go with some fresh new faces, would once again buoy optimism within the county.

Seamus Bonner would depart, deservingly leaving with three Ulster medals in his back pocket. The likes of Lafferty, Keeney and Griffin would remain on but their game-time was, McEniff explained, going to be limited. Brian laid his cards out early and decisively. But there was no surprise when McHugh was handed the captain's armband for the new year. He'd earned it.

We'd five league games pencilled in for before Christmas, which mightn't have been a bad thing given our previous festive escapades. Things opened brightly with a 3-6 to 3-3 win away to Wexford. Although a 10-point lead late on was allowed to slip to just three in the final two minutes with a pair of late goal concessions.

I was again having some bother with my knee… nothing too serious but it was felt that a little break would be the best thing for it. Still, I didn't want to be sitting around too long and allow someone else to come in and make a name for themselves. Next up was a home clash with Mayo in Ballyshannon, All-Ireland semi-finalists the previous year, and I was again absent from matters. McEniff kept insisting, not just to me but quite a few others, that his intentions were to use the first number of league games to blood new players. But I was a little sceptical.

The wolves were at his door so he couldn't afford a bad start to matters. He just didn't have that luxury. And this was Division 2, the last port of call before Division 1, the place we always wanted to be.

McEniff has always had balls, even in the face of adversity. And I was concerned that this 'temporary approach', which was what he called it, was in fact one last ballsy and left of field roll of the dice. The fact that we held Mayo in a fantastic spectacle didn't ease my worries. In our third outing, we went to Cork and came away with a 2-4 to 1-6 win that put us top of the table.

Our enthusiastic and early bubble was finally burst by Dublin, at that most unhappiest of hunting grounds, Croke Park, when we went down by 0-15 to 0-8. It was a setback of sorts but for me, it at least meant that I might finally be given the green light to come back in. The knee, to be fair to McEniff, was responding brilliantly.

Again, he reassured me that I'd be in his plans when it really mattered.

Still, I was again made wait as Longford were easily swept aside in Ballybofey by 1-11 to 0-5. It was also a win that meant we broke for Christmas in second place in the standings, a point ahead of Dublin and just two behind leaders Mayo.

McEniff was a big fan of trial games and he continued to run A vs B encounters in the lead-up to Christmas, and even into January. He was leaving no stone unturned. My own clubmate Martin Gavigan was one of those that had caught the eye and I was delighted to read that he was one of the handful signalled out at the end of the entire process by McEniff.

I was also told that I was to finally be taken back into the mix. McEniff continued to make the right noises in the papers. But one headline in particular caught a lot of people's attention. *'Prohibition imposed on Donegal footballers,'* announced the *Donegal Democrat*.

'Drinking is out, totally,' Brian insisted, in the same newspaper article. *'People are going to have to measure up if they are to stay on this panel. After our recent talent-seeking exercise, I have plenty of young and hungry lads who will fight strongly for a place on both the team and panel. No one is assured of their place from here on in.*

WE WERE FINALLY scheduled to get back down to league business on February 3, of 1986, against Cavan at Breffni Park. Thirty players were summoned to a get-together in Bundoran and the word was that five more would get the cut as Brian and his management team settled on a final 25. It was a crucial juncture in the season. With just two league games left, we were all in little doubt that this was going to be the final opportunity for some to stake a claim ahead of the serious business of championship. And getting to Division 1 was firmly in our sights. As well as Gavigan and Kieran Keeney, Martin's younger brother Luke was also in the late mix. It was great from an Ardara perspective.

John Cunningham had already made his senior debut, but his cousin Barry was now also in the reckoning while other precocious underage talents like Manus and Declan Bonner had also made real impressions up until that point. I was back in the mix as well but if I was to get game time, it was going to be in off the bench late on. That's what I was told beforehand.

But a 2-7 to 0-7 shocker against Cavan, coupled with Dublin beating Galway, meant we would drop to third by the end of the day. It was another one of those abysmal showings that we seemed to serve up all too frequently. I got a late runout, but by that stage our goose was well and truly cooked. We'd need a minor miracle now if we were to be promoted.

Brian labelled the side's efforts a, *'disgrace to the county'*.

He pulled apart certain sections of the performance and one area that got it with both barrels was midfield. Truth be told, underneath it all, that probably meant the door could be instantly opened back up to me. But I was rusty and very short of match practice.

I was still named to start in our final league outing against the Tribesmen in Ballyshannon. I did okay and lasted right up until the 50th minute. But against an already relegated Galway we again had our struggles and actually found ourselves behind going into the final moments. Leslie McGettigan, who coincidently had just replaced myself, managed to get himself on the end of a McHugh run and fired in the goal that would snatch the victory, 2-8 to 1-10.

We were straight into a McKenna Cup campaign that yielded an opening 0-14 to 1-5 win over Derry in Ballyshannon. Not that it felt like that big of a deal, but our aspirations, if we even had any, of holding onto the McKenna Cup were foiled by Armagh at the Athletic Grounds when we were edged out by 3-8 to 1-13. It was a game that could have gone either way so there was no real criticism. It just meant we'd a little more time to knuckle down and focus in on Down and the start of the Ulster Championship.

An issue that had cropped up immediately after our last league outing against Galway was finances. We were basically running on empty, or so the county board said.

We were more or less told that there was no money to train the team. Martin, as captain, took it upon himself to train the side and car pools were hastily organised to ferry small groups to our new base at Inver Beach. McHugh had led Kilcar to a Donegal championship the previous year so he'd experience of putting lads through their paces.

And it was gruelling. But it was an avoidable situation. Martin should never have had to put himself in that position. And there was a feeling that the board just didn't see us as a worthwhile investment at that point.

We eventually moved things back to Ballybofey six weeks out from Down. McEniff's tenure was coming to a close regardless. And he'd have to stand for re-election if he wanted to go again. A bad championship would only put pressure on the outcome of such a scenario being successful. So his job was on the line, there was no doubt about that.

And the team he was putting his faith in against Down, the side pinned to the MacCumhaill Park dressing-room wall on the Thursday night prior was: Gary Walsh; Tommy McDermott, Des Newton, Matt Gallagher; Michael Carr, Brendan Dunleavy, Eunan McIntyre; Anthony Molloy, Michael Lafferty; Sylvester Maguire, Donal Reid, Joyce McMullin; Martin McHugh, Charlie Mulgrew, Leslie McGettigan.

Our record in Down in championship, the *Democrat* said, wasn't good. It was terrible in fact. We'd never won a game at senior level there. *'McEniff's job on the line in Newcastle'*, read the same newspaper article headline. Final words were delivered by Brian as we huddled up. And as we made our way out onto the field we were left in no doubt whatsoever that Brian's head was on the block.

Lose and he'd be gone.

The middle 80s proved a struggle for Donegal, but for club and county Anthony continued to grow and command as a footballer. Here he is in action with Ardara (top and middle), and also in the best of company, with his brothers Lanty and Connie.

« CHAPTER 6 »

'Discipline is the soul of an army'
– George Washington

TOM CONAGHAN WAS destined to manage the Donegal senior footballers. His zero tolerance for bullshit and excuses ruffled feathers and split opinion, but Tom cared little for reputation and even less for what people thought of him.

The truth hurts, but the cold fact was there were things we, as a squad and as individuals, needed to hear and be told. Tom's parting words to many of us, as under-21 All-Ireland winners four years previously, was that standards had been set and as a result, objectives and even dreams were achieved. His formula was simple but very effective.

Everything that Tom despised and stood so defiantly against was there present, and to the fore, in that dressing-room as we went about trying to save Brian's skin. But a 2-8 to 1-10 Ulster opener defeat to Down, in Newcastle, sealed McEniff's fate. His six-year reign had come to a sad end. But the truth is, Brian's hands were clean of that failure and the players, to a man, carry that stain. In our hearts we knew we'd let him down but the easiest thing was to hide behind the many excuses that were thrown about after in the local and national press.

Brian, after some thought, did decide to throw his hat back into the ring once again. But as soon as Tom made his intentions clear, there was only ever going to be one winner there. And again, that's not a reflection on Brian at the time. At that stage, there was just this feeling amongst supporters that a change, even for the sake of it, was needed.

But in Tom, supporters had an individual they felt would bang heads and, at the same time, deliver success. There is this narrative that Tom ruled with an iron fist. But he didn't. First and foremost, he looked to be a problem solver. But if he couldn't solve that same problem, then he'd eliminate it.

And Tom was box office.

And by that I mean, what he said was to the point… sharp, and often delivered with cutting wit. His methods were exactly what fed up supporters wanted to see implemented. Weeks of speculation had passed but come June of 1986, Tom finally broke his silence and at the same time, fired his name into the reckoning. As well as his big success with the under-21s in 1982, he'd also brought his club Four Masters to the Promised Land for the first time ever that same year. He then backed that up with another county title in 1983. This was a serious operator.

Tom – to Donegal supporters back then – was what Jose Mourinho represented to Premier League fans when he first landed in England. As well as being a brilliant manager, there was never a dull moment or comment. And so he was always going to be pushed favourably by the press. McEniff, that little bit more understated and guarded, just didn't throw them those kind of verbal bones.

BUT THE HARD truth of the matter, regardless of all of that, was that Tom deserved his shot. It's a fact and it's also a measure of the man, but he had also been pushed and pressed behind the scenes, in 1983, to make the step up.

Tom declined.

McEniff's three-year tenure was up at that stage, but Tom being Tom, said that Brian deserved another shot off the back of landing the Ulster title and taking the side to within a whisker of a first ever senior All-Ireland final. Tom was tough, but he was also fair. And that typified him. The thing was either black or white, and the individual right or wrong. In Tom's mind, to run against McEniff at that time would have been the wrong thing to do. And that simple creed of Tom's is still the only way to manage a football team. You don't have to like your manager, but you must respect him. And respect can be earned in so many fashions.

I spoke recently to an ex-player – a double All-Ireland winner. And the talk got up about his very famous and heralded former manager. The same individual said he owed that manager his two Celtic Crosses but, without breaking breath, he also said he couldn't stand him on a personal level.

He was, *'A complete arsehole!'* And because of that, the same player didn't invite him to his wedding. And that little insight is what usually sums up and separates the very best of them from the rest.

If you get too close to players, they'll use it against you. Believe me, I've been on both ends of it. Ultimately, you can't sack a team and the easiest decision in that instance is to offload the boss. That's what happened to Brian back then.

And, at the subsequent August sitting of county committee, Tom would score a sizeable 33-19 win in the head-to-head vote. Pressed on how he was going to approach the new post he told the attending journalists, *'If any player steps out of line, he'll only do it once!'*

It was a typical Tom line. And it was obvious to one and all that he hadn't changed a bit in his approach to football.

WHAT HAD CHANGED for Tom in the time since I'd last had him as boss was something very personal and so tragic. On December 23, 1984 Tom lost his 14-year-old son Kevin. The car in which Kevin was a passenger had been travelling to Dublin, but collided with a fire engine truck on a stretch of road between Maguiresbridge and Lisnasksea.

And on Christmas day, Tom and his lovely wife Celine would bury their beautiful wee boy. *'A cloud of tears hangs over Donegal Town'* was how it was described in the local paper and that was exactly how it felt.

Kevin was a little gem. And he went everywhere with his daddy.

He worshipped the ground Tom trod and the feeling was mutual. Kevin was also a brilliant young footballer. And he was a very important part of our 1982 success. He was only 11 years old at that time, but he was one of the boys. He sat on the bus with us, to and from the games and after every single training session he'd collect balls, cones and water bottles.

There was never a lost cause! and each night without fail, he'd account for every single one of the above.

He was his father's son no doubt.

My admiration for Tom is even greater now than it had been when he put a first All-Ireland medal in my hand. The way he's carried himself and continued on … for any parent that loses a child too early, so many of my prayers at night go out to those same people.

A GOOD CHUNK of us had already experienced Tom and his ways. But we were grown men now, prouder and a little bit stubborner as well. And the older boys in the squad were on red alert that some of the previous ways, the copping out that had gone on at times, just would not be tolerated from here on in.

And it was obvious now that Tom viewed the under-21 crop as men as well. So the small bit of slack that was afforded to some of us wasn't going to be there this time out. Back then, it was often an arm around the shoulder father-type talk that you got from Tom. And some of those olive branch tales from that previous regime were hilarious. There were days we tried to take liberties or break out, but Tom was more often than not a step or two ahead of us all.

One time during that under-21 campaign, the Four Masters boys Cornie Carr, Michael Kelly and Joyce McMullin had decided they'd had enough. They were getting out of town! Their plan was elaborate and, it seemed, fool-proof.

There was a very famous dance going at the time just outside Castlefin, The River Club. And the boys were sure that if they went that far there was no way in hell that Tom would ever find out. The lads had managed to get a lift over. But as they approached the pay box at the door and handed their few pound through the hole, who was inside reaching out to grab the fiver off Joyce, but Tom!

Tom, like he always did, had got wind of what the lads were up to and got there just before them. In front of everyone, he frogmarched them back out the door to his car and landed them home to Donegal Town!

There was another occasion in 1982, around the Ulster semi-final time, where myself and Paddy Gavigan had met up in Donegal Town. Both Ardara and Glen had played club games that evening and we'd arranged to have a few pints after. McGroarty's Bar was the spot back then. But Donal Monaghan, another shrewd operator, was one of Tom's selectors and he'd spied us sheepishly around the Diamond there and, from a distance, tailed us all the way up the street.

I'd parked my car up behind the old fire station, just across from Tom's house. I figured we'd be hiding in plain sight. But Tom again landed at the scene of the crime and both of us were directed straight out the main door in front of everyone.

I knew I'd done wrong. But for some reason, Tom had huge time for me, even then. There were no repercussions. Because the way he was operating, if anyone else had to have acted like that I'm sure they'd have been gone! Tom drove my car down the road and he dropped both it and myself off at Bart Whelan's, the then county secretary.

That resulted in another chewing but like I said, there was always a way back at that stage. But times had moved on and so had Tom. This was senior county football now and Tom was even more serious. And his sole aim was to deliver an All-Ireland title.

TOM'S FIRST ACT was to launch a sort of trial competition, the Inter-Divisional Senior Championship between the four regions within the county. The Inter-County Summer League was also running at the time. So between the six weeks until our first National Football League outing, Tom intended to spread the net far and wide.

I'd planned to take a sort of sabbatical to the States, and that decision was taken long before Brian moved on or indeed Tom had come in. Once it was confirmed that Tom was the new man in charge, it wasn't long before the phone rang. Tom of course diverted this spreading of the wings intention once before, when he convinced me to come back in from the cold for the under-21s. We talked and again, he knew it was something I just needed to try and, he hoped, get out of my system.

I'd a bit of work lined up in New York, which Connie had organised. Tom wanted me to stay but conceded some ground on the promise that I'd be back before Christmas. It was flattering I suppose, that he said he needed me and, like I said, we were very close. I gave him my word that he'd see me again in December and when he did, I'd be in good shape. But just before he hung up he explained, in no uncertain terms, that this was the best window to impress and that he couldn't promise that others wouldn't move ahead of me in the pecking order while I was away.

And it was a comment that bugged me and fell about my head the entire time I was away. Again, it was a deliberate seed planted with intent.

If Tom was mildly inconvenienced by my plans, Martin's September bombshell that he also intended to take some time off rocked football followers within the county. It was dressed up as Martin not wanting to play winter football and worse, not having the stomach for it. That was pure bullshit, but that was the accusation thrown at Martin from some quarters and it was wrong.

Martin loved football and if he had a fault it was that he sometimes cared too much. He was obsessive at times. He'd also been picking up injuries and at that stage, I felt it was the right thing for Martin to do. He needed to recharge the batteries.

But again, the knives were out in many quarters when it broke that he was turning out for St Catherine's FC, the local soccer club in Killybegs. No one should have had any issue with that. He was staying sharp and there just wasn't the same pressures placed on him. It was, I'm sure, fun.

Martin, to be fair, did say that he'd be back and ready to go in the Spring.

Tom, though, didn't see that point of view and in the *Democrat* expressed his disappointment in Martin. And it was his opinion that it wouldn't be fair to let anyone, even the great Martin McHugh, just waltz back in without having put the hard yards in. And having pinned his initial and sizable training panel to the wall or, more accurately the sports pages of the local papers, Martin's name was etched upon it. It was a sort of... *I dare you to defy me* kind of act.

But of the 40 or so names put through the ringer during Tom's first get-together, McHugh and Des Newton were the notable no-shows.

Pressed by members of the local media on whether he'd now drop them, Tom's short response was, *'No, they've just dropped themselves'*. Tom's other big initial statement was to discard the services of Ballyshannon men Brian Murray and Gary Walsh. Tom wanted all his panel to be working and living within the county and complete attendance was needed at our three weekly training sessions. It was another one of those decisions that put more than a few noses out of joint.

Tom's reign would eventually open with a 2-11 to 1-10 NFL loss away to Kildare on November 7. By all accounts in the Thursday *Democrat*, which I was able to purchase in an Irish store in the Bronx by the following Wednesday, Donegal were unlucky not to leave Newbridge with at least a point.

As well as the paper, a box of Barry's teabags and a pack of Emerald sweets would also become regular buys in my short few months in New York. The first thing I'd scan towards, and it would become a habit when I was away, was to see who Tom had paired in midfield. Munching away on my Emerald sweets, something I never once ate at home, I was delighted to read that, *'The new midfield pairing of Declan Bonner and Barry Cunningham worked hard but never looked an effective combination'.*

And the gist of the same journalist's thoughts was that if a better handle could have been got on that middle third, then Donegal would have nailed two good opening points to the Division 2 board. Tom himself was also quoted as saying our shortcomings at midfield were his one concern. *Good news… I thought!*

The following Wednesday, off I went again in hunt of the weekly local newspaper from back home. Connie was my foreman on-site, in the city, and the routine was for the big brother to chew me out in front of a few others before ordering me off to pick up something or another in the local hardware up the street.

But Connie was just as interested in events at home as I was and this ruse of sorts was his idea. And I was only too happy to play my part.

It's fair to say I nearly choked on one of those damn Emeralds when I read that Tom had decided to go with a combination of big Griffin and Joyce around the middle this time out. And both men had been highly influential in a 0-8 to 0-5 win over Cork in Ballyshannon. In our third league outing and our second last before Christmas, a hard-earned point was taken against Tyrone in Ballybofey. On a 1-6 to 0-9 scoreline, a young Manus Boyle had made an impression with 1-2 of our total.

On December 19, Donegal went to Longford and a fine 2-7 to 1-4 win meant the side sat third in the standings on five points and just one behind the joint leading pair of Cork and Derry. I'd only touched back down in Dublin the day before, but I was pleased to read a footnote on the same *Democrat* page, now back at base in Leamagowra, that Tom's intention was to bring me straight back into the fold.

We wouldn't get back underway in the league until February 8 and that gave me enough time to try to get up to speed.

ONE OF THE things I'd taken a passing interest in during my short stint in the States was American Football. Connie and a good few of the other boys were big fans and because of that I sat through a number of games also.

Now the game itself, as a spectacle, was a bit dull. But Americans and now the initiated Irish, just weren't content unless there was copious amounts of food and beer to accompany the drama. And it lasted the entire day. Truth be told, it helped break up the boredom of the actual game.

And these sessions would eventually end up being serious craic. But the analysis before, during and after the games was seriously interesting. It was so far ahead of what we were used to at home, at the time, in terms of GAA or soccer.

There was this coach, Jimmy Johnston. And he was in charge of the Dallas Cowboys. One night I'm watching this profile on him and his ways. He was ruthless. He was a Tom-type that didn't deal in bullshit or slacking. Anyway, video analysis was and no doubt still is huge in the sport. There was this one early morning session where Jimmy dimmed the lights, pulled down the blinds and replayed the previous night's game on one of those big old projectors.

By the end of it, as he brings the lights back up, Jimmy notices that both his first and second choice running backs have nodded off to sleep.

Jimmy wades down towards the back and kicks the chair out from under the second string player and tells him to pack up his shit... he's cut! He then proceeds back up to the top of the room and gently shakes his first choice man, a marquee player that went by the name of Emmitt Smith, and gently says, 'Emmitt, wake up!'

The truth is, and Jimmy knew this, was that he needed Emmitt if he was going to challenge for and win Superbowls. And Emmitt also knew as much.

And closer to home, the reality was that Tom knew he needed Martin if he was to have any chance of creating history and leading Donegal to Sam Maguire glory. A wave of relief reverberated around the county, come January, as the news broke that Martin was coming back. As well as that, Des Newton, one of the team's most consistent players in previous years, was also welcomed back in from the cold as were myself, big Dunleavy and John Cunningham.

However, any notion that Tom had softened somewhat over the Christmas holidays was put to an immediate bed the evening we regrouped as a squad.

A number of the panel had been dipping in and out of the local soccer and rugby ranks throughout the county and Tom was now putting an end to the practice. Manus was forced to miss out on a very important FAI Junior Cup game for St Catherine's, while the likes of Charlie Mulgrew and Martin Carlin, important cogs for Letterkenny rugby club, were also told that they wouldn't be turning out for the side any more. Letterkenny were on the verge of a massive Forster Cup semi-final themselves, so all of this inevitably hit the headlines.

Quizzed on the so-called tough new line, Tom insisted he'd issued no ban. He stated that the lads were free to play whatever sport they wanted, but it had to be one or the other. Again, there were mutters of discontent, but few to his face.

However, both the rugby lads decided to defy Tom's order and played their game. They still reported for training on the Tuesday night, but they were turned at the gate. Come the Sunday, and with Cavan coming to Ballybofey, the other big revelation at the time was that Griffin had been relegated to the subs bench for what Tom would only label as a 'discipline breach'.

Straight into the team came Newton, Dunleavy and McHugh. I had to make do with a place on the bench having picked up a thigh injury the previous Thursday. But Tom had made his point emphatically. However, a 1-8 to 1-8 draw against Cavan left many wondering just what was going on with this team. *Democrat* reporter Connie Duffy certainly felt he knew.

Fair play to Connie, he at least was putting his name to his reports and that wasn't an all too familiar practice back then. Connie's summary in the following edition of his paper was scathing. As well as his damning report, he carried a sort of whispers piece where he quoted a number of apparently disgruntled players, whose names were not as forthcoming as their opinions. I've no doubt Connie talked to a few lads but for those same fellas to hide behind those words and their identities to remain in the shadows, was inexcusable.

'One player commented that respect was a one-way thing at this moment', the piece read. *'Players are disillusioned with the lack of a game plan or tactic of any kind. There has also been the suggestion that county training sessions were exceptionally punishing whenever members of the county executive or others were present, as if geared to impress them.'*

On Duffy continued, *'Matters came to a head on Wednesday night last in Donegal Town. Charlie Mulgrew and Martin Carlin's futures on the county panel were at stake. It is understood the other players refused to train until a guarantee was given that both men would be restored to the panel. Manager Tom Conaghan was not available for comment this week. But no doubt he will not like what his players are saying.'*

It was a damning moment and it was the start of an ugly stand-off between Tom and the *Democrat* who were, at that time at least, still the premier GAA newspaper in the county. Tom and his backroom team would refuse to engage with the paper for the remainder of the season. Which meant that the scrutiny was even harsher as a direct result.

Training and our discussions before, during and after, were heated and contentious for a while. But Tom demanded, to a man, that we park the practice of snipping behind each other's backs and if anything needed to be said. it was thrashed out between the group and not the pages of the *Democrat*.

And we seemed to fire the perfect retort to the doubt and criticism next day out, away to Derry, when we recorded a very fine 1-9 to 0-7 win at a bare Greenlough. The reality of the matter was that promotion to Division 1 was still on the cards going into our final game at home to relegation threatened Laois in Ballyshannon. But our chances of going up were blown to pieces when we suffered what was a humiliating 10-point hammering. To make matters worse, a sort of free-for-all erupted at the final whistle as frustrations boiled over.

WE TOOK A number of weeks off, to cool down really, ahead of the McKenna Cup. The time away was needed. I'd been used off the bench ever since my return from America but in what was a largely experimental McKenna Cup team, I was named to start at midfield in our clash with Tyrone in Omagh come mid-March. My clubmates Martin Gavigan and Patrick Gallagher had also been handed opportunities to impress.

The hosts though would prevail 0-9 to 0-7 and the pot-shots from the local papers continued to be fired. The real concern though was that we'd now have no competitive football until our Ulster first round opener against Armagh on June 14.

Tom would name a 25-man panel for the Ulster Championship and again, most of the talk centred on the continued omissions of Carlin and Mulgrew. Both men had come back on board for the McKenna Cup and it seemed the slate had been wiped clean. But again, a clash over their rugby commitments meant they were gone just as quickly as they'd reappeared. The other big shock was the dropping of former captain Michael Lafferty.

Michael was only in his early thirties and was still good enough to play for Donegal. But himself and Tom were clashing frequently and that inevitably came to a predictable conclusion. Gavigan was also cast aside, and I felt that wasn't the right decision. But I was in no place to be pressing Tom on it given the injuries and lack of fitness issues I'd been having since I'd come back into the fold. Before long, big Griffin was also shown the door when he opted to play a soccer game instead of a challenge match against Kerry in Ballybofey.

The Kingdom were, of course, managed by Mick O'Dwyer at the time and believe it or not, Tom and Micko were big buddies. 'Micko 2' was our name for Tom.

And while it was far from a full strength Kerry, our 1-20 to 4-8 win did lift morale. Truth be told, Tom probably needed Micko's counsel now more than ever. Tom would often quote Micko and one of the lines he'd use was, *'Just being good enough isn't near good enough at all'*. And their meeting that weekend certainly put a little pep back in Tom's step. The other big news, as our clash with the Orchard men loomed, was that the under-21s had landed an Ulster title and had taken Kerry to a replay in the All-Ireland final the week before our provincial senior opener.

We'd to make do with another challenge, this time against the visiting Donegal club from New York that was touring the country at the time. A dull enough 0-10 each draw in Ballybofey played out with the highlight being a predictable dust-up between the sides just before half-time.

And off the back of that Tom and his management team would sit down to plot both his team and the manner in which he felt a win could be secured over Armagh in the championship. To say there was pessimism in the air would be an understatement. The wisdom of fielding without the likes of battle-hardened men like Lafferty, Carlin, Mulgrew and Griffin was questioned by both the papers and supporters in the lead-in.

But the team Tom would put his faith in, for his first shot at championship glory was: Michael Kelly; Tommy McDermott, Sean Bonner Des Newton; Eamon Breslin, Corny Carr, Matt Gallagher; Sylvester Maguire, Anthony Molloy; Declan Bonner, Joyce McMullin, Martin McHugh; Kieran Keeney, Brendan Dunleavy, Manus Boyle.

In what could only be described as a dreadful game of football, the visitors would score a 1-8 to 0-6 win as we made our Ulster exit at the very first hurdle. Gerry McDermott, another *Democrat* scribe would label it, *'One of the worst games of football ever witnessed at this level'*. It wasn't great, but it was far from that.

The infamous 'Player Ratings' – which are carried to this day – were also rolled out in the aftermath of this defeat. I very much doubt anyone gives a damn about that kind of grading now, but it carried serious sting back then.

Michael Kelly and Corny Carr were, *'not up to inter-county standard'*, McDermott would harshly write. Sylvester Maguire apparently, *'ran around thinking he was Rambo'* while Dunleavy, at full-forward, was *'a duck out of water'*.

This was just a taste of some of the criticism that came our way. But the sharpest barb was reserved for Tom. *'Tom Conaghan has the most important job in the whole of Donegal. All that is asked of him is to produce a successful team. The supporters want success, the county needs success and if Tom Conaghan can't provide it, or even show signs of being able to provide it, then the County Board must look elsewhere. We cannot spend the next two years watching football like this!'*

The under-21's subsequent All-Ireland replay win over Kerry would provide some respite for Tom and the team as their success rightly came under the spotlight. But when he was pressed on the loss and the manner of it at the subsequent month's county board meeting at the beginning of July, a calm and defiant Tom would simply state, 'The only thing I ask for is patience. Donegal will get success'.

It was a comment and line that typified Tom.

There was no doubt his detractors were sniggering and enjoying the pressure he now found himself under. But Tom was about to ram those comments and column inches straight back down the throats of all those who questioned his methods.

Tom Conaghan was 'box office' as a manager and highly admired by Anthony and most of the Donegal players, but his ambitious plans did not get off to a smooth start when several players, including a young and mercurial Martin McHugh, and also Charlie Mulgrew and Martin Carlin, decided to take a break from winter football and play soccer and rugby instead.

REFLECTIONS

'God Almighty himself wouldn't deliver success with this current team'

– Anthony Molloy

DONEGAL'S SECOND ALL-IRELAND crown, delivered in 2012, was brilliant for so many different reasons. The fact that it had seemed so unlikely just two short seasons prior, made the feat all the more special. And the truth was, for myself and the Class of 1992, a horrible monkey was finally dragged from our backs.

We had been put on ridiculous pedestals, for the best part of 20 years. It was powerful and our achievements, as time went on, began to cast a real shadow. And I'm not just talking about Sam Maguire.

Donegal would also not deliver another Ulster crown for 19 long seasons. It became overwhelming in many ways. And, in time, we became a stick to beat all subsequent Donegal teams with. It was so unfair.

Because believe me, we had our fair share of disappointments and hammerings along the way as well.

JIM MCGUINNESS CAME on board in late 2010 and the Anglo Celt was finally secured once more the following summer. His arrival and impact was seismic. And when Michael Murphy climbed the steps of the Hogan Stand a full 20 years after I did, a Donegal man once again lifted Sam and a weight... the bag of rocks we old men had been carrying around for too long, was gratefully tossed aside.

We'll always be the first, but now someone else had achieved that same feat, it just spreads some of the load.

People talk about pressure or attention in the likes of Kerry and Dublin. But there are so many triumphs and medals floating about those counties. Being the first, and the only men to claim an All-Ireland title… at the time it was crazy stuff.

People lost the run of themselves. It was bedlam. We were like rock stars. Everyone wanted a piece of us. Years after our actual feat, we were still the ones being asked to turn up to events, cut ribbons or hand out medals. In the end, when we eventually did become too far distant in the rear-view mirror, present and playing GAA stars were asked to come on board to fill the void.

The only problem was that the lads now turning up in Donegal were from outside the county.

I vividly remember Tyrone's Sean Cavanagh coming down to Ardara in 2010 to see all the youngsters in my own club and hand out their end of year accolades. The sentiment was good, no doubt. But it probably was indicative of just where we were. I felt for the likes of Damien Diver, Eamon Doherty and Brendan Boyle. They were Ard an Rátha men, all dedicated in the extreme when they represented Donegal, but success had eluded them all.

I'd been there myself.

In 1991, Downmen Ross Carr and DJ Kane took Sam Maguire to Ardara. I stood beside them and smiled for the photographs but inside I was hurting. I couldn't have contemplated – not in my wildest dreams – that I'd have that same cup in my hands, on my own terms, soon enough.

But at that stage I had decided to hang them up with Donegal and I truly believed the end or, my end at least, had come at that level. Things, like I said, did finally work out for me and my vintage. But like I alluded to also, for what came between 1992 and 2012, the majority of those lads just weren't so lucky.

But all of that was finally water under the bridge in 2012. I can look back now and appreciate all over again that we made real history. And when people want to talk about it, that's no problem.

That wasn't always the case, but I enjoy the reminiscing and the looking back now all over again. So much changed for the '92 lads because of what Jim and those boys did. And both Jim and Michael remain two of the most sought after men in the country.

Jim changed Donegal's approach to football for ever... that's his real legacy, I believe. Regardless of how they fail or fall now, no one can say they aren't putting in the yards. On and off the pitch, Donegal players now carry themselves in a way that it's easy for supporters to make peace with the bad days that will still come.

There are no guarantees in sport, that's the one thing that doesn't change.

AND MICHAEL MURPHY, what a captain and leader he is!

He's a special guy. My admiration for him is immeasurable. And as Donegalmen, we share something uniquely special. But the truth is, the years book-ended by those All-Ireland wins were shambolic. There simply is no other word. And they were shambolic both on and off the pitch. Managers came and went, good men too that just simply could not get a hold on what was painted as a wild group... a motley crew. Outside men, quality operators like Mickey Moran and Brian McIver, were brought in, but to no avail.

And the manner in which McIver was eventually ousted in 2008 was nothing short of embarrassing and a disgrace.

The position of Donegal manager had been in disarray since early September of that same season when Brian was forced to resign from the post after certain club delegates tabled a motion of no confidence in his abilities at a fiery county board meeting. In the end, both the Gaoth Dobhair and St Eunan's clubs were forced to plead their innocence in the matter, and insisted that their delegates had acted on their own accord.

Regardless, McIver had washed his hands of the scandalous mess, walking off into the darkness never to return.

When the noise eventually began to die down, 1992 teammates John Joe Doherty, Declan Bonner and Charlie Mulgew as a joint ticket, and a certain Jim McGuinness all threw their hats into the ring. In the hunt to find McIver's successor, John Joe was initially offered the job. I believe John Joe looked for certain assurances which the county board took issue with. And as a result, Declan and Charlie were then informed on the very same evening, that they were in fact now going to be put forward for ratification.

In the end, the clubs chose to vote in favour of giving John Joe the job. But

Donegal were again the laughing stock of the entire country at that stage. And again, when my phone rang at that time, be it a local or national journalist, they were usually looking for an opinion on the latest controversy. Even though I've had various run-ins at times with certain writers, I've always answered the phone. But it wasn't nice talking about what was happening. And some of the stories floating about during that wild period were crazy.

But this latest instalment... it was all of our own making, off the pitch, at county board level. And for once, the players couldn't be blamed. But lost in the cracks of that much publicised debacle, was Jim's application. It was pushed to the very bottom of the pile.

Jim had apparently attended his interview armed with a PowerPoint display but there was no plug socket in the room for the projector. Rather than move next door, where his presentation could easily have been facilitated, the interview panel at the time dismissively asked him to instead state his case. Jim would eventually get the job two years later, but for the simple fact that no one else wanted it.

It was viewed as a poisoned position and no one in their right mind was looking to touch it, even with a barge-pole.

But that whole episode was unsavoury and it left a really bad taste. It pitted friends and former teammates against one another, and it had the potential to cause irreparable damage. To the best of my knowledge, the important people in all of that, the ones I cared about, have thankfully moved on.

But from root to branch, back in 2010, Donegal football was in complete disarray... one big joke. But thank God for Jim's perseverance. At the third time of asking, nearing the end of that same year, he finally found himself as Donegal senior football boss. Coming in off the back of a superb under-21 campaign, a brilliant number of weeks where that young group and its charismatic manager captured the imagination once again of the Donegal football supporters, an Ulster title was landed.

They would eventually make their way to an All-Ireland final, against the Dubs, but were squeezed out when a cruel twist made all the difference. With only seconds remaining in what was a compelling encounter, Michael crashed a last-minute penalty against the crossbar. It was later revealed that almost half of Donegal's team were on antibiotics that night after a viral bug had invaded the camp a few days earlier.

Still, Jim had whipped them into such a frenzy that only the width of a crossbar denied them the ultimate glory. Before that All-Ireland under-21 decider, I remember talking to two young lads in my own club that were part of the starting team – Paddy McGrath and Conor Classon. There was almost this hypnotic coldness to how they answered my prodding and poking line of questioning. 'How far would you go for this man?' I asked.

'As far as is needed!' replied Conor.

A few short months earlier – and Jim frequently tells this same story – he'd gathered his young Donegal team into a huddle. He eyeballed them all and told them they would win the Ulster title. One player apparently started to laugh… the giggles bursting out before he'd even realised it.

But McGuinness spun around on his heels, with finger pointed, turning to the others to say, 'Do you see that? This is what Donegal football has become. A joke.

Once he'd got the senior gig, both he and his ways were finally going to be taken seriously at the very top level. Like I said, throughout all of that turbulent period, I was often asked by journalists for my tuppence worth. And having seen how John Joe had fared, the big problem, I believed, remained the players.

BUT INSIDE TWO short seasons, Jim not only transformed Donegal as a team but also people's perception of them as individuals. His passion, conviction and sheer defiance led Donegal back to the very top. I'd famously remarked at the time, in print, that, 'God Almighty himself wouldn't win anything with this current team'.

In the same article, printed in the Irish Examiner, I went on to add, 'The other thing I have to say about the current squad is, it does not seem to hurt them enough when they lose. Everything is fine and dandy with them when they win but when they lose it does not seem to bother them. And it doesn't matter who comes in, that isn't going to change any time soon.'

But Jim saw it all so differently.

He changed the mindset, rallied a county and helped Donegal's future finally catch up with its past. I vividly recall passing Jim in the tunnel back in 2012, just after they'd beaten Cork to secure their place in the All-Ireland final.

I was doing some media work. But he grabbed me by the arm and asked me to come into the dressing-room and say a few words.

I was taken aback.

Very few of that squad would have had any real serious recall of 1992. They'd have only been babies. Patrick McBrearty hadn't even been born!

I asked Jim was there anything in particular that he wanted me to mention? But all he said was, 'I trust you!'

Three words. Jim was able to put me on a pedestal inside my own head, one I hadn't been on in a very long time, just outside that dressing-room door.

And that is his gift. He'd just lifted me in a way that brought me back to that place. In I stormed and laid it out in black and white.

'Nothing has been won yet,' I warned them. 'Make your own history, let us '92 men finally rest easy!' I demanded… begged even. I hope I lifted them. But there was no doubt that gesture from Jim certainly lifted me, at that time.

And maybe that was the real point of Jim's request. I was on cloud nine for about a week after.

I FIRST GOT to know Jim when he came onto the Donegal senior squad back at the tail end of 1991. As a scraggly-haired 19-year-old he never actually played in the All-Ireland winning run, only making his debut in '93. He was quiet, timid even. He was very humble and mannerly.

He was still a kid really. Life shapes people and I have no doubt that life was still in the midst of shaping Jim at that time. He was only 12 years of age when he witnessed the death of his older brother Charles, who passed away from a heart defect when he was just 16. More tragedy was to come his way in 1998 when a second brother 'the Giant'… big Mark died following a road accident.

A few weeks after the 1998 Ulster final, one which Joe Brolly won with a last-minute Derry goal Jim, like so many of us had previously done, decided to head off and kick ball in America. Mark, being the absolute gentleman that he was, offered a lift to Dublin Airport. The pair of them were almost inseparable, more like best friends as well as brothers.

But at Lisnaskea, barely 10 miles from St Tiernach's Park in Clones, their car was hit by a lorry and Mark — who was just 27 at the time— was killed.

I remember reading Jim's own book, his excellent memoir, Until Victory

Always and feeling my heart break for him all over again. Because I've always had a really good relationship with Jim. I cannot begin to imagine what that must have been like for him. He was entitled to be angry, to cave even. But what he decided to do, and how he went about educating himself, becoming the man he is today... he's an absolute inspiration.

The journey he's been on, moving out of his comfort zone, his arena in the GAA and into the world of soccer, has been fascinating to watch. Again, the bravery of such a move, the want and will to test himself is a serious example to set for others.

LIKE I SAID, myself and Michael share a very unique distinction as Donegal men. I now have company on those same walls I'd lonely hung upon, by my own, for two decades! For a long time there was word about this youngster in Glenswilly that had serious potential. And as he rose up through the ranks it became pretty apparent, from very early on, that we had a potential great on our hands.

And in great, I don't mean a Donegal great... I mean a length and breadth of the country great.

At just 17, he was already a mountain of a man. The skill levels he had and the natural framework he already had to go with it... Brian McIver soon came calling and took him into the senior Donegal squad back in 2007. And while the team continued to falter, Michael still managed to pick up the Young Footballer of the Year award in 2010. That same season, Cork had annihilated Donegal at Croke Park in the All-Ireland quarter-final by 1-27 to 2-10, with two injury time goals putting just an ounce of respectability on the scoreline.

But Murphy had given Michael Shields – who would go on to be named at full-back on that season's All Star side – the absolute run around. But with a county seemingly going nowhere, Australian Football Rules vultures suddenly began to seriously circle.

Our seemingly one glimmer of hope looked like he was going to be snatched away from us. It was a real concern for so many inside the county. I recall talking with Martin McHugh and he was furious, as were a number of others who would only have had Donegal football's best interests at heart. Martin, to his credit, was very vocal at the time on the subject and the manner in which this Aussie agent, Ricky Nixon, a combative and controversial character, was openly just showing up at GAA games.

A year or two later, myself and Martin attended an Ulster secondary schools game in Irvinestown. Donegal's Colaiste na Carraige were involved, a school that Martin's son Ryan was playing for at that time. But a 16-year-old Patrick McBrearty was also in their line-up. It was drawn to our attention, after about 20 minutes, that this Nixon fella was in the stand, video camera in hand, trailing McBrearty's every move.

Patrick would, it seems, flirt with the notion of going Down Under as well but thankfully quickly moved on, as did Michael.

But at the time, in Michael's case, he'd been pictured attending some kind of AFL trial in Dublin and it seemed to confirm our worst fears. I remember talking to Brendan Devenney in Letterkenny one morning. Mine and Brendan's paths never crossed on the field, but I'd got to know him over the years as he became one of Donegal's stars.

Murphy idolised Brendan as a youngster... he was his hero. And in the midst of all this noise about Murphy going to Oz, Brendan was confidently able to tell me not to worry. Brendan had it on good authority that Michael had no interest in heading off, that he was a real home bird. And the only reason he was at those trials was to brain pick the Australian experts in an attempt to obtain a nugget or two that might, if it was at all possible, improve his own game. Sure enough, even if it was a week or two later, almost word for word what Brendan had told me appeared in the newspapers and the quotes attributed to Michael.

SO, WE'RE PROBABLY really only talking about a matter of months, possibly a year really, between Jim McGuinness letting bygones be bygones with the bungling Donegal County Board and a teenage Michael spurning the advances of the Australians.

It's an intersection in time that is rarely looked at, if at all, but it was a period where the two most important pieces in the resurrection of Donegal football somehow fell into place. And the truth is, Jim putting his hand up for a third time for the senior gig and Murphy deciding to stay put, that was simply down to their love for their county.

And it's funny how life goes.

We're 30 years down the track now from 1992, but we're also 10 years removed from 2012. Time waits for no man. Donegal supporters demand success now, simply because they've become so accustomed to it. 1992 was our fifth provincial title win.

We didn't claim a sixth until 2011. But we've added four more since as well as that second All-Ireland win.

Still, I don't think the 2012 vintage feel like any kind of a monkey on this current crop's back. Inter-county football now, its preparation and the time and effort that goes into it… it's all or nothing. And you simply cannot burn the candle at both ends any more.

It just would not be tolerated or entertained.

PART THREE »

« CHAPTER 7 »

'Through it all, when there was doubt,
I ate it up and spat it out'

– Frank Sinatra

WITH THE DUST settling on the exploits and All-Ireland success of PJ McGowan's under-21s, it was finally time for Donegal to get back down to business at senior level in late October of 1987.

The big question being posed at that stage was, what bridges between some players and management, if any, had been mended in the few short months since we went our separate ways after our Armagh embarrassment. Looking around the Abbey Vocational School gym during our first number of quiet get-togethers, the answer was pretty obvious.

And when Tom finally did release his National Football League panel, it only served to raise eyebrows, as well as plenty of heated debate alongside the usual negative commentary. By now, the *Democrat* had enlisted the talents of the *The Follower* – a cloaked columnist whose identity was initially kept a secret. Over time it would eventually be revealed that the individual in question was Cormac McGill – a very talented writer originally from Convoy but, at that time, residing in Leitrim. Cormac was a Donegal GAA historian who had the most impressive recall and knowledge of all sporting matters.

His turn of phrase and his ability to blend English, Irish and even Latin quickly became the must-read piece in the local paper. He quoted Caesar, Mussolini and even Frank Sinatra. And his debut submission coincided with Tom's first official panel ahead of the new season. The truth is, I had to read it a number of times, break it down, go back to the start and even then... so much of it flew right over my head.

'Jacta est alia,' said Caesar, as he left the confines of his beloved Empire setting, his foot in Caul. So upon reading the panel to represent us in the forthcoming league series, I join with Caesar saying in translation, 'The die is cast'.

Cormac or, should I say, *The Follower* went on, 'The manager has made the choice. He is democratically chosen to lead Donegal out of what some thought had been a footballing wilderness into a promised land. I could not even in the wildest flights of imagination agree with the panel he has chosen. I will vouch for his honesty, his integrity and his commitment to do what he thinks is best for Donegal football. But still I will not agree with the panel chosen.'

The usual suspects were all back on board, but there was no place for the likes of Noel McCole, Michael Lafferty, Martin Griffin, Kieran Keeney, Des Newton, Martin Carlin and Charlie Mulgrew. There was an influx of under-21s but as well as Manus, only four more in the form of John Connors, John Joe Doherty, Diarmaid Keon and Tommy Ryan would be drafted into the senior ranks.

AHEAD OF OUR Division 2 league opener against Kildare in Ballybofey, the *Democrat* turned the screw in their preview with the dramatic line, *'It comes down to this: if Tom Conaghan does not inspire the Donegal team to new heights on Sunday afternoon in their opening contest with Kildare then we may have to sit back and watch the systematic annihilation of the side for the rest of the season.'*

Talk about being dramatic. Yes, the pressure was on but the newspaper was laying it on a bit thick here. I was named amongst the substitutes as Tom went with a midfield pairing of James Carr and my own clubmate Martin Gavigan.

Led by new captain Brendan Dunleavy, we managed to secure a very encouraging 1-10 to 1-3 win. But Kildare had been poor and no one was really too sure what to read into the victory. Ahead of our trip to Roscommon, Bart Whelan, the county secretary and a fellow Ardara man, resigned from his post. His gripe was a valid one, however. He'd taken his eight-year-old son along to the Kildare game the week previously, but some clown of an official at the gate refused the pair entry to the ground. Unbelievable stuff.

Bart's entry was fine he was told, but his young fella couldn't follow. How in under God did that same official expect a father to let his eight-year-old son wander the streets on his own as he conducted business inside? And this kind of thing, even now, rears its head in the GAA, where common sense and even manners just goes out the window.

Bart had been very good to me and he was also a close friend of Tom's, and this made both our bloods boil.

My mood lifted somewhat when Tom told me I'd be in from the start at the weekend when we went to Hyde Park to take on Roscommon. Still, my enthusiasm waned somewhat when he told me he wouldn't be breaking up last week's winning midfield partnership. Instead, he said, I'd be going in at full-forward. And, he warned, as he left the dressing-room the Thursday night before, 'Don't even dream about roaming!'

On a dour afternoon in Hyde Park, we claimed a second league win thanks in large to a very fortuitous McHugh goal. A free from very deep was battered into the wet and windy air and with conditions so, so poor, the ball somehow made it the whole way into the back of the net. It was a crucial score and it would mean we'd eventually win by 1-6 to 0-8. I didn't get on the scoresheet, but I still managed to secure a reasonable enough 7/10 in the following Thursday's *Democrat*.

Still, there were understandable groans of concern when Tom decided to stick to the same team for our next outing, an away trip to Tuam to take on Galway. We were still relying heavily, too heavily it had to be said, on Martin for scores. Manus had been absent due to a club suspension but that had now lapsed. Both supporters and the local media were adamant that he should be sprung immediately back into the mix.

The season before last, in McEniff's final league outing in charge, we'd relegated Galway to Division 3. They made an instant return, going through their entire campaign unbeaten. So there was going to be an inevitable bite to this.

'**Tuam belongs to Molloy**' read the headline in *The Follower's* subsequent column. We would secure a draw that sat us alone on top of Division 2. But the truth is, and the warming local media agreed, we should have taken the two points on offer.

The game would finish 0-11 to 2-5 and that leaking of two quickfire second-half goals were the only real blips on our 60-minute effort. We had trailed by 0-3 to 0-1 inside the first quarter, when Tom signalled to me to head out to the middle of the field. And I knew this was my chance to stay there, so I intended to grab it. We managed to surge one ahead in the half and with Manus sprung into the mix, the momentum was with us.

But no sooner had he appeared, Martin departed to injury. It was rotten luck. We were still looking good halfway through the second period with a two-point advantage. Disaster struck however as Galway, with some help I felt from the match officials, pounced for a goal.

A '45' that we seemed to have dealt with was ordered to be retaken, as our physio John Cassidy had encroached ever so slightly onto the field to treat one of our players near the end-line. Still reeling from that decision, we dropped our concentration and the retaken kick was somehow flicked to the back of the net by Gerry Burke. We barely had time to collect ourselves when John Joyce added a second Galway goal.

In the blink of an eye, we'd allowed a two-point lead to turn into a four-point deficit. It asked a serious question of us – had we the character to now dig ourselves out of trouble? With little over 10 minutes remaining, we gained so much more than just a share of the spoils. Without McHugh, we dug in and by the end we salvaged a brilliantly satisfying point.

Doubting Cormac, *The Follower*, was now *The Believer* and the opening paragraph to his next article would read, *An old song went thus: 'If they ask you what your name is tell them it's Molloy.' Somehow I could not get that tune out of my head leaving Tuam on Sunday last. This was a veritable tour de force by the Ardara man, playing football that we always thought he had within his capabilities, and which he did not show us since the historic year of '82. Normally John Joe Doherty would have been man of the match if Molloy had not decided to play football that would have paled Jack O'Shea at his best into insignificance.'*

I'LL BE HONEST, it gave me a huge lift.

And for the first time, others were finally seeing what Tom was attempting to drag out of Donegal. The shite that had previously went on wasn't now going on and no one was taking the easy way out. 'Accountability for yourself and your efforts, take individual responsibility for all of that and the rest will look after itself.' Those were the words that Tom used to preach to his young under-21 boys and we ate it up… we blindly and in complete and innocent trust, swallowed it every single night.

But pride and to be honest, becoming men, meant our first instinct now was to swim against any kind of authority or order. We'd become sceptics. But Tom was making good on his promise to drag us, if he had to, to where he wanted to take us. But the hope after Tuam was that there would be a little less dragging from now on. *The Follower* was certainly on board.

'Stand up Tom Conaghan and take a bow as you accept our thanks. You have got the attitude right. You seemingly have instilled the requisite never say die spirit into this dedicated bunch of players. If your wry smile widened once again in Tuam let's hope it will grow to a grin after the Clare game come February 28th.'

When we regrouped on the Tuesday night, the gravity of Martin's shoulder injury, picked up in a 50/50 that he didn't hold back in, became much more apparent. It was a long term one and if we were to fire our way to Division 1 for the first time ever, we'd have to do it without our main man. The Christmas break was on the horizon and our last outing was a home match against bottom of the table Clare. The opportunity to end the year on a high was more than within our reach.

For some reason on Sunday, December 13, in Ballyshannon, we decided to make hard work of the matter and only just got out of there with a 1-7 to 0-9 win. Declan Bonner posted 1-2, while Manus also chipped in with a couple of valuable points. I was happy once again with my efforts around the middle, this time from the very off. It was also an opportunity to draw breath. We'd three league games to contend with in the New Year against Cavan at Breffni, Down in Ballybofey and Laois in Portlaoise. But we were in the driving seat as regards to securing automatic promotion.

And what an endorsement that would be – a first ever visit to Division 1 – of Tom and his ways. *The Follower* continued to wax lyrical about the side's turnaround in fortunes and his writing filled the gaps between the break in the league. Pontius Pilate, Macbeth and even John Wayne were quoted as he pondered and speculated about what lied in store for Donegal in 1988.

I'D CHECKED IN with Martin to see what he was making of it all and, more importantly, how his own injury was. Martin liked the direction we were going in. Tom was giving new lads like Martin Gavigan, John Joe Doherty and Tommy Ryan their chance. But Martin still felt there were fellas out in the cold that needed to come back into the fold. And, he explained that Tom's hard-line approach wouldn't be questioned from here on in, as long as we were winning games.

But, he warned, it still had the potential to be divisive if there was a sharp downturn in fortunes.

Martin said he'd no doubt we were good enough to get into Division 1 but, he warned, we'd need reinforcements to stay there. And if we had serious designs on both an Ulster and All-Ireland title then some fractured relationships would need to be mended as soon as possible. What struck me most about Martin's comments was that he referenced an All-Ireland. I was walking around with my chest out off the back of my Division 2 performances but Martin put some perspective on all of that.

But like Micko often told Tom, management wasn't a popularity contest. So if we wanted the status quo and current harmony within the group to remain the same, the answer was simple… we had to keep on winning. And Tom might be more likely to offer olive branches if things continued to point in the right direction.

Christmas and New Year is usually a quiet time on the sporting front. And given that we were top of the Division 2 standings, we could for once bask in the reward of tranquillity all of that would surely bring.

But our moment of calm was brought to a grinding halt on January 1 as the first *Democrat* of 1988 hit the shelves. A broadside from an unlikely source had made the local paper when the out-of-favour Des Newton decided to transfer back to his native Roscommon.

Des was no doubt one of those that Martin was referencing when we talked quietly about the absent quality in the squad over a Christmas cup of tea in Melly's Cafe, Killybegs. But this type of salvo was just the kind of thing we didn't need and it had serious potential to cause disruption. In Connie Duffy's 'exclusive' with the disgruntled Des, who had been playing his club football with Carndonagh, he'd let fly at Tom with a real barrage of criticism.

'The past 14 months have been a nightmare in my career. The disgraceful handling of the Donegal county team has made it impossible for me to continue as a player under the present manager.

'I had made this decision last summer so it came as a bonus to me when the new Roscommon manager approached me in early September to rejoin his squad. I made that decision in the hope that I could continue to play county football for a few more

years and be happy in doing it. My decision proved a wise one when the present squad
was announced. I had not made known my intended transfer to Mr Conaghan but his
decision to drop me is just another chapter in what has now become a comedy.

'*Mr Conaghan's ego trip since last September has left the career of many good players*
in tatters. I am lucky and fortunate to have an alternative. In leaving I wish the team
well in the future. I have had many happy years here. If all does not go well then I
can't say I'll have any sympathy for those clubs who chose to elect Mr Conaghan to the
position of county manager.'

I have no doubt Des felt the need to get all that off his chest but his decision
to do it on the back page of the *Democrat*, on New Year's Day was, for want of a
better word, rash. He'd already high-tailed it out of there so it was easy enough to
be brave at that stage. Why didn't he tell Tom all of this to his face?

Or if he did, why not just let the rest slide and think of his former teammates?
We were top of Division 2 at that stage for heaven's sake.

Coincidently, just a week later the *Democrat* was speculating that the likes of
Carlin, Mulgrew, McGettigan and both Cunninghams, John and Barry, might be
coming back into the mix. And as it would turn out, the *Democrat* was correct.
But it's only right that it's pointed out that the first move came from each one
of those players, and not from Tom. From the outside looking in, for those lads,
they obviously felt things appeared to be moving in a direction they liked and,
thankfully, they all wanted to be a part of that. And outside distractions like
soccer and rugby Tom was assured, wouldn't be an issue this time out.

Traditionally slow New Year starters, our trip to Breffni Park would answer
some questions. The big news in the lead-up was that Martin's shoulder injury
had mended well in the off-season and come Sunday, February 7 of 1988, we
took to the field against Cavan bidding to claim two more very important league
points to pin to the board.

From the off, Tom went with a team of: Gary Walsh; Sean Bonner, Brendan
Dunleavy, Cathal Campbell; John Joe Doherty, Brian Tuohy, Martin Shovlin;
Martin Gavigan, Anthony Molloy; Donal Reid, Charlie Mulgrew, Declan
Bonner; Martin McHugh, Manus Boyle, Tommy Ryan.

It was a skilful but hardened fifteen and it was a side good enough to down
the hosts in their own backyard. In dreadful conditions we out-battled Cavan 2-6
to 0-11. Manus grabbed one of those goals, while the other came about after a

goalmouth scramble, where the ball came back off a Cavan man and ended up in the back of the net. Our drenched supporters who had made the journey rose to their feet as we made our way off to an appreciative round of applause.

The win meant that we'd stayed ahead of Down by just a single point in the standings. With just two rounds to go we sat alone on nine points, with Down second on eight. Behind that came Roscommon on six. Cavan, Galway and Kildare sat on five, with Clare and Laois cast adrift at the bottom with just a single point each.

As fate would have it, Down were up next but crucially, we felt, the game was fixed for Ballybofey. Our supporters were now firmly rowed in behind us and they were no doubt going to make it as uncomfortable as humanly possible for the footballing aristocrats from the Mourne county.

On Valentine's Day, February 14, 1988, very little love was shown by either set of players. As usual, the conditions were atrocious and the contest quickly developed into a wrestle in the mud. The sides were locked at 0-5 each at half-time. By the end, we'd only add two more to our tally as Down won out 0-11 to 0-7. They would also leapfrog us in the standings as we slipped to second.

Crucially though, our hopes of going up still rested in our own hands. And our final game was away to already relegated Laois, who had failed to win a single game in their previous six outings. On Sunday, February 28, 1988, Tom Conaghan wrote his own little but significant piece of Donegal footballing history when he led the side to a first ever promotion to the National Football League top flight. All was well that ended well, but there was no doubt we did things the hard way in O'Moore Park. With the gale force breeze at our backs in the first-half we only mustered two points on the scoreboard. A disaster, it felt, was on the cards.

Believe it or not, both those points came from myself, as I looked to make the most of the elements when I raided through from the middle. As well as that, Gary Walsh was called upon in spectacular fashion to deny the home side a certain goal.

Our problem in that first-half was that we tried to find our inside men and more often than not the ball carried in and over their heads. It took the locals what seemed like forever to retrieve those stray balls and all I could think to myself as the half-time whistle blew was, *we're screwed.*

As we dried ourselves off and settled in for an almighty chewing, Tom, as was his way, quoted Micko. 'If you play against crap, you'll stay crap', or something along those lines. He laid it on the line and in clear terms. The simple fact was that if we wanted our championship performances to improve, we had to be playing Division 1 football. And here we were in 'Port-f***ing-laoise' as Donal Monaghan aptly described it, level-pegging with relegated Laois at the midpoint having played with the wind.

The gameplan was torn up before we went back out.

Our wing backs Shovlin and Reid were told to empty themselves into the mouth of the breeze from now on and carry the ball into an area where it could be worked over the bar. And given the day that was in it that meant we almost had to go right into the '21'. Martin or 'Rambo' as he had now been christened, was told to hold the middle along with Dunleavy if needed and I was to keep doing what I was doing. Our inside men were ordered to drop deep to aid this running of the ball.

And with those simple enough instructions, keep ball if you will with very little kick passing, we were a side transformed following the restart.

Laois would finish the game with just three points while we'd add another 1-3 to eventually win out on a scoreline of 1-5 to 0-3. Charlie grabbed a crucial goal with a typically fine bursting run while McHugh, Bonner and Manus nailed the other points. Surprisingly, Down had only drawn in Clare, so both they and ourselves ended up locked on 11 points each. But their better scoring average sent them up as champions. It wasn't something that annoyed us too long and as the significance of our achievement dawned on us pretty quickly, it felt amazing.

TOM, HIS METHODS and his ways had been slaughtered for so long. But he'd delivered on his promise. And no one could blame him when he availed of the opportunity to bask in a little of all of that. At the subsequent week's county board sitting he had one or three cuts at his detractors. Donegal, he said, were now Division 1 quality footballers and paraphrasing what he asked of the press, he basically challenged them to step up their own game from here on in.

Of course, the *Democrat* carried all of those quotes on the following Thursday's back page. To be honest, we all got a great laugh out of it that same evening at training. We were looking forward to a league quarter-final clash with Monaghan, so the mood was jovial as we headed out onto the training pitch. Even Tom and the management team of Donal and John Cassidy found the article funny, but soon enough it was crumpled up and binned as Donal brought an end to the shenanigans.

Our mid-March tangle with Monaghan was fixed for Omagh. They had finished third in Division 1 and were, of course, a rival for the Ulster title so a few different things were on the line at Healy Park. By the time we pulled into the venue on the day of the match the weather was worse than usual. And there was even talk that the game might be called off. But it eventually got under way and from very early on, I sensed that Monaghan just weren't at our level. We were fitter and it seemed much more determined to prolong our stay in the league hunt.

We did ship a careless goal when Eamon Murphy netted inside the first quarter after a very rare mistake from Gary, but we would clip two successive points through Martin to come back to within a point. We could even have had the lead had we been more accurate in front of the posts. But there was no doubt we were first to every ball and winning most if not all the individual battles.

One man proving particularly hot to handle was Manus. He was giving Gerry McCarville the run-around at full-forward. But on 24 minutes an off-the-ball incident between the pair was flagged up and the game stopped. Gerry looked like he'd been taken out of it by a sniper. He wasn't moving.

Monaghan lads were crowding the referee and it was painfully obvious that something underhanded was going on here. Some of the bigger lads waded in and when order was eventually restored, Antrim official John Gough went to the foot of the posts to talk to his umpires. Finally, Gough makes his way back out towards Manus and brandished a straight red card.

An obviously dejected Manus pleaded his innocence and I could tell by the now 'conscious' Monaghan man, that little or nothing had occurred. At half-time the score was level at 1-1 to 0-4. As we made our way in, to a man, Manus explained that he did not touch his marker and that McCarville had simply flung himself to the ground. We didn't need much talking to at the break and the motivation for the second-half was easily sourced.

We threw everything we had at Monaghan, but down a man we just couldn't drag ourselves over the line and were squeezed out by 1-5 to 0-6. Tempers flared outside the dressing-rooms and it was very close to completely kicking off. But both sides were eventually bundled inside by a variety of officials. Tom let rip at the antics of McCarville to the waiting media. He was like a bull in the corridors and continued to let his feelings known as he came back in and closed the door.

But he settled instantly, and insisted to all of us that we'd passed another significant test. His rationale was lost on many of us but he said the battling qualities we'd shown in the second-half were exactly what he demanded and asked for. He insisted that we would have easily won the game with fifteen men on the pitch. And with a little bit more luck we could still have won it down to fourteen.

His point was that we'd given it everything and for that he could not be mad or critical of us. At a subsequent disciplinary hearing, Manus was handed a three-month suspension. But he'd be back for our Ulster Championship opener with Armagh. We'd have the McKenna Cup to contend with in between and that got up and running pretty sharpish, the very next week, after our league quarter-final elimination.

WE WERE, OR at least we felt, primed and ready to throw the kitchen sink at the rest of the season. The bandwagon had momentum and was hurtling down the road towards our destination of the Athletic Grounds and Sunday, June 12.

But the wheels were about to wobble worryingly at the most unlikely of junctures.

Tom Conaghan was a friend and admirer of the great Mick O'Dwyer (top) and appeared to take his advice. In building his team, Tom also offered Anthony's clubmate Martin Gavigan and John Joe Doherty opportunities to build their great county careers.

« CHAPTER 8 »

'Never apologise and never explain...
it's a sign of weakness'

– John Wayne

NO ONE COULD have imagined just how bad, pathetic even, our subsequent collapse would be. Even now, being asked to recall or source a reason or 'the reason', it's impossible to put one finger on it. I couldn't grasp it then and, to this day, it still grates at me.

A McKenna Cup defeat to Antrim, in Belfast, tipped the first domino. As a consequence of that, we would have no competitive action again until our championship outing in Armagh. There were some comings and goings in the nine or so weeks of build-up but there was no major upheaval.

We trained hard and we trained well.

Tom picked a good side, a team that would include 11 players who would go on to start and win the 1992 All-Ireland. In the lead-up, even Tom's fiercest detractors in print felt he'd got it right with a selection of: Gary Walsh; John Joe Doherty, Brendan Dunleavy, Matt Gallagher; John Cunningham, Donal Reid, Martin Shovlin; Anthony Molloy, Martin Gavigan; Martin McHugh, Charlie Mulgrew, Tommy Ryan; Declan Bonner, Joyce McMullin, Manus Boyle.

This was our chance to make a statement and progress into the Ulster semi-finals. It was also an opportunity to seek vengeance for the manner in which Armagh humiliated us the year before in our own backyard. The stage was set... the afternoon baking hot and the terraces full of noise, mischief and anticipation. Our supporters, won over by the way we went about our business in the league, rewarded our efforts by making the journey in their droves.

The national soccer team had made history by qualifying for its first ever major tournament, the European Championship, which were being held in Germany. Our own Packie Bonner was in goal and the interest in all of that was huge.

There was just this real energy and hope to the day from very early on.

Wireless radios were being held to the ear by many, but there was no doubt that by turning up in Armagh instead of hitting the pubs to take in the Republic of Ireland's opening group clash with England, our supporters had paid us the ultimate compliment. Believe me, that meeting and the build-up to it in Stuttgart was massive. So there was an air of expectancy and hope at the Athletic Grounds.

AND THEN, A very strange thing happened.

The ball was thrown in and we simply wilted. We folded completely... from the very first minute. By the quarter hour mark, the game was already on the verge of slipping away from us as we trailed 1-4 to 0-1. It was still only six points, but to a man... the white flags were going up.

We finally pulled together some kind of response as we added three points to the board before half-time through McHugh twice and Joyce late on. We managed to hold Armagh scoreless for the entire second quarter, meaning just a goal split the teams at the break. However, the capitulation we feared was coming at one stage in that opening half did arrive in the second and, in the end, Armagh stuffed us 2-10 to 0-8. It was an eight-point humiliation.

A loud cheer broke out at one point in the second-half and that only meant one thing – that Ireland or, more to the point Ray Houghton, had just put the ball in the English net.

As I looked around the pitch following the final whistle, I just couldn't fathom what or who was to blame for this embarrassment. Tom though certainly did. And immediately after, as we filed past, both he and the press and onto the bus, it was clear that he was washing his hands completely of our sorry collapse.

'There's no point in blaming the referee, no point in blaming the county board or management. The players have to carry this one, that's the way I would see it. On different occasions in the past we, the management, have accepted responsibility for different things which have happened.

'I'm not offloading the blame to anybody, but to go out and give the performance

they gave after the way they were prepared by Donal and myself, there can be no excuses unless the players can make some.'

I didn't blame Tom and I couldn't entirely disagree with him.

Tom had his faults and he certainly had his critics. But there was nothing in that hour or so of football that resembled anything he represented or stood for. The pride and maybe hope we'd managed to build up in the league was ripped from us in the most demoralising of fashions. And I just knew the knives would be out.

Four was the highest mark awarded by the *Democrat* in their ratings scheme. I was afforded a two, which I no doubt deserved. Of course, those knifes that continued to be sharpened for the next couple of weeks were finally put to use at the July county board meeting. There were personal vendettas and scores being settled with some of the criticism.

Clubs that felt they should have had players on the county team, like Aodh Ruadh were, through delegate John Travers, particularly scathing. My own clubmate John McConnell had his say, stating, *'Donegal are now bottom of the pile'.*

Tom, going by the newspapers, was a little subdued in delivering his report. He'd usually come out swinging, so I didn't know what to really read into that.

The club season proved to be a welcome distraction and we eventually edged a marathon three-game saga with Naomh Columba, a tie that was only decided after extra-time. The games were the talk of the county for a number of weeks. But we eventually made it through to the semi-finals. But despite an heroic effort, eventual winners Killybegs would account for us 1-9 to 0-10, and that was that.

THE NATIONAL FOOTBALL League fixtures for our first ever Division 1 campaign had been released and with the curtain down on club football, attention once again began to veer towards the Donegal team. So much of it was negative.

'Papers are inventing stories,' county secretary Bart Whelan would fume on local radio. And he was adamant that, *'A vendetta was being carried out against the county football team manager by one newspaper in particular'.* Bart raged that if there were certain disgruntled players carrying stories behind Tom's back then they were not the kind of men Donegal needed to get back on top.

And, in the midst of Bart's barbs, *The Follower* got the blame for stirring up or giving a voice to what he labelled, *'player-power'.*

On top of all of this, Tom was about to name his NFL panel. When that landed, it only served to endorse much of the previous newspaper gossip. A number of challenge or trial matches had been played. But those conspicuous by their absence meant that there was a fair idea some big hitters had checked out.

And when Tom finally did release his 25-man squad, most of the talk centred on those who were absent... Declan Bonner, Sean Bonner, Matt Gallagher, Manus Boyle, John Cunningham and Barry Cunningham had, for one reason or another, opted to not play senior county football that term. The Cunninghams were emigrating and Manus had some knee issues. A young and up-and-coming Barry McGowan had said he'd be interested in coming on board after Christmas, but that was never going to be entertained by Tom. All of that meant Killybegs, the reigning county club champions in Donegal, would have no representation on that season's county squad.

Sean Bonner had given a flat no when approached by Tom, while brother Declan intended to play soccer over that winter as well. Matt also, it seemed, just wasn't interested in playing for Tom. Now, I'm sure all those guys would have different recollections of that time. And they would all come back into the fold down the line to become All-Ireland winners. But the fact was Donegal needed them there and then.

And I will always wonder what might have been achieved in 1989 had we kept everyone on board.

I firmly believe we'd have won Ulster.

We could and should have won it without them. And I've no problem saying we would have gone seriously close to an All-Ireland title. We were in our pomp and prime. Ironically enough, Tom decided to sit down with the *Democrat* and, on the record, lay his cards out on the table ahead of the new season.

'From the day I took over there was an anti-Tom Conaghan thing in the camp, at least with a few of the players. I know quite well there were players speaking behind my back trying to stir things up. I knew there would be a certain amount of this, I suppose it was only natural with new management. They had been around a while and weren't going to be pushed around.

'I made an effort to discuss these problems with the players who seemed unhappy but it didn't seem to clear the air with a few of them and it steadily got worse.

'It was a known fact there was a certain element of player power within the county

and maybe that was one of the reasons I was given the role to get Donegal football the way it should be so that players would have pride wearing the county jersey.

'In my opinion The Follower was a mouthpiece for these players who weren't prepared to come out into the open themselves. Without being too harsh on the man, he has given me a fair whack since I started. I don't think a person like this can class himself as a true follower of Donegal. From day one it was obvious that this man did not agree with my style of management and his outpourings are nothing short of a joke.'

If anyone had felt Tom's previous sombre or downcast end-of-year report hinted that they were now dealing with a defeated man well, they were left in no doubt that nothing could have been further from the truth. This was Tom backed into a corner, but now coming out swinging.

'We're in Division 1 now and I would like to say to the supporters, give the players that are here a chance. They are the committed ones and that's what Donegal football needs. Get behind the players and give them the respect they deserve. At least they are prepared to wear the jersey. We did something in last year's league campaign that was never done before. And none of those players being talking about were involved.

AS FATE WOULD have it, our first taste of Division 1 football would come back at the scene of our Championship crime the season before, as Armagh played host at the Athletic Grounds. Unlike our June debacle, we stepped up to the mark here, at least in terms of the effort and desire needed. But some old failings were still evident as we went down 0-10 to 0-9. Unfortunately, we'd lost big Dunleavy, our captain, to a bad hamstring pull and the management just weren't sure how long Brendan would be absent.

Still, one of the biggest and most important moments of my career, the one that opened up the door to everything else, came about because of Brendan's misfortune. On the Tuesday night when we gathered once again for training, Tom casually announced that I was going to take over the role of captain... that I was going to now lead the group.

I'd done the job so often for club and underage Donegal sides and, I suppose, it was something that I probably felt might come my way at some stage. But this was out of the blue and it caught me by real surprise.

Some perhaps felt that the armband should have gone to Martin. And it was something that did cross my mind, to talk to him about it. But I decided not to. The truth is, Martin didn't need to be captain of this group. He was already leading by example and was never shy in having his say. Tom knew what he was getting from Martin every single time he put him out on a pitch. Perhaps this was a challenge being laid down to me. Tom was looking for consistency in my performances and maybe that extra responsibility, that sense of duty, would bring that week in, week out.

All-Ireland and NFL champions Meath were on their way to Ballybofey the following Sunday. I knew right away I'd be up against Liam Hayes. Being made captain ahead of such an assignment had me trembling from head to toe. But it wasn't nerves, it was adrenalin. Again, I remember Micko addressing us, as a group, one time Tom had taken him up to Donegal to watch an under-21 training session many years previously.

Micko explained that adrenalin had gotten a bad rap over the years. That people were wrongly dressing the sensation up as 'nerves' when it was, in fact, your body preparing itself for combat or some sort of stress or challenge. Adrenalin, Micko said, was what made us run faster, hit harder and jump higher. I recently read a Roy Keane article where he described a very similar reaction to whenever Manchester United were on the verge of facing Arsenal. Keane knew that the Gunners were the biggest threat to United's title aspirations and he also knew that a certain Patrick Viera was going to be his direct competition.

And I've no doubt that my body was already in preparation mode for facing down the best side, and best midfielder in the country, in five days' time. I grew to love the onset of that first little leg tremor. I waited for it, and sometimes grew anxious if, a day or two out from a big game, it hadn't kicked in.

Yeah, I was sometimes nervous about not being nervous. But it always came. It didn't happen every single week. But when it did, it was because you knew something big or special was on the horizon. We were like men possessed on the Thursday night. I addressed the group. I tried to do it from the heart. I spoke my mind.

I might not have been the most eloquent man in the room, but I wanted to be the most determined and passionate. When we huddled up, I squeezed the man to my left and, like a chain reaction, waited until that same squeeze had made its way all around the huddle before finally arriving back at source and burying deep into my own right hand side.

Then, and only then, did I say my piece.

We delivered spectacularly on our pre-game promise and beat the Royals 0-15 to 1-6. I was awarded the 'Man of the Match' in the *Democrat* and given a lofty 9 in the Player Ratings. The usually hard to please Connie Duffy commented that I was, *'Two steps ahead of Hayes for most of the hour'* and that, *'were I to describe the Ardara man's contribution on Sunday, I'd run out of superlatives'*. On the way back to the dressing-room Martin whispered to me that I should dampen enthusiasm straight away, as soon as the door was shut. And he was right. Unlike Divisions 2 and 3, there is never an off week in Division 1, or a Sunday that you can ease off.

Next up was Kerry in Killarney.

That was big enough but there was also the sub-plot of Tom coming up against his friend and great confidante Micko. I wanted to win this one for Tom. That was my motivation. Jack O'Shea and a young Maurice Fitzgerald were the midfield pairing Kerry were using. We knew all about O'Shea but Tom had already told me a year or two beforehand that Micko had described this young 'Fitz' lad as, *'sent from the heavens'*. He was two-footed and doing some outrageous things with a football. Myself and Gavigan knew we'd have to bring a certain physicality to matters, if we were to put him off his game.

Getting togged, it only dawned on me that there would be a colour clash with both counties traditional green and gold jerseys. I could see Tom and Donal locked in deep conversation with the match referee at the door. As captain, I felt I should wander over. It soon became apparent that Donegal had been issued a directive midweek to take their away kit or, provincial colours with them.

Tom though, and this was so out of character that I almost laughed at the insincerity of it all, could only offer his apologies for such an oversight. We were over 200 miles from home so it wasn't like he could spin back for them. In the end, it was Donegal that ran out in Tralee in their familiar colours. Kerry were the ones that had to change and, in the blue of Munster, they just didn't seem as imposing or that celestial.

Tom had pulled a fast one on his great mentor and it set a brilliant tone in the dressing-room just before we ran out.

'In the air, Molloy climbed higher than the mighty O'Shea and on the ground his dedication was the keystone to this victory.' The *Democrat's* lavish praise continued to flow my way and I felt empowered. But not in an arrogant way… I just felt that

at 26 years old I was approaching my peak. I pushed myself as hard as I could in training. And in games I genuinely feared letting both the team and Tom down.

How could I, as the group's leader, give instruction before, during or after, if I wasn't delivering myself? Honest to God, that dread buried deep in the back of my head was what drove me on. And it was powerful fuel.

Towards the end of the year, the endorsement of all of that arrived in the form of the Donegal Player of the Year award.

A 1-11 to 2-12 loss to Down in Ballyshannon – a game where we'd gone seven clear at one stage – dampened the mood somewhat as we broke for Christmas and New Year. When we got going again at the start of February another loss, this time to Derry in Drumsurn, meant that we were now in real danger of slipping back down to Division 2. A much needed 1-6 to 0-5 win over Monaghan in Ballyshannon steadied us somewhat but with a final league outing away to Dublin in Croke Park, we still had it all to do if we were to fend of relegation.

In the end, despite a battling effort, our Croker hoodoo remained intact as Dublin squeezed us out 1-10 to 0-9. Thankfully, Kerry and Micko showed that they bore no ill feeling towards us for our antics in Tralee and with the Kingdom downing Monaghan that same day, we managed to survive, just about.

WE'D BEEN DRAWN to play Cavan away in the championship and a dress rehearsal of sorts awaited us in Ballyshannon in the first round of the McKenna Cup. We got over the line, barely, at 1-10 to 1-9. But we'd led at one-point early in the second-half by 10 points. So again, there was plenty of criticism.

In the fortnight's break between the end of the league and the start of the McKenna Cup, the local papers again picked at the scab that was those players who were absent. Tom had actually entertained asking the likes of Manus, Matt, Barry Cunningham and Barry McGowan back in and giving some weary legs a much-needed rest. But there was a kick back from the squad.

I'd no reservations about the recalls, I felt we needed the lads. But others strongly believed that those who had earned our stay in Division 1 deserved to be the ones that got a rattle at the Ulster Championship.

To be fair to those same lads, the ones that were objecting I mean, I could see their side. They'd stuck to Tom's severe rules, they'd hung in there and they felt he was now going back on that word. I didn't feel threatened by any of the possible recalls and, as captain, I felt our needs were best served with the boys back in tow.

But the names being mentioned… I'd no doubt every single one of them would have been coming back into the team, not just the panel and that, in the end, was the bone of the rejection.

Tom, to be fair, was prepared to bend. But on this occasion, the majority of the players simply weren't. It was an opportunity lost. And in siding with the players Tom, in a way, went against his own creed. I've no doubt had that crop come back in we'd have won the Ulster Championship and it would have taken something really powerful to stop us after that. And in a way, even though we didn't know it yet, it was a decision that probably cost Tom his job.

But at the time, what the team needed to do was back their stance up with a performance that endorsed the decision. But a shambolic 5-7 to 1-14 McKenna Cup loss to Down, after a drawn encounter in Ballyshannon, meant that the talk of those absent continued to dominate the local papers.

WE'D SEVEN WEEKS to get our act together before our Championship bow at Breffni Park. We returned to the unforgiving sands of Murvagh Beach. It was horrible work. It was hell on earth, to be honest. But the longer evenings and lead-in to summer meant it was much more bearable that the pre-season slog done at the same location. It was also galvanising and you knew with each passing session that you were edging closer to the level needed.

But, in mid-April our focus was shattered, blown to pieces really, when the news came through that Pauric Gallagher, our former teammate and friend, had died tragically in a road traffic accident in Boston. It was heart-breaking and it was something that left a good few of us, especially the ones that had soldiered with Pauric at under-21, in a very sad and lonely place.

Matt of course wasn't with the group and it felt even lonelier because of that. We wanted to be there for him and, of course, we were. But it just felt like such a blow. We'd this huge match just around the corner but in an instant the importance or significance of that seemed to evaporate. When we did meet back up after Pauric had been laid to rest, you wondered what it would feel like.

To be honest, and it wasn't something we discussed, but it seemed easy to throw yourself back into it.

There were no great declarations or anything like that but there probably was a comfort or distraction in going at it again, hammer and tongs. It was probably quiet enough work for those first few sessions. But soon enough, the old noise and instruction began to grow loud once more.

We had a serious amount of work banked.

And the truth is, that's where real confidence and belief is forged. If you know you have the work done then there is no reason why the hinges shouldn't be ripped from the dressing-room door on the way out. That's the point we were at.

I've often run out onto a football pitch when the exact opposite was true. And that old saying, *'They were beat before they went out'* is a real thing. It's never uttered beforehand, but I've seen men sometimes come to blows after, when that home truth is thrashed out. First and foremost, before anything else… have the work done.

We were back on the grass of Townawilly now but the punishment didn't end just because we'd relocated. The hill there… it was like something out of the TV show *Gladiators*. 'The Travelator' I think, is what it was called. That's what those endless runs up that hill resembled.

Men caving in at different spots on its elevation. But desperate times called for desperate measures. Donegal hadn't won an Ulster Championship game since 1985. And throughout the torture, Tom kept yelling at us, *'DONEGAL WILL BE NO THREAT COME CHAMPIONSHIP… DONEGAL WILL BE NO THREAT COME CHAMPIONSHIP!'*

When we finally caught breath during the warm down, big Brian Murray, barely able to string the words together, because he was so exhausted, asked, *'What the hell was Tom going on about?'*

Murray, like a few men, wasn't actually aware that Cavan boss Gabriel Kelly had told the *Anglo Celt* newspaper, after that previous McKenna Cup game, *'that Donegal wouldn't be any kind of threat in the Ulster Championship'*. So we had our ammunition and motivation. But we didn't have to go as far as Cavan to find newspaper articles that doubted us, even ridiculed our chances. There were plenty of those much closer to home.

But it was all fodder.

Breffni Park was parting at the seams come Sunday, May 21.

Tom had decided he needed to push 'Rambo' back to No 6 – a position he'd make his own and, in the process, give us the authority and steel we'd been perhaps missing in that area. It was another very important piece of the jigsaw that was now slowly coming together.

Because of that, Tom tasked Glenties' Michael Gallagher with the job of partnering me around the middle. 'Big G' was what we called him. Michael was late coming on the county scene but here he was making his Championship bow at the age of 27. And you know something, he didn't let anyone down.

We were up against Vivian Dowd and Stephen King, a fearsome pairing that Cavan had confidently pinned so much of their hopes upon. But myself and Michael didn't take a backward step and even before King departed in the second-half through injury, we had that battle won.

Joyce was immense and tore through the Cavan defence to hammer in two goals and a point in a 3-12 to 0-14 win. McHugh and Tommy Ryan also stood tall. We were now just 70 minutes out from the Ulster final. In our way stood a very good Derry side that had just put 4-15 past Fermanagh. Plunkett Murphy and Brian McGilligan manned the middle for Derry but I certainly held no fear of those two. And Big G... well, he was running around in training and taking plenty of heads in the process. So I'd absolutely no issues going into battle alongside Michael once more. I'd played regularly with G in New York and I knew just how hardy a bit of stuff he was.

Like I said, 'Rambo' seemed to have found his home at centre-back and he just offered this sense of safety and presence that both myself and Michael felt. We'd openly talked about it after and how you could commit fully to a kickout or aerial duel, because you just knew this animal was behind you ready to mop up if we'd come up short. And knowing that and without apprehension, we seemed to get to ball against Cavan that we just wouldn't have got to in the past.

But even with things going so well, the *Democrat* tried to stir matters up when they published an interview McEniff gave to the *Anglo Celt* prior to the Cavan game, where Brian named-checked the players that weren't there or who Tom hadn't chosen. We'd got the win, so what was the point of putting out those week-old comments Brian had given before the game? If we'd lost, I could understand a little better, but this was just another effort at poking the bear... the bear being Tom.

But it was all fuel, because in a way some of the lads that had got the job done against a lauded Cavan were still being told they weren't good enough. In our semi-final against the Derrymen, Martin was the one stepping up and a super haul of 2-2 went a long way in helping to secure a 2-8 to 1-9 win. And Martin was lucky to be involved at all as he suffered a work accident in the lead up where some sort of sign came off its station and his shoulder bore the brunt of its fall.

But the 'Wee Man' stood tall and the likes of John Joe, Shovlin and Reid also injected some serious energy and pace.

Standing in our way, between us and a first Ulster title since 1983, was the province's residential hard men, Tyrone. They'd laid plenty of markers on their side of the draw and stories of how they dished out some real batterings, both on the scoreboard and on the field of play, to the likes of Armagh and Down were widely being told. They revelled in that reputation as well. But we weren't going to Omagh and if Tyrone wanted to bang heads in this game of football, then I had every confidence that our boys wouldn't be found wanting.

We didn't have to dress ourselves up as hard men.

But believe me, we had our own collection of bruisers and tough nuts who could all look after themselves. All we were asking for was a fair crack of the whip. And if we got that we'd go close.

Being appointed Donegal captain was the greatest honour of Anthony's football career, and in his first season he knew he had to lead by example, which he did by outplaying the magnificent Jack O'Shea, amongst others, in the 1988/89 National League. But Tom Conaghan still was struggling to come to grips with his strongest squad and amongst those who didn't fall into line for the manager were Barry McGowan, Declan Bonner and Manus Boyle.

« CHAPTER 9 »

*'The trouble with referees is that they know the rules,
but they don't know the game'*

– Bill Shankly

THE NAME MICHAEL Greenan probably doesn't ring too many bells with Donegal supporters but for the group of players that contested the drawn 1989 Ulster final encounter, it will forever be etched at the back of our minds.

For some, the Cavanman is a former Ulster Council president. But for me and those boys of that time, he's the man who cost us an Ulster medal.

Had we not finally got our act together in the following years, the late events of that controversial draw with Tyrone would probably have been more openly spoken about. We'd have remained very bitter. But the truth is, I still haven't forgiven him.

This was a far from pretty game of football.

And over the course of it we kicked 14 wides – many of them poorly executed opportunities that should have hit the mark. In what was a clumsy, and stop-start affair, I don't think the man in the middle intentionally swayed one way or the other. But there is no doubt he got a massive call very wrong at the end.

In the dying seconds of injury-time, we somehow had managed to find ourselves 0-11 to 0-10 in front, with Tommy posting what seemed like a sure-fire winner. As the resulting kick-out came booming out from Tyrone stopper Aidan Skelton, those seconds where it hangs in the air are surely going to be interrupted by Greenan's final whistle… but, for some reason, on we go.

Damien O'Hagan finally finds possession but he's a fair enough distance from goal. John Connors – a superb and very underrated player from Donegal's past

– looks to hold firm and stand his man up. A desperate and no doubt frustrated O'Hagan tries to drive at him but it's a charge where John backs off at just the right time, and the Tyrone man simply falls over. It was evident in real time and it was even more evident when we watched the incident back later on that night.

I glance towards Greenan and I immediately see his hand signal Tyrone's direction before he even blows the whistle. And we're absolutely furious, livid. I'm looking at the posts, it's something like 35 or maybe 40 yards out and there's an angle to the kick that appears tricky. Stephen Conway has kicked well enough all afternoon but he looked nervous here as he's told, *'This has to go dead… it's the last kick of the game'* by the referee.

I offer my own whispered 'encouragement' as he goes through his kicking routine. My first instinct, as it leaves his boot, is that he hasn't caught it right. The loop of it looks off and I wait for it to tail away.

But it somehow catches the upright at a fortunate angle and falls back between the posts. My immediate reaction is to usher the likes of 'Rambo' and Shovlin, men foaming at the mouth, away from the referee. *There's going to be another day out here and we can't give him the opportunity to further wrong us.* The others are in a state of shock.

There is no doubt we all believed we were about to be crowned the new Ulster champions. The noise that greeted Tommy's point was deafening, but it also felt like an acknowledgement from our supporters that the job was done… we were finally over the line. But in the cruellest of fashions our desperate want and need for an Ulster title was taken away from us.

THE HEADS WERE completely down in the dressing-room.

That was understandable, but we'd drawn the game, we hadn't been beaten. After a cooling off period, attempts were made to lift spirits and cries of *'WE GO AGAIN'* soon echoed around the room.

Again, our local papers chose to centre in on the negatives and one even ran with the headline, **'Heroes or Villains?'** In whose head or mind did that seem like a suitable or even legitimate question to pose of a team that had almost delivered a first provincial title in six seasons, and a side that still had another bite of the cherry in front of them?

Yeah, there were men outside the wire that should have been playing and yes, had we them in our ranks and in the starting line-up we'd have been a much better side, good enough to beat that Tyrone anyway. Those same men were and still are, to this very day my friends, really good ones at that. But I still believe that if you want to play for Donegal... you play! You put personality clashes and differences of opinions to one side, and you turn up and tog out. On one hand, Tom's iron fisted approach had almost reaped its reward. Here was the example of what a total buy in approach could achieve.

Shy of up to a half dozen genuine contenders for starting places in our team, we'd almost got over the line. There had been no shortcuts taken that year. But in the end, the lack of genuine options, competition and perhaps killer quality in the team was what proved to be our undoing.

On what I can easily describe as one of my worst days in football, Tyrone would hammer us 2-13 to 0-7 in the replay. It was embarrassing stuff. It was one of those games where you just wanted to curl up in a ball after and hide. Events just seemed to conspire against us from very early on. Martin had kicked the game's opening score but a targeted take out on him soon after, a shoulder injury that should have seen him go off, limited his impact from that point on.

On 23 minutes, Tyrone were holding a 1-2 to 0-3 lead after Stephen Conway had earlier slotted home a penalty. But the tide really turned when Brendan Dunleavy and 'Rambo' both went to contest the same ball but inadvertently crashed into each other. The thud of that dangerous coming together was deafening. With that pair worringly stretched out on the ground, Damien O'Hagan took full advantage of the situation to palm in a second Red Hand goal.

The rest of the contest is a bit of a blur but the sight of some Donegal supporters funnelling out of the ground midway through the second-half was a difficult watch.

The post-mortems began right away.

Some felt that the running sessions undertaken between both games, on the training field, had left us sapped. I didn't buy that. The disappointment of the previous week had cut deep. And I think deep down we simply knew that our chance had probably slipped. We didn't go out to lose but there just wasn't that belief within the group, collectively, that we could come back again and claw ourselves over the line. Regardless of the drawn game being scrappy, and despite the wides tally, we'd given it absolutely everything that first day. The end was within seconds of justifying the means as far as Tom's hard-line approach was concerned.

The failure to back that up and the nature of our collapse in the replay meant that Tom simply wouldn't survive. His three-year term was up and while he intended to seek re-election the fact that a recharged McEniff was also back in the running meant that vote was only ever going to swing one way.

As well as Tom and Brian, PJ McGowan and Hugh McClafferty would also put their names forward. But this was a two-horse race from the very start. Brian politicked and canvassed the clubs and there was no doubt the delegates were with him. Tom just wasn't going to play that game.

And, in the end, with eight votes to spare, McEniff was back at the helm of Donegal football. Supporters of our county team wanted to see our best side take to the field and the belief was that there was a better chance of that happening under Brian.

They were right, but there was also the real chance that we could easily slip back into that undisciplined comfort zone that had been prevalent in Brian's last tenure. 1992 did come along, quite soon in fact, but the truth of the matter is that 1991 was a complete disaster. But 1990... there is no doubt that Brian walked into a set-up that was ready to be led.

Under Tom we were conditioned to within an inch of our lives, like broken horses. The very least that was expected of us now was that we showed up and we trained. And because of that base, McEniff could bring to the table his real skills and expertise. The irony in all of this was that Tom's shortcoming, the sword upon which he fell in the end, was that he wasn't a little more like Brian.

And Brian's failures in the past could have been transformed had he been a little more like Tom. We're talking about two great men here but two very different individuals all the same. I've told both since that they would have made a brilliant and very formidable 'good cop/bad cop' duo had they decided, at the time, to put their heads together.

RIGHT AWAY, BRIAN set about mending bridges and as quick as a flash he'd managed to entice most of the prodigal sons back into the reckoning. Barry McGowan, Declan and Sean Bonner, Sylvester Maguire, Manus Boyle and Matt Gallagher were all present at our first get-together. Barry and John Cunningham, when they returned from England, and Tommy Ryan, in the States, would also be drafted back into the mix down the line.

Imagine any GAA transfer window delivering such a cluster of talent to one team? I looked around that squad, when all the pieces were finally in place, and I felt it had the potential to take us to the very top. And I wasn't just thinking about Ulster titles. Again, one of the opinions or, the opinion that really counted for me was McHugh's. I pulled him aside and we talked.

And the nub of that conversation was that markers had to be laid down… standards had to be kept. If these lads could be whipped into shape, like the previous group had, it could yield awesome results. McEniff's assembled backroom team included Naul McCole, my own clubmate Anthony Harkin, Seamus Bonner and Mickey Lafferty. The first obstacle both the team and the new management had to contend with was a new set of experimental playing rules which would be trialled in the National League. Frees, sidelines and kickouts were now going to be allowed to be taken from the hands. The motivation behind those changes was to speed up the game. The kickout one especially was going to have an impact on midfielders as the trajectory of those kicks was going to change significantly.

The games were also going to be split up into four quarters.

Brian was very vocal about his dislike for the changes right away. But we had to quickly set about getting used to things in training. In Division 1 of the NFL we'd be locking horns with Armagh, Cavan, Kerry, Down, Derry, Cork and Dublin, and in that order. All the big hitters were there and with a pair of Ulster opponents up first, before a clash with Kerry, two opening wins were immediately targeted.

Armagh, a bit of a bogey side for us in recent times, were downed in convincing fashion, in Ballybofey, by 3-12 to 0-13. The new rules and the ferociously quicker restarts seemed to suit us. 'Rambo' of all people nailed the first goal there, while Joyce and Martin Carlin also found the net. I particularly enjoyed my own tussles with big, bad Mark Grimley. Hard but fair is how I'd describe most of our exchanges.

It was, as the *Democrat* labelled it, *'A five-year bogey'* off our backs. Before our trip to Breffni Park, we played a specially arranged match with an All Star select to honour the memory of Pauric Gallagher. The likes of Paul Earley, Liam McHale and Ciaran Duff all travelled up to Ballyshannon to take part. It was a really special day. It was potent and I could feel it galvanising us even further in a certain kind of way.

In a dirty and niggly contest in Cavan we just about got the job done, with a McHugh goal proving decisive in a 1-12 to 0-13 victory. Manus kicked six of our points but it was 60 minutes littered with off the ball clashes. Mickey Kearins failed to stamp any kind of authority on matters and had to be escorted off the field at the end as both sets of players and some supporters looked to express their annoyance with the Sligo referee.

There was some criticism about the performance but sometimes those behind the pen or typewriter miss the point completely. There are just some games that you simply aren't going to be allowed to win pretty. We'd embarrassed Cavan the previous summer and they were intent on seeking some revenge here.

And there was real value to standing up to that premeditated aggression, especially in Breffni Park, and actually turning the tables. We were infuriated coming off but once settled we were quite happy with how we'd just acquitted ourselves. As well as securing two very valuable league wins, with Cavan drawn at home in the championship we'd also laid an important marker ahead of summer. But those points all seemed to fly over the heads of the local 'experts'. With Kerry scheduled to come to Ballyshannon next, just where we were at, footballing-wise, would surely be much clearer after that high-profile clash. Fr Tierney Park was understandably packed for the visit of the footballing aristocrats from the Kingdom.

Manus once again stole the show by kicking the winning point in a brilliant 0-11 to 0-10 victory. As well as our obvious big hitters, other lads were really stepping up to the plate. Gerry Curran was back in the mix. He truly was a footballing enigma and in no small way reminds me of current sometimes Donegal star, Odhran MacNiallais. 'Free spirits' is how I often see their like described. They play in a way that often makes no sense. But there is just this natural ability that allows them to be so impacting.

Here Gerry was terrorising a Kerry side possessing the likes of Jack O'Shea, Maurice Fitz and Charlie Nelligan, having not been involved at county level since McEniff last sprung him, out of nowhere, on the morning of the 1984 Ulster Championship loss to Armagh. And he would help himself to three sublime points on his own home patch. Paul Carr was also making a real impression in the middle of the half-back line. Barry McGowan made his senior debut that day, while James McHugh also caught the eye when sprung in the second-half.

Three games in and with as many wins, we were sitting top of the table.

Our last league outing before the Christmas break was away to Down, in

Newry, on Sunday December 10. We seemed to be in the driving seat shortly after half-time when a point to the good, the hosts lost Eamonn Burns to a second yellow card. We let our concentration drop and even with a man less, Down capitalised when Ambrose Rodgers' goal pushed them from one down to two to the good. In the end, the sending-off seemed to work against us as we were defeated 1-15 to 0-14. At the time it was a really frustrating way to go into Christmas but, in another way, it did ground us.

Four wins from four and there would have been that sense of entitlement – the one where you felt you'd worked hard and deserved a blowout. But there was no doubt we were far from the finished article at that point. Again, there still was a comfort knowing that the likes of John and Barry Cunningham, John Connors and Tommy Ryan would all be making returns from abroad in the new year. John Joe, someone I expected to start for Donegal come summer, was almost back from injury, while a certain Tony Boyle was also about to be unleashed on a national scene.

Again, McEniff and his management team held some trial games between then and early February when our NFL campaign would get going once again. As the 1980s prepared to roll into the 90s, I'd already made the decision that I wasn't going to sit idle and let my fitness slip. I was captain now and I had to approach things differently.

I continued to train. No one could ever say that about me, that I took the easy way out as far as the hard yards were concerned. In the end, it probably was to the detriment of my knees. But in 1990 I was injury free and in my prime. And I felt that as a side so too were so many of the others. And like I said, I fully expected our young guns, the missing puzzle pieces like John Joe, Tony Boyle, Barry McGowan and even an emerging Noel Hegarty, to show their worth during the rest of the league.

WE HAD TO stew over Christmas but I still firmly believed that something special was just around the corner or it was, at least, very close. As punishment for our slip against 14-man Down, McEniff decided to return a little earlier in January, which was a cute enough idea. In that A vs B game, the B side would also come out on top, which was also a cause for concern. McEniff had taken a look at close to 50 players in those few weeks and the truth was, the loss to the B team, coupled with the poor showing against Down… no-one returned to training that first week in January with any kind of spring in their steps.

Men were coming in the door grunting at each other, togging out and heading straight out into the sleet and snow. We were all intent on hitting the ground running. John Bán Gallagher, a new but very instant threat to my position, had taken three points off me in that so-called trial game.

At Ballyshannon, in early February of a brand new decade, all that simmering tension came to a perfect boil as we annihilated Derry by 0-11 to 0-3. It was a result that not only secured our top flight safety but pushed us right into the mix for a place in the quarter-finals. Conditions were atrocious but we dug in and earned a fine win.

Next up was a trip to Páirc Uí Chaoimh where reigning All-Ireland champions Cork awaited. The Rebels and Larry Tompkins, a legend of the game and a man I'd played beside in New York, would again help reveal that little bit more about the side collectively and, of course, myself as an individual force. Despite the distance involved, Donegal supporters travelled south in their droves.

Heavy rain had been forecast and there was an immediate doubt about the venue's ability to hold the fixture. No alternative was arranged and, in the back of your mind, you wondered if this could transpire to be the most wasted of journeys.

Landing at the famous old ground, it quickly became apparent to all that this game wasn't going to be played. Referee Tommy Sugrue admitted as much to both myself and Tompkins even before he had his walkabout. Already our board and the Cork board were at it and there was a palpable anger that we'd found ourselves in this ridiculous predicament at all. Cork, like ourselves, needed the win if they were to have a hope of advancing to the knockout stages. But they had a number of injuries and the immediate accusation was that they deliberately didn't arrange an alternative ground and let the Donegal team and their supporters travel, at great expense, to Páirc Uí Chaoimh knowing full well the pitch wouldn't pass its inspection.

Both their manager Billy Morgan and, at the time, their very outspoken secretary Frank Murphy, made half-hearted apologies to us as we stood about looking and very much feeling like dummies.

But there was no doubt whatsoever that we'd been hoodwinked.

The game would eventually be refixed for a fortnight later at Ballincollig, with assurances from the Cork County Board but, more importantly, Croke Park, that a number of alternatives were also in place should the weather intervene once again. Plenty of noise was made by Donegal officials about the entire farce and rightly so. But it was headlines and coverage that Cork, with all their big guns back in tow, would easily use.

There was an edge to matters now and a dark vibe in the air when we ventured back down to Munster a fortnight later. Because of the rearranged fixture McHugh had to cut short a holiday in Spain that clashed. That made the papers but, for some reason so too did the question of whether or not the county board would be funding his flight home? Who gave a flying f**k if that was the case or not? It wasn't Martin's fault and it was a huge declaration of his own commitment to do such a thing.

For 56 minutes, our angry efforts looked like they were going to get their desired and indeed deserving result. At the end of the third quarter we led our Rebel hosts 2-9 to 1-8. McHugh and John O'Driscoll traded points and the gap remained four going into the final 10 minutes. Joyce had a half-chance to net after he'd been teed up by a very tanned McHugh. But a brilliant save from the Cork 'keeper denied him.

In one final flurry a Tompkins sideline into the area was somehow slapped home by Shay Fahey – a contest under a high ball I was close to and should have taken a better command of. We didn't manage to win the subsequent kickout from Gary and the same Cork player levelled the game. These are the moments and scenarios that to this day, despite all the changes to our game, still separate the men from the boys. And worryingly, our old failing of folding when it mattered most, would once again come back to haunt us.

A cheap free coughed up gifted Tompkins the chance to push Cork ahead. He'd add another, as we again struggled to win our own kickout. Now caught in a real spin, Teddy McCarthy and Larry would drive the final nails to complete an eight-point swing as we somehow lost out by four on a scoreline of 2-10 to 2-14.

It was a huge setback for us. Cork were both league and All-Ireland champions, but we didn't care. We didn't want anyone saying to us, *'Ah, but you ran them close'*. We did, but when it really counted they stepped up and stepped on the gas. It was what the best teams did to us. We weren't ruthless enough.

Cork were gracious in victory – this was just another day at the office for them.

There was just an inevitability about those kind of scraps back then as far as Ulster sides were concerned. The sight of Frank Murphy fist pumping towards the home support afterwards particularly grated at me. We'd been taught a lesson on and off the park, no doubt about that. It meant that our entire hopes now rested on winning our final league outing, at home, against Dublin.

The latest offering from the local paper back in Donegal wasn't kind but those same doubts, that complex of inferiority that seemed to be in our heads, was also evident to their scribe.

'I don't know about the supporters' viewpoint but I'm sure the players and manager don't like being thrashed in the dying minutes of a game they should have won. Indeed, it's downright embarrassing and surely a pointer that says: 'We're good enough to put up a reasonable fight but that's about it'. Hopefully, players and manager will want to prove they can compete with the best when this Sunday they face the might of the Metropolitans. Realistically who wants to be known as the team that can frighten champions? Who can continue to follow a team that promises so much but delivers so little?'

I LOOK BACK at certain moments in time, turning points or forks in my career that had an impact. And there is no doubt that our performance, as well as the result in our 1-10 to 0-9 win over the Dubs that March day of 1990, had a significant impact on that group of players. Not in the sense that it was any kind of springboard to an eventual All-Ireland success; it just seemed to inject some much-needed confidence and even viciousness to our mindset.

We'd been called out, rightly it has to be said, after Cork. But here we were now into the quarter-finals of the NFL having finished just a single point off the coattails of Division 1 winners Cork. Regardless of what would come our way next, what had we to truly fear in Ulster?

Coincidently we'd finish the Dublin game with 12 of our starting All-Ireland winning 15 from 1992 on the field. We were pitted against the mighty Meath in the last eight... a game fixed for Clones on April Fools' Day. Martin McHugh lit up St Tiernach's Park that afternoon, giving Liam Harnan the absolute run around on his way to kicking nine points.

The team itself had performed very well, right up until the last quarter as we led by six points. But the roof caved in on us once again and the Royals were allowed to somehow pull things back and actually win by 0-13 to 2-12. David

Beggy's two goals in that final 15 minutes cost us dearly. And it wasn't as if they'd earned the win. We, as was often our like back then, just seemed to hand it to them on a plate.

What exactly did our National League campaign mean, in the greater scheme of things? Not much, as far as I was concerned. Our goal was to win an Ulster title and losses to Cork and Meath weren't going to have an impact on that ambition. True Down, who unbeknownst to everyone were on the verge of paving the way for the rest of Ulster, had taken us in Newry very early on but we certainly didn't fear them.

We didn't fear anyone in Ulster but there were just some teams, outside of our province, that somewhere in the backs of our minds we seemed to feel we just weren't entitled to beat. We were seen as, and very much felt like, second-class footballing citizens.

Democrat expert Connie Duffy, who would have made a great Donegal manager, felt that some of the lads needed to, *'have 'sell by dates' stitched onto the backs of their jerseys as it might spur them into action'.* It was a sharp cut. Maybe some of us did have big miles on the clock. But this was still the best squad of players at the manager's disposal. And the great thing was that there was still the chance to prove everyone wrong.

We quickly licked our wounds but, like I said, there wasn't really any kind of residual hurt or doubt in our minds about our Ulster chances in 1990 because of what had happened against Meath. We still felt we were the best team in the province.

Ulster was very much viewed as a poor relation when it came to the other provinces and the battle for the All-Ireland. No one could have imagined what was just around the corner.

But, similar to Jim McGuinness likening the Donegal team he inherited to a 'beaten dog', Ulster sides had shipped so many blows over the years in the All-Ireland stages, mostly semi-finals, that there just wasn't any real belief that the glass ceiling could be shattered.

The last northern team to go the distance was Down way back in 1968. And there was nothing to suggest things were going to change any time soon.

But we all cherished the one piece of silverware that was up for grabs... the Anglo Celt.

I CAN ONLY speak for myself, but I always felt that psychological hang up was very much a collective thing. I never once went out on a football pitch, pre-1992, thinking anyone was better than me. Regardless of who I was in direct competition with, I fully expected to get the better of them or at least break even. But team sports are a funny thing. It takes so much to get the whole thing right. There are just certain players and even human beings that you simply do not have to worry about. And they mightn't always be the best players in a dressing-room.

Some lads can take the smallest thing to heart. I'm serious. I knew players that if they won their first ball they were up and running... off to the races. If they didn't, the head often dropped and that was it.

And my heart would sink a little on each of those occasions. *That's him f***ed*, I'd think to myself, and the game often only seconds old. I genuinely didn't care too much if I was beat to the first ball, which was usually the throw-in. I wanted it more than anything but if it didn't come my way, I parked it and just got on with it.

But as a unit, we still had a little way to go in that sense.

The seven-week countdown towards our Ulster SFC opener with Cavan, in MacCumhaill Park, was now well and truly on. Sunday, May 20, was circled on the calendar, right away the Tuesday night we met up after the Meath loss. A spanner threatened to be thrown into the works with the news that both Martin and Donal Reid had been selected as All Star replacements for the trip to New York and San Francisco. *Lucky bastards* was all I thought, good luck to them. The first game, on the west coast against All-Ireland champions Cork was to take place on May 6 in San Francisco, and the second contest a week later in New York.

Those kind of perks back then were seldom and especially unique as far as Donegal players were concerned. As captain, I didn't have any issue with it or feel the need to pull rank. Martin was... well, *Martin* and Reid with his athletics background was one of the fittest men in the squad. He'd probably end up running up and down the famous hills of San Fran or swimming out and in to Alcatraz... or so a few of us joked!

There were no real tactics meetings or plays to be rehearsed on the training field back then. So the truth was all they'd really miss was running and more running. And sure they could do that Stateside. Of course, the only concern we did have was that they might pick up injuries. But that could easily happen just as handy at home.

And anyway, there were five of us, myself, Gary Walsh, Martin McHugh, Martin Gavigan and Martin Shovlin who, before all of that, were going to be attending a Compromise Rules training trial camp that also involved physical and sometimes nasty provincial battles of the hybrid code. The reward at the end of all of that was a place on the squad that would go to Australia the following autumn.

So there was time and scope for plenty to happen, and even not happen, between then and our clash with Cavan. In the end, we all came through our Compromise try-out unscathed but, only one man was selected by Ireland boss Eugene McGee and that was 'Rambo'. Martin was an animal of a man and in his pomp was, to coin a well-used phrase, built like a brick shithouse. And none of that muscle or girth was gained or fabricated in a gym. It was constructed in the fields, the bog and on the building site from a very young age. Martin also rowed competitively.

It's an unforgiving sport but it was another thing that helped pile muscle onto muscle. He was a frightening specimen. And again, I don't doubt that being selected to represent his country helped buoy Martin's belief in his own ability and push him to the next level.

As for the matter at hand, and just a week out from our Ulster opener, Martin and Donal returned from the US and the news wasn't good. Martin had picked up a groin injury and would not be available for our massive Ulster opener with Cavan the following weekend.

Donegal were at the top table in gaelic football, but the biggest games were squeezing out of their grasp and, twice in 1990, in the National League quarter-final and the All-Ireland semi-final, late goals from Meath proved the vital difference. Anthony (top) wins possession against Liam Hayes and (bottom) Bernie Flynn beats Matt Gallagher to possession.

REFLECTIONS

'You will always have to go wire to wire...
that's the one thing that never changes'

– Jim McGuinness

I'M OFTEN ASKED what do I think of our modern game of gaelic football? And I always try to be careful on how I answer that question. The easiest way not to offend anyone is to simply say, 'Football back then wasn't as great as some like to remember... while football today isn't as terrible as some like to think'.

The simple truth of the matter is that they are poles apart on a number of levels. Life has changed so much over the last 30 or so years, on and off the pitch. And I'm sure if you attempted to compare the Liverpool side of the late-80s to the one now you'd also find huge differences in both how the game of soccer is played and, indeed, how lads behave and look after themselves off the pitch.

On the odd occasion I'm prepared to be completely honest about the same question, I try to explain how you need to compare the complete package... life and football. Because it was beautifully intertwined for my vintage. The scrapes and carry-on that I got up to, for club and county, they're memories – documented only in my mind – that I gladly share with old teammates and friends whenever we do meet up.

And so much of the fun is piecing all our differing versions together in an attempt to find some kind of middle truth! But I'm also glad some of those same tales are either forgotten or just don't leave that same trusted circle.

Because nothing is off limits for today's generation, simply because of the internet and social media. They are both extremely powerful tools and can be constructive and destructive in equal measure. They can let you know instantly how a club championship game might be going at home, or they can be used to completely humiliate or throw some young person under a bus. Some of the things I see passed about and sniggered at – blips and mistakes we all made ourselves back in the day – it is used now as giggle fodder. But the strain or impact it probably has on the unfortunate individual in the same picture or video could be catastrophic.

I see concerts and sports fixtures on TV where very few of those in attendance are living in the actual moment. They're too busy trying to post the experience on social media. If you truly stop and look around at it all, it's quite bizarre. I wouldn't swap my experiences growing up and playing football for what young men have in their lives right now.

And that no doubt works both ways. I've no doubt if you could somehow parachute a modern 21-year-old back into early-80s Ireland, they'd be looking for the first route back to the future!

BUT WHAT I loved about my youth, my prime even, was that every single moment of life was there to be truly lived. And I had a life on and off the field.

I'm not saying that modern footballers don't, it's just a very different landscape. They are professional athletes now and the standards they adhere to goes way beyond what was ever asked of us. In terms of the actual product, it can be fascinating. And so much is made of how modern sides set themselves up. It's a game of systems now. There is no right or wrong opinion on the matter.

My belief, and it's just my opinion, but I still believe a bad game of systematic football is still much sorer on the eyes than a bad game of man-on-man football ever was or could be. When you take spontaneity or off-the-cuffness out of the equation on a sports field, then what are you really left with?

And I do miss the responsibility that used to go with gaelic football... players being completely accountable in their respective duels and having to win them. It was very easy to go to a game back then, and come home and say who played well... who edged their battle and why a game was either won or lost.

I go to games now and I truly never know what quite to expect. And I sometimes find it difficult to point out or pinpoint exactly why a team might have won or lost a game. Take for example the 2020 Ulster SFC final between Cavan and Donegal. It was played behind closed doors because of the Covid pandemic.

I had to watch it on the TV, which is never the greatest vantage point to call the action. But speaking to very good footballing people that were very close to the action that night, they were still at a loss as to just how Donegal were defeated by what was a very poor Cavan. And after that kind of contest, there is very little personal accountability. Yes, the management will get criticised but it's almost impossible to say, with any degree of absolute certainty, who actually didn't uphold their end of the bargain. Whatever about the fare on offer, like I say, I'm just not a fan of that.

I BUMPED INTO Jim McGuinness a while back. We spoke about some of those contrasts between the old days and the new. He bridges both, so it goes without saying I value his opinion. Our not too serious conversation veered towards fitness and how hard players are actually pushed now on the training field.

We didn't talk about gym work or strength and conditioning, as the truth is we just didn't need it back then. I'm not trying to sound macho here but almost to a man, our 1992 panel were all employed in some form or fashion in work that required a certain degree of manual labour. We also had a large chunk of fellas that farmed and so on.

The demands of the modern game just don't facilitate that kind of lifestyle now. Go through the pen pics in any championship programme and you'll do well to see anything other than 'student' or 'teacher' beside occupations. And that isn't a criticism. The route to education and third level schooling now is there for almost everyone and that's a brilliant thing. But what I really wanted to know from Jim, in a sort of Neanderthal kind of way, was... are modern players putting harder or more yards in on the training field that we used to?

My initial point was that it wasn't humanly possible to push players any harder than we were pushed in 1992. After our Ulster semi-final win over Fermanagh a few of us, led by McHugh, had famously asked for training to be ramped up. For a period of four weeks, between that dressing-room confrontation in Healy Park, and the Ulster final win over Derry, we were flogged into the ground.

The ball was put away and we went wire to wire, every single night. Wire to wire was what you called visiting the four corners of the training pitch or, in our case at that time, MacCumhaill Park. Men crumbled over on their knees, often vomiting but unable to complain as the severity of it all meant you were in a real struggle just to catch breath. Those sessions usually began with 15-minute runs with pacers making sure there was no drop off. We were then subjected to other various running drills that ranged between 800, 400 and 200metre distances.

We'd asked... actually demanded this. So no one was entitled to complain.

And despite all the weights, protein shakes and living a completely disciplined life off the field in today's era, the one thing that never changes, Jim grinned, is that you still have to go wire to wire. And I think back to the shape so many of us used to turn up in for pre-season... it was reckless, dangerous even... when I look back.

Today's players tick over 24/7 and for the entire 12 months of the year. They'll never know the torture of being put through the ringer with sometimes up to two stone of winter weight to shift. And while there is a fair degree of science applied to how teams now go about their field sessions, the hard yards still go in.

But there was no such thing as sports science, diet or any kind of nutrition back in our day. It just wasn't talked about. Even up until 1992 we were all still eating things like fish and chips most evenings. Fitness is a strange thing. It can be attained by almost anyone and so much of it depends on what you ask of your body and are prepared to put it through.

But not everyone is the same blank canvas.

THERE ARE SOME strange exceptions to the rule.

I saw so many coming and I saw so many going in my time with Donegal. But Martin Shovlin was the stand out freak of nature. A complete scientific contradiction. Martin and myself were on the batter one Sunday night... we'd at least 10 pints each.

And we were down to train in Ballybofey on the Monday evening.

This was 1993. And my own clubmate Damien Diver had just come onto the fringes of the panel. Damien at that time was just an animal for the yards, a thoroughbred. Obviously, he was extra keen to make his presence felt that evening as we went into our 15-minute runs, which were held at the end of what had been a very tough session.

Towards the end, Shovlin as usual was leading the charge. It was his thing and no one ever dared to attempt to upset that tradition. They couldn't have even if they wanted to. That is when Damien, ticking along nicely at the front of the middle third, decided to make his move. Off he tore like a cheetah. It was a sight to behold.

At that stage of my career, I was usually nearer the back of it all. So I had a real bird's eye view of this unexpected duel. Reputations counted for absolutely nothing here. It wasn't disrespect either.

Damien's ambition was to play senior football for his county and he was giving this drill, like he did with every drill throughout his career, his absolute all.

Shovlin had to have heard the steps and no doubt felt the vibrations coming up on his inside. And just as Damien gets within touching distance, Martin, 33-years-of-age at this stage, finds another gear to somehow pull away and still cross the line first.

Stamina is something you can build, but only to a point. Ultimately, from my experience, you either have it or you don't. You couldn't train or replicate what Martin had just done. You either had it... whatever 'it' was, or you didn't. Donal Reid and Joyce McMullin, were others that just had it.

My take on today's scene, is that we're looking at a collection of serious athletes first and foremost. They all have to have that kind of stamina. It's the basic requisite managers first look for, but are they gifted in the true sense of the word... as footballers I mean? I don't know if they are or aren't.

I'd love to see how those same players would perform 15 on 15. It could well be spectacular. With the power, pace and athleticism they have, I'd imagine we'd also finally get to see that they are, in fact, supremely talented 'footballers' as well.

Football really is a game of yards and percentages now. Often, who wins comes down to who's best at eliminating mistakes. I'm not saying that is wrong, but it's not the game I grew up to love and play. My argument is that other field sports, like soccer for instance, have become even easier on the eye as they've tactically evolved. Liverpool, who I just mentioned, and Manchester City, do quite amazing things. Gaelic football has certainly changed as a spectacle but is it more engaging for supporters as a result?

I listen and read some absolute tripe in regards to where the blame for the current direction of gaelic football lies. Ulster gets the finger pointed at it unanimously. For some, it's Armagh or Tyrone's fault… for others it's Donegal and Jim's fault. But those men were innovators. They found a contrast to what was going on elsewhere at the time and they found a way to win. And I found the manner in which all three of those teams went about their business both fascinating and easy to watch.

I can safely say that if Jim McGuinness came back into an inter-county job now the way he'd look to guide his team to the top would be much different to the manner in which he did it over a decade ago. He'd have moved on, because he's smart enough to know it just wouldn't work now.

The problem is that others haven't left it behind. And it has to be flattering that so many others have just tried to imitate his old template. It's mirror image tactics we're seeing so much of the time… especially at club level.

We are in a constant state of flux regarding rule changes but few if any of them tackle the real issues. It would be comical if it wasn't so depressing. Why can't the GAA put a committee together, fresh and pragmatic minds like Jim McGuinness, Jim Galvin, Kieran Donaghy and say a Ciaran McDonald, and just see what they can come up with?

At the root of it all there are probably four or five areas that could do with being addressed in gaelic football. Blanket defending, cynical fouling and running down the clock with 'keep ball' are the ones that I feel most of us would like to see addressed. Now tell me this, would a shot clock, no back passing once you reach halfway and, possibly, having to keep say three men up all the time really veer us in a direction that would have people up in arms?

I don't think so.

What we currently have with offensive and defensive marks, I genuinely fail to see how they've impacted on our game for the better.

I hope my concerns or suggestions don't paint me as some sort of crusty old schooler pining for the good old days. I've already pointed out that there is a certain degree of myth attached to the fare we often cooked up. I believe we're all on the same page when I say I want to get back to going to games that I simply can't take my eyes off.

Because they did exist. And they still do at times, but they just aren't as plentiful.

That's not opinion this time, that's just fact.

PART**FOUR**»

« CHAPTER 10 »

'I'm the best, I can take it more than anybody.
So give me a stage where the Bull can rage'
– Jake LaMotta, *Raging Bull*

IF I'M ASKED when my pomp was, without hesitation or doubt, I'd say 1990. My knees weren't any kind of issue for most of that entire year. It was… I can only liken it to some kind of freedom, or release from something that had always held me back.

They'd caused me pain for most of my entire adult career.

But for some reason that season, they decided to take a break. God knows both they and I needed it. It took some time for me to realise this as it was just something that was always in the back of my mind. When I planted my left knee I was cautious of it and, if I had to turn sharply to that same side, I always made a point of lifting my studs.

I knew that whatever cartilage remained needed very little encouragement to pop or tear. I was always hindered or playing through the pain barrier.

But that year, as the league progressed, I could just feel it getting stronger. There was less and less heat coming from it and the painkillers I'd been swallowing by the fistful, I just didn't need them as much. I can't explain it. But I took great confidence from it.

'The Doc', Austin, would further ease my concerns explaining how building muscle up around the leg, just like he'd advised, was stabilising it. That probably seems like obvious enough instruction in this day and age but, back then, strength and conditioning or resistance training wasn't really a thing. But I kept throwing myself into training on the field and even embracing, to some degree, a new weights machine that the local community centre in Ardara had just purchased. It was a big, blue multi-purpose contraption that had everything you needed. I had a key to the premises and I'd come and go as I pleased.

WE WERE INTO May now and we were all moving very well, together. In the past, under Brian, some were often moving better than others and a distinction was probably easy to make. But we were in real sync now. To be quite honest, it was difficult to gauge who might be in and who might not, as we edged closer to the start of our Ulster campaign.

In the end, Brian's first championship team named, since 1986, to face Cavan was: Gary Walsh; John Cunningham, Matt Gallagher, John Joe Doherty; Donal Reid, Paul Carr, Martin Shovlin; Anthony Molloy, Martin Gavigan; James McHugh, Brian Murray, Joyce McMullin; Declan Bonner, Charlie Mulgrew, Manus Boyle.

In a sometimes nervy encounter, we'd eventually prevail by 0-13 to 0-9. Again, there was some criticism, there always was. But as *The Follower* noted, *'Any Ulster Championship win is a good win'.* There was some real dirt in this one with outstanding scores to be settled from the previous league outing earlier in the year. Championship football was so much better when there were still league scores to be settled! Paddy Downey, in *The Irish Times*, would label the game, *'disgracefully dirty'* and that was hard to argue with.

The big blow for us after was that Bonner had got his marching orders and that meant a month's suspension. Declan had given Barry McArdle an almighty roasting for most of the first-half and a late switch was made with Pat Faulkner taking over that responsibility, just before the break. Out of the corner of my eye, I see Faulkner immediately drill Declan in the side of the ribs and they lock up. All of a sudden my man, Seamus Gannon, looks to make a move in that direction and wade in.

I take control of that situation in my own blunt way and the handbags between Declan and Faulkner quickly becomes the side-show. Like a scene from a Wild West movie, it's an almighty dust up that is very hard to actually take command of, and even though it's nasty, it's over as quickly as it started. I receive a booking… happy to, as I'd helped stop Cavan's attempt to lay some kind of marker at a crucial time.

But to my amazement and disgust Declan, as clean as they come, is sent off along with Faulkner.

Cavan went in 0-6 to 0-5 in front at half-time, and we'd just lost the game's form player. We'd level matters after things got going once again but a full 22 minutes would go by before we'd claim another point, through Manus, to square things once more at 7-7. In the final five minutes, after a game where we produced 14 wides, we'd finally get our act together as Manus twice, 'Rambo', Mulgrew, James McHugh and late sub Gerry Curran all hit the mark to make the scoreline look a little better.

As we settle down in the dressing-room after, McEniff soon does the maths and it's quickly figured out that Declan won't, in fact, miss the semi-final with Derry after all. It's explained that his four-week sentence doesn't bridge the gap between then and our late June encounter with the Oak Leafers. It will actually end at midnight, just hours before throw-in.

We get back down to business on the Tuesday and McEniff pulls me. He's in jovial enough mood but he informs me that my coming together with Gannon had been caught on video and it didn't look good. Trial by TV wasn't a thing at that stage, or so I believed.

But McEniff says a precedent had already been set in Munster earlier in the campaign and that the Ulster Council would likely follow suit. But again, *'Don't worry'* he says. *'They can't actually hurt you.'*

THERE IS A hearing later in the week that myself and Bonner will have to attend. But McEniff once again reassures me, if there is punishment, like Declan, it'll be a month and I'll still be available for the Derry clash. *Grand,* I thought, and off we went laughing and sort of joking about the matter. I didn't know it then but the entire episode would come back to haunt both myself and Declan much further down the line, that same season.

Later in the week, off the pair of us headed for the Four Seasons Hotel in Monaghan for our disciplinary hearing. We walk into the lobby and already sitting beside the big open fire are Gannon, Stephen King and Mickey Faulkner. They are out of the championship and have pints in their hands. 'What are ye having?' says big King, in an admirable attempt to break the awkward ice.

And sure enough and soon enough, we're all laughing and having the craic together. We eventually go in to face the firing squad but like McEniff said... *they can't hurt us.* Fr Dan Gallogly was provincial president at that time. Under normal circumstances, he could have been described as a stern and intimidating figure. But his sanctions and words are falling on deaf ears this time.

We smile and take our pointless punishment and soon get back to matters at the bar. To this day, Gannon and King, lads that we were on the verge of despising at that time simply because of the bad blood that existed on the field, remain very good friends of mine. We'd had a light session on the Tuesday... they'd call it a recovery session today, no doubt. But by the Friday when we met up again, the mood had very much changed with the management.

They'd watched the video back and it was now time to get to work. God knows there was plenty to address. To my delight though, a very familiar voice could be heard holding court in the dressing-room before hand... the hearty laugh was unmistakable. It was big Martin Griffin! With some injuries and perhaps doubts to contend with, McEniff had sent the call out to MacCumhaills' pair Griffin and Michael Lafferty to come back into the fray.

Griffin was 36 at this stage but as captivating and impressive as ever. He was a real cult hero on the terraces and a powerful man whose reputation, even then, still had the power to precede him. He just had this fear factor and that reverberated around the province. You simply did not mess with Martin Griffin. It gave everyone a lift.

One of my abiding memories of Griffin, on the pitch, is of him holding both the mighty Armagh twins, John and Mark Grimley, in separate headlocks under each arm and winking at me! He was a living legend.

COINCIDENTALLY, AND THE sad thing is, just as we're touching on this, for the book, it's November 2021. And just two days later the news comes through that Martin has passed away.

It hits me hard and I'm sure it was a huge blow to so many others that soldiered with him. You see, Griffin was simply a God to us younger lads when we first came on the senior scene, back in the early-80s.

He got a Donegal crowd going like no one ever did or has since. There was just this crazy connection. They loved him too. He was wild... untamed. We couldn't get down the back of the bus quick enough to sit beside him... we were in awe of him.

We'd heard all the yarns at the time, so we wanted to see and hear for ourselves. We were like giddy children down around him, almost sitting on his knee. His one-liners were classic. One time, we were training on the old pitch beside MacCumhaill Park and off he disappears down behind the ditch, beside the Finn River.

He suddenly reappears with a huge salmon bouncing around in his hands! He'd been out earlier that morning to set up his net! We were all rolling about laughing as McEniff both scratched and shook his head all at once.

On a Division 2 League trip to Wexford back in late 1985, when the thing was still so mad, he pulled another famous stunt. He was named to start at full-back. And as we're preparing to go out the door he puts a headband on with a feather in it and some black shoe polish under his eyes! He's yelping like an Indian!

McEniff can only shake the head again and insist that Martin takes it all off! But that was Martin. And we all loved him. Without ever taking the thing too serious, he was still an amazing player. He was All Star material in 1983 but he was wrongly overlooked.

And Brian was very good to Martin and knew how to manage him. But Brian was good to all of us. And as we set about getting ready to face Derry in the Ulster semi-final at Clones, even though I was suspended for my club Ardara, I continued to train at a ferocious pace. In the end, Derry were so poor on the day that we cruised back into an Ulster final. A 1-15 to 0-8 win saw Bonner post 0-4 and Manus hit 1-4.

And to give the thing a real boost, at the end McHugh, back from injury, climbed off the bench to nail two points.

OUR INJURY LIST had already widened alarmingly before the Derry game because of the Donegal club championship, with the likes of John Joe, Gerry Curran, 'Rambo', Shovlin, Reid, Mulgrew, John Connors and Paul Carr all picking up knocks. Some were sidelined and some needed rest. But we were in a worrying state as far as injuries were concerned before the Ulster final.

Things came to a head behind closed doors between McEniff and the Donegal board, and the decision was eventually made to put the club championship on the back burner, even though we were looking at another four-week run-in to the Ulster final. Still, it meant we could really put the heads down with Donegal and there'd be no distractions. Besides injuries, those club games, especially at that time, had the potential to be divisive and cause disharmony that we just didn't need at that delicate stage of the inter-county season.

It was something that had also made national headlines with former Donegal star Pauric McShea, a close friend of Brian's, having a serious cut at the county board for their staging of the first round so close to the Derry game. Against better opposition, it could have cost us dearly. But we'd got the desired outcome in the end.

We just had to hope that some of the knocks weren't too serious.

The good thing was that time was on our side.

Because of some of those injuries, there had been a reshuffle of sorts with 'Rambo' once again dropping back to centre-back to fill in for Carr, and Murray pulled from wing half-forward to the middle, beside myself.

That triangle would not change again, from that day forward.

Again, the exploits of the Irish national soccer team – this time at their first ever World Cup finals – was threatening to overshadow that summer's GAA championships. A very small crowd had turned up for the Ulster semi-final and the coffers of the association were no doubt taking a real battering.

Packie and the Irish team had earned threes draws in the group stages with England, Holland and Egypt, and it was enough to send them through to the last 16.

In a dour enough game, extra time couldn't separate Ireland and Romania, and the contest would have to be decided on penalties. To be fair, the excitement and drama of it all was captivating.

And when Packie finally managed to stop one of the kicks, it set the thing up amazingly. David O'Leary would secure Ireland's progress to the dizzy heights of the quarter-finals, but there was no doubt Packie was the hero.

Donegal went bananas. You couldn't escape it… you didn't want to.

It was just mental. And I was so pleased for him. Packie had been involved with Donegal at underage and was a friend. And here he was, on a global stage, setting Ireland up for a shot at hosts Italy in the last eight. Diminutive Italian forward Totò Schillaci would eventually send Ireland packing but it was a time in everyone's lives, who were fortunate enough to live through it that is, that'll never be forgotten.

A WEEK LATER, after arriving back home in Donegal, Packie dropped into MacCumhaill Park in the lead-up to the Ulster final. He even joined us in a training session where he played outfield! Word quickly circulated and the place was soon besieged with autograph hunters and fans, eager to get a glimpse of their hero.

With the hysteria eventually subsiding and Packie departing, we got back down to business in our attempts to plot Armagh's Ulster final downfall. We were made favourites for the game and that didn't sit well with McEniff at all.

He was so guarded against any degree of complacency, but the cold truth was we'd no reason in the world to be getting ahead of ourselves. We were nervous in the lead-up but, like I've always preached, nerves are a good thing. If that adrenalin isn't flowing then something is wrong.

We knew just how much was on the line.

We wanted and we needed an Ulster title, but we also knew it was the gateway to an All-Ireland semi-final and we wanted to see just exactly where we were at, at that level, more than anything. I certainly did anyway.

Finally, on the Friday night before the final, the starting team was revealed. With Charlie still injured, back in McHugh came to the starting line-up. The other man who didn't make it back in time from injury, John Connors, was replaced by John Joe Doherty. That meant McEniff would go with a team of: Gary Walsh; John Joe Doherty, Matt Gallagher, John Cunningham; Donal Reid, Martin Gavigan, Martin Shovlin; Anthony Molloy, Brian Murray; James McHugh, Martin McHugh, Joyce McMullin; Declan Bonner, Tommy Ryan, Manus Boyle.

Over the course of a pulsating 70 minutes the sides were level on six occasions. But, crucially, we never fell behind once. Armagh were always chasing. We started quickly and Manus had us up and running inside 30 seconds. Ollie Reid posted a free for them but we jumped in front once more thanks to another Manus over, this time from a free. Martin managed to widen the gap to two, on 16 minutes, but a pair of Reid frees again squared matters at 0-3 each.

Nearing the midpoint Donal Reid and Bonner (free) were both on target but Armagh found a reply on each occasion. But with McHugh and Murray clipping fine points late on, we managed to reach half-time in a deserving 0-7 to 0-5 lead. A brilliant interception by Reid at the start of the second-half, where he cut across the middle at a miraculous pace, prevented John Toner from picking up possession on our '45'.

We were getting stick for this style but cared little as we intricately moved the ball down field, through the hands, before Martin finally tapped over from close range… 0-8 to 0-5 up, the next score if we could get it, would have a real impact.

However, a soft free was gifted to Armagh by referee Damien Campbell and Toner again pulled us back to within two. A beautiful Tommy Ryan point, where he'd little or no option but to take a swing, again made it a three-point game. Gerard Houlihan responded but so too did Manus from a free. It's 0-10 to 0-7 as we passed the three-quarter hour mark.

Bonner converts a free and we finally put four between the teams.

We're on the verge of deciding this, I can feel it. But we seem to falter or hit some kind of wall and Armagh strike four times on the trot through Shane Skelton, Jim McConville, Kieran McGurk and Houlihan to somehow level matters up at 0-11 each, by the 58th minute.

They are in the ascendancy now.

I'm looking around as Gary hesitates with his restart. Nothing is on and no one is showing. *'Are heads going to drop here?'* I bark. *'Are we going to… ROLL OVER FOR THEM?!'* Someone needs to step up. And our saviour at that moment, the one pushing back against the orange tide, is 19-year-old substitute Tony Boyle. He's just come in for Tommy and immediately makes an impression with his directness. Shovlin sends a ball into the corner that Tony gathers. He drives along the end line before setting up Bonner to once again push us in front.

There was no doubt that Tony's impact, at that moment, saved us. It was inspirational and lifted us all. Skelton levelled it up at 0-12 apiece but another Donegal replacement, John 'Ban' Gallagher, shows a good understanding with his Killybegs' club men John Cunningham and Manus, as the latter again gifts us the lead. We're pushing now and McHugh lands a quite brilliant '45' to leave it 0-14 to 0-12, with little over three minutes to go.

We manage to turn Armagh over on their own kickout and, as I look up, I see that eager wee head of blond curls desperately fending off his marker to once again get out in front. Tony loved the diagonal ball into the corner and was superb at making my stray outside of the right boot passes look so good. So I send in another one of my specialities, and he does the rest. He chases it down like a mad man and somehow manages to collect and turn his marker… who at this stage is hanging out of him.

With Gareth O'Neill on his back, Tony eventually goes to ground but the spilled ball lands perfectly in Manus' hands. Manus was a brilliant lurker, always in the right place at the right time, and he did the rest. Armagh rally with two late efforts, but it's over. The scoreboard reads beautifully… **Donegal 0-15:0-14 Armagh**. We're once again kings of Ulster.

Getting my hands on that cup, sticking two fingers up at the doubters… we had so many reasons to feel proud that day. We were in no hurry to pack up and ship out of Clones. Once we did, we knew it would be crazy. Those few hours togging in and packing up, amongst ourselves behind closed doors, were always the real special moments for me.

We already knew an All-Ireland semi-final date with the champions of Leinster was on the cards in four weeks' time and some loose chat kind of turns towards that.

OUR COUNTY CHAIRMAN at the time, Charlie Faulkner, saw this as the perfect opportunity to whip out a copy of *The Sunday Press* and centre in on what he felt was a less than complementary article by Meath midfielder and sportswriter, Liam Hayes. Meath were superstars at that time, with the likes of Hayes and Colm O'Rourke regularly featured in national print and on our TV screens.

Naturally enough, they'd given their tuppence worth on the Ulster final beforehand. The Royals still had to overcome Dublin in their own provincial decider but they were that good, cocky even… that Charlie felt they were already availing of their chance to stir the pot for down the line. We had been everyone's favourites, but Hayes went against the grain and tipped Armagh.

I didn't think there was anything malicious in it. In fact, Liam was, at that time, one of the few enthusiastic voices out there on Ulster football and its potential.

Charlie's stunt, as good as the intentions were, might have had a much bigger impact had it been kept under wraps until the morning of the actual game. With a few beers already opened and the steam of our sweaty gear still rising in the middle of the floor, we were in much too good a humour to even attempt to care.

We eventually made our way down the hill towards the Creighton Hotel. We were in our element but after some food and a few more beers, McEniff began to round us up. 'Don't let yourselves down before we reach home… there will be a big crowd waiting for ye this evening.'

He was right, but when we finally did land in Donegal Town – the unofficial homecoming welcoming spot – there was no stage or lorry bed in sight. A band and a platform had been in place the previous season after the drawn game. And the accusation going around was that the local club side Four Masters, perhaps annoyed that their own man Tom Conaghan hadn't gotten another term in charge, simply didn't bother erecting one. If that was true then it was petty. It certainly wasn't Tom's style or doing, but others may have felt, misguidedly of course, that it was some kind of display of support for their man.

The Four Masters club pleaded their innocence in the following Thursday's *Democrat* and blamed the apparent snub on *'a breakdown in communication'*. Someone obviously forgot to tell them that day we'd just won the Ulster Championship!

Once we realised there was no official reception for us, we all slipped out into the crowd and got lost in the many small corners of Donegal Town's many bars. It was a great few days… really satisfying. Worse for wear but happy to do so, we got back down to business on the Tuesday night, a beach session in Murvagh. It consisted of frequent dips in the ocean and a bit of light running.

Some initial talk centred in on the possibility of training at Croke Park in preparation for Meath or Dublin, but that request was apparently blocked. Out of nowhere, it was announced by Brian that he'd secured two high-profile challenge games against both Cork and Kerry. The even better news was that we were headed south for an entire weekend.

It was madness, but there were no arguments from the players. Our game with Cork was fixed for the Friday evening in Castlehaven, and the Kerry one the following evening in Killarney. On the Sunday, McEniff's plan was to take us all up to Croker to see the Leinster final.

In what turned out to be a lively and competitive tussle against the reigning All-Ireland champions Cork, we were just about beaten, 2-11 to 0-13. No injuries were suffered but a five-point showing from Tony Boyle was the talk of the entire venue immediately after. He was just superb. And there was no doubt that night, when myself, McHugh and Shovlin spoke, that we were looking at a certain starter in the All-Ireland semi-final. But the big question for us was… who would be making way?

The Kerry game was a bit of a farce with little of the Kingdom's top talent lining out. They had been hammered by Cork in the Munster final and few of their really big stars were on show here. McEniff was livid as he said he had assurances before travelling that wouldn't be the case. We earned a facile 0-17 to 1-8 victory but, on the whole, the weekend had been a really enjoyable experience.

We certainly bonded, but what we actually gained from it, from a footballing point of view anyway, I wasn't too sure. Today, to do something similar on the eve of an All-Ireland semi-final would be branded ludicrous!

But we had an absolute ball.

One of the stand-out moments for me was coming face-to-face with the Sam Maguire Cup, our first night out in Castlehaven. We were in awe of it. Standing so close to it was a surreal feeling. There's a famous Dubliner's song, *I Loved the Ground She Walked Upon*. There's a line in it, '*She was not mine to hold, but it was easy to pretend*'.

And that's what we were all doing that night, imagining she was ours.

WE LET OFF some more steam on the Saturday night, in Killarney, before eventually departing for Jones' Road on the Sunday. Blocked booked into the lower end of the Hogan Stand, we watched as Meath and Dublin collided.

It was tight, physical and extremely close.

But the Meath of that time were a much different animal to most. They took no prisoners. They were fierce. And at the end of that titanic tussle, a Colm O'Rourke goal would prove to be the decisive score in a 1-14 to 0-14 victory.

On the Thursday before our semi-final clash, the *Democrat* carried a full back page article of Liam Hayes, picked up from the previous *Sunday Press* edition. It was difficult to know what to make of it. There was again some serious praise for Ulster football and how Ulster sides went about their business. Meath had gone back-to-back in both 1987 and '88. They were uncompromising and there were some who felt they went about their business in an unsavoury kind of way.

But that was absolute bullshit. It just didn't sit well with the likes of the Dublin, Kerry and Cork that Meath had re-emerged, and were once again winning the big one.

Offaly had dared to poke their heads above the parapet in 1982 and halted Kerry's famous 'Drive for Five'. The happy establishment had their friends in the press and I have no doubt Meath, and their style, drew unfair criticism.

Meath certainly had a reputation, but it wasn't something that concerned us. Every game in the Ulster Championship was a war and there simply wasn't anything Meath could throw at us, in those stakes anyway, that we hadn't already seen. We were more worried about just how good they were. Sean Boylan would no doubt have had his own worries in the lead-in, especially given the manner in which we ruled such a large portion of our NFL quarter-final meeting... a full three-quarters of it, earlier in the season.

We'd also downed them in Ballybofey the previous year.

'I know that Donegal are a good team,' wrote Hayes. *'Not from '89, when Meath showed less stomach against them than the average Christmas turkey. But from this season's National League quarter-final when Donegal outplayed us for 45 minutes, and then, inexplicably, froze. That was a strange victory for us.*

'We kept plugging away during the first-half and early in the second, because that's the nature of Meath football teams. But we never smelled victory, there wasn't even the slightest whiff, and then suddenly we were handed the game... like a sumptuous plate.

'Donegal will not do that again, and if they did they might never forgive themselves. We don't expect them to. I don't expect Anthony Molloy to be any less competitive or confident than he was that damp afternoon in Clones. He is one of the great midfielders of our time.

'We have played Donegal twice in the last two years, and on each occasion, in our hearts, we were beaten. Yes, that includes Clones, because the Meath dressing-room wasn't dripping with satisfaction after that victory. Why should it, we were handed the game. We hadn't earned it.

'I'm not just saying that. It's the truth, and that's why Meath are looking forward to playing Donegal next Sunday. We want to beat them. We feel we never have.'

We were pumped. Not because we wanted to take heads off Meath men but simply because we felt an All-Ireland final spot was now within reach. Meath were simply in the way. The entire county was behind us... no doubt the entire country was as well. The build-up was mental. But it was enjoyable and certainly wasn't any kind of a distraction. There was an unprecedented interest in us from all kinds of media.

The big news emanating from our camp was that Tony was going to be handed his full championship debut at Croke Park. In an All-Ireland semi-final. Even though he was still a teenager, Tony already had knee issues and he had a cartilage problem in the lead-in to Meath. Thankfully, with the right treatment, he was declared fit. John Joe wasn't so lucky and an ankle injury, on the Thursday night before the game, cruelly ruled him out. It was a massive blow for us.

In the end, the side put out aimed at pushing Donegal into a first ever All-Ireland final, was: Gary Walsh; Matt Gallagher, Paul Carr, John Cunningham; Donal Reid, Martin Gavigan, Martin Shovlin; Anthony Molloy, Brian Murray; James McHugh, Martin McHugh, Joyce McMullin; Declan Bonner, Tony Boyle, Manus Boyle.

We tore into Meath like animals.

We were at it. When I say 'we', I mean both myself and Brian, in the middle of the park, were on our games. We weren't budging an inch against Hayes and sidekick Colm Brady. Indeed Brady would be called ashore with a quarter of an hour to go, with the game still in the melting pot, such was our grip there.

'Rambo', Shovlin, John Cunningham … they were meeting iron with iron and Meath were coming off second best in those coming-togethers. Matters were delicately tied at 1-4 each at half-time thanks to a goal and a converted free from Manus, while Tony, Martin (free) and Bonner kicked the other three overs. Our big problem, and it was one I simply couldn't understand, was that our forwards, as a unit, were failing to fire.

Still, we were grinding towards the finish and just one adrift at 1-7 to 1-6 as the game went into its last 10 minutes. But Martin, our orchestrator, was being marginalised brilliantly by Meath throughout. And that old failing of ours… where if the 'Wee Man' was being targeted or couldn't pull those strings, then no one else could either.

He had a chance for a goal that might have pushed us in front for the first time in the contest but it was cleared off the line by Kevin Foley. The issue needed to be forced at that stage and we just didn't know how to.

Meath did.

And they'd eventually have eight points to spare at the final whistle, on a group of lads that wanted to win so badly but just didn't know how to get the job done at that level. 3-9 to 1-7 sounds like a bit of a hiding but, the truth is, we kicked 13 wides that day to their three. A point adrift bang on 60 minutes… we'd gifted two absolute howlers of goals to Meath, back-to-back.

And inside the space of two and a half minutes, the dream was shattered.

O'Rourke, as their captain, came into our dressing-room after. And while his words were no doubt genuine and well meaning, I didn't hear a single word.

I was devastated. It was real pain. In 1983, as a much younger man, it just didn't hurt as much. But this time, I could genuinely feel my chest threatening to cave in. This was our chance.

Meath had been there for the taking. But we let the moment slip.

The criticism was cutting. And the local media in particular went after our half-forward line of Martin, James and Joyce. It was sickening stuff. And you know what, many of those same individuals criticising were some of the very first looking to shake those same lads' hands just two short years later.

Packie Bonner was a welcome and surprise visitor to our training camp in 1990, after his heroic exploits with the Irish team (above) at the World Cup finals in Italy. But the man who made an even bigger impact upon his arrival was our all-action full-forward Tony Boyle.

« CHAPTER 11 »

'It's not over till the fat lady sings'
– Charlie Redmond, April 5, 1992

A LOT OF fuss was made about the National Football League reshuffle ahead of the 1991/92 campaign. Having battled for so long to establish ourselves as a Division 1 team, many felt aggrieved that we were now suddenly Division 1B tenants, alongside the likes of Leitrim, Longford, Roscommon and Wicklow.

Personally, I felt it was a shake-up that might actually benefit us or, at least, benefit me. I needed to get up to speed and I'd be able to feel my way through those games much more comfortably, something I just wouldn't have been able to do against the so-called big guns.

Perhaps underwhelmed about the prospect of the league and the tests that may or may not lie ahead, McEniff lined up some meaty challenge matches. A high-scoring and heated draw in Parnell Park against Dublin, was followed up by wins over both Derry in Celtic Park and Mayo in Ballyshannon.

In late October and early November, opening league victories would be secured away to Antrim and at home against Longford in Ballybofey. I didn't feature in either and there was nothing spectacular about the manner in which those wins were secured. The boys simply beat what was put in front of them.

I made a first appearance of the new season, late on, off the bench against Leitrim in MacCumhaill Park. But the 0-7 to 0-4 scoreline certainly didn't suggest that anything spectacular was stirring in Donegal.

1992 rolled around but we didn't get going again in the league until late

February. Away in Aughrim against Wicklow, I started at midfield. But we'd suffer a 2-6 to 1-6 loss, which was an embarrassing result for Donegal. Still, a win the following week against Roscommon in Ballybofey helped qualify us for a league quarter-final against Dublin in Breffni Park.

Some sparks had flown a few months earlier in that drawn challenge encounter up there. Dublin were simply a side that we did not like. We didn't like how they carried themselves against us.

They looked down their noses at us. But who the f**k were they to be doing that? Yeah, historically, they were a big deal but they'd achieved nothing as a group of real note. Kerry didn't do it, Cork didn't do it… nor Meath, by that I mean view us as something stuck to the bottom of their boots. But there was an unearned arrogance about that Dublin side.

Pat Gilroy inherited a similar Dublin with a similar attitude much further down the line. But he rooted it out. And it would eventually take Pat O'Neill's intervention to straighten out this lot in 1995.

BUT AT THAT stage of the season, April, and with Paddy Cullen at the helm, those lads were there to be taken down a peg or two. They were already strutting around like All-Ireland champions in waiting. There certainly was talk at that stage that 1992 was going to be their year once again. But you could see right away, the change in attitude and mindset with us, now that a real big dog was finally on our radar. I was moving really well. And that soft league schedule had the positive impact I hoped it would.

Despite conceding the first three points inside six minutes to the Dubs, we'd soon find our feet to move 1-6 to 0-3 in front towards the end of the first-half. Joyce scored a blistering 12th minute goal, on the run, after Tony had broken a raker from 'Rambo' into his path.

Dublin clawed it back to three at the break with Charlie Redmond picking up the pieces to slam a loose ball home for a goal in first-half injury time. We steadied in the second period, winning the majority of our individual battles, to lead 1-10 to 1-4.

Jack Sheedy and Dessie Farrell pointed but the Dublin deficit would remain at four points until the final 90 seconds, when two substitutes struck a goal apiece to turn things on its head and dump us out at 1-10 to 3-6.

First, Vinnie Murphy outfielded Paul Carr to set up Paul Clarke to fire past Gary. Carr was then unfortunate in an attempted block that took the fizz out of a Farrell effort, at a levelling point, and it fell into the gracious arms of Murphy to shoot a goal that would prove to be the winner.

We couldn't believe it… we were devastated.

We were devastated we lost, but we were also broken that we'd lost to that lot.

And true to form, Dublin didn't let us down or our opinions on them thaw as a gloating Redmond sung, *'It ain't over till the fat lady sings'* in the ear of a young Noel Hegarty as he jogged on past. Smirks, smiles, winks… their gloating had it all.

'UP THE F***ING DUBS!!' roared Keith Barr as they finally departed the scene having milked maximum pleasure from our obvious dejection. There was a way to win but that certainly wasn't it.

McEniff called an impromptu session for the following day, where the rain would fall in sheets, at the Holmes, the base of Donegal Town Rugby Club. In atrocious conditions we ran ourselves into the ground, as the wind and rain completely muddied the playing pitch by the time we'd finished.

Once inside, McEniff instructed that no one showered.

As we sat shivering, we mulled over what had happened less than 24 hours previously. I had my say.

'We need to remember that last night, the way we lost and the way they rubbed it in our faces. That, right there, is a hateful shower of p***ks. And the incentive now going forward for us has to be to get our hands on them when it really matters.'

A four-point McKenna Cup loss to Monaghan was our last competitive action until our Championship opener away to Cavan in late May. It was still a worrying enough wobble, especially after our grand promises just made. But we set about getting to work… getting our Championship yards in so to speak. But just as May arrived, Padraig Brogan decided to depart. Bizarrely, the enigmatic Mayoman just upped sticks and left without a word to anyone, including Brian.

At that stage he'd started almost all our league games and beside myself around the middle, we'd just taken Dublin pair Paul Bealin and David Foran to the cleaners. Padraig had also enjoyed Railway Cup success with Ulster.

He was finally finding his feet, or so it seemed.

The truth is we, as a group, didn't make things easy for Padraig for long enough. But as much of that was his fault, as it was ours. But it felt like we were moving on from all of that nonsense. Had he remained put, I've no doubt Brian would have stuck to his guns and stuck with Padraig. But what that did mean was that a starting spot was suddenly up for grabs just three weeks out from the start of the Ulster Championship.

AND ONE OF those immediately putting his hand up was the recently returned Barry Cunningham. Barry, disillusioned about his prospects and aggrieved that Mayomen were being parachuted in ahead of him, had headed for New York. But McEniff somehow managed to bend his ear the week after Brogan departed and Barry was on the first plane home.

In challenge game wins over the likes of Galway in Tuam and Wicklow in Donegal Town, the Killybegs man did enough to earn a starting spot against Cavan. Declan Bonner hadn't played a game all season because of a pelvic injury but he was nearing a return at just the right moment. The other good news was that John 'Razda' Cunningham had also returned from a spell working on the construction of Euro Disney in Paris.

With plenty of options at his disposal, the side Brian named to open in Breffni was: Gary Walsh; John Cunningham, Paul Carr, Matt Gallagher; Noel Hegarty, Martin Gavigan, Martin Shovlin; Anthony Molloy, Barry Cunningham; Declan Bonner, Tommy Ryan, Joyce McMullin; Martin McHugh, Tony Boyle, Manus Boyle.

In what was a truly spectacular game of football, Cavan emptied every single ounce they had into matters and thanks to the brilliance of Damien O'Reilly we were right in the mix going into the final moments. The Cavan attacker had somehow managed to volley over, soccer-style, from near the end line to tie the game up. It was an amazing score. But deep into injury time, from the guts of 55 metres out, Martin boomed over an absolute monster of a free to nudge us back in front.

But that man O'Reilly came up with the goods once more for Cavan, right at the death, and a 1-15 to 1-15 draw was secured.

It might have been cracking fare but the truth is we were well off the pace on a number of levels. We kicked 17 wides and I have to admit, Stephen King had given me a bit of a run-around. But there were quite a few others that also came off second best that day. Because of that, for the replay in Ballybofey, in came Murray beside myself, while Barry went to centre-forward. Donal Reid was named instead of Paul Carr in defence. That reshuffle meant that Matt could slip into full-back and Bonner went back inside to where he belonged, in the corner, instead of Manus who also dropped out.

Those changes worked a treat. And just a week later, back on our home patch, we dealt comfortably with them, 0-20 to 1-6. I managed to kick two points and it was a victory that eased us into the last four in Ulster. Bonner also looked back to his best with a fine six-point tally to his name.

All that now stood between us and a place back in the final was what we viewed as a very poor Fermanagh. When the final whistle signalled in Healy Park in our semi-final, the scoreboard read 2-17 to 0-7. But the truth is we were abysmal. Fermanagh actually led at the break by 0-7 to 0-6 but went in a man down after Michael O'Brien had been sent to the line for a head high tackle on Bonner. We fumbled through the third quarter before finally painting over the cracks in the last 10 minutes with a late scoring blitz.

Once we got inside the dressing-room in Omagh, McEniff had his say. It was barbed and pointed… it had to be. Martin hadn't started the game because of injury but he was sprung in the second period. So he'd had a bird's eye view for most of it all… the entire s**t show. Coincidently, as I'd been making my way off, I was stopped to be presented with an award to mark my 100th appearance for Donegal.

And then it suddenly dawned on me…

A century of appearances but, it seemed, none the wiser. I couldn't be, as here I was presiding over the same kind of crap that had cost us every single time in the past. And believe me, despite the promises of late '91, here we were in the midst of throwing it all away once again. In the kind of manner only we ever did.

We might have won by 16 points, but now was the time to thrash it out. It just wasn't good enough. I settled myself in beside the others and waited for McEniff to say his piece. And just as he finishes, Martin is the one that stands up and speaks up. And in the next half hour, Donegal did something really special… we won the All-Ireland.

By that I mean, the most significant element of what was coming down the line was put in place right there and then. A players meeting was called.

And everyone else, bar Brian, is politely asked to leave the room.

Martin, standing up on the bench now, tells it like it is.

'If this s***e carries on we're going to be hammered, for the second year in-a-row, in the Ulster final. We're still a fucking laughing stock after last year. We are not fit enough to play the game we want to play... the short, running one. We're only fooling ourselves. Look around, some of us are done after this season.

'This is the last chance for a good few of us.

'That's the cold truth!

'So we have to up the ante and by that I mean by at least thirty percent. The balls have to be put away, lads. We have to f***ing go for it... wire to wire at training.

'And this is on us, we have to be the ones that ask for it.

'The talent is there. Believe me, I know it is. Things have to be driven harder, in training.

'But every single man here has to be on board from this point on.

'ARE WE ALL ON BOARD?!'

WITH MY BACK up against the door, I have my say and Brian also had his.

But it's short and it's sweet because Martin has already covered everything that needs to be said. I move back and invite everyone else back into the room. Anthony Harkin, our trainer, was told exactly what we were demanding and that it would have to start the following Tuesday night.

And, to be fair to Anthony, what he came up with was pure hell. But it was labour that would push us across a number of thresholds. We'd start off with 15-minute runs to wake the legs. Then we were straight into our four x 800metres, four x 600metres and, to finish... six x 200metre runs.

The rest of the session was always unique and varied, and that was a great help to the mind as we never knew what to expect. Sprinting drills and more stamina runs usually followed and, at the end, men were on their knees, always gasping, sometimes vomiting... and a few often close to passing out.

It was an absolute shock to our systems.

But with each passing session, we grew closer as a result. It bonded us in a way that, up until that point, we simply hadn't. We were gaining each other's respect, real respect I mean, by going to the well every single night together.

If a cone was cut, a yard stole... then everyone was punished.

It might have happened once or twice the first week, but that was it. Choosing the selfish route cost the entire team and the drill would have to start again. And that was a lesson that was easily transferred into games.

We were priming ourselves up for a shot at All-Ireland champions Down. After what they did to us the year before, we so badly wanted them. But in the other semi-final Derry would topple the Mourne men by 0-15 to 0-13 and, as a result, instantly inherit the favourites tag, alongside the Dubs, for Sam Maguire.

We were ... devastated might be too strong a word, but we were in the middle of building up a vicious head of steam with real retribution in mind. Now, we needed to flick a switch and divert all that emotion towards Derry.

AGAIN, IT JUST went to show how difficult it was to come back in Ulster. Not even an All-Ireland medal in your back pocket was enough to propel Pete McGrath's men back to our province's pinnacle. Well, at least not straightaway anyway.

By now Martin was having some difficulty with his ankle and had it plastered for a week. The picture made the papers but we knew it was only a precautionary measure. That was good news. And the other piece of really good news was that John Joe, whose own pelvic trouble had sidelined him ever since he'd returned from working in Paris, was tearing it up in training. And he was the real standout operator as we obliterated Louth in a challenge match.

Looking at the Derry side that was named in the lead-in, Brian McGilligan and Dermot Heaney were a formidable midfield partnership. As well as that, I'm looking at Anthony Tohill and Dermot McNicholl just in front of them in the half-forward line. Myself and McGilligan... our duels had always turned into battering matches. And this would be no different. We just liked to bang into each other. But it was a duel that always had a huge bearing on our games' results.

It was again going to be an almighty battle for our middle line and our other muscle that hugged the fringes of that area. There was much talk about 1992 being the last hurrah for many of our lads, including myself. And that's how it felt.

And each night you went to training that was the thought that occupied minds. The journey to Ballybofey was often a blur. In an amateur sport, that's serious pressure. But there was genuine fear that the next game could well be your last. That contemplation had the potential to cripple your efforts, or inspire. For me, at that stage, it was a real mixture of both.

But it's something that was openly talked about and as more of us actually spoke about it and addressed the feeling, the less daunting or intimidating it became. In the end, it felt like we were all in this together, on a real mission. And going into that Ulster final against Derry we felt we were right where we needed to be. The one time it again felt lonely or, that every man was for themselves, even if it was for just a moment, was when it came to Brian naming the team. There were always going to be changes after Fermanagh.

And because of that you could just feel the tension as we all leaned in after training on the Friday night. So much had changed in such a short period of time since our semi-final win. In the space of a month, we were a completely different group.

Physically and mentally, we were poles apart.

'Rambo' had sat out Fermanagh through injury and would definitely return, while McHugh and Shovlin were also straight back into the mix. Out went Michael Gallagher, Barry McGowan and Barry Cunningham. It was tough medicine and for the lads that didn't make it, you could see they were devastated.

But they sucked it up for the good of the group. Like I said, things had changed and everyone was on board. You didn't have to agree with the decisions being made but you had to respect them.

The team McEniff would go with from the beginning against Derry was: Gary Walsh; John Cunningham, Matt Gallagher, Noel Hegarty; Donal Reid, Martin Gavigan, Martin Shovlin; Anthony Molloy, Brian Murray; James McHugh, Tommy Ryan, Joyce McMullin; Martin McHugh, Tony Boyle, Declan Bonner.

TO SAY THE first-half in Clones didn't go to plan would be an understatement. Kicking with the breeze, we eventually went in level at 0-5 each, but a man down after John Cunningham picked up a second yellow just before the break. Derry had systematically targeted us.

Martin was being interfered with by Brian McGilligan and Tony Scullion before we'd even lined up for the throw-in. And after losing 'Razda' late on in the half, we suffered another terrible blow as Tohill swung a reckless boot at Tony Boyle's kneecap and, right there and then, ended his participation in matters.

Jim Curran, the match referee, unbelievably failed to take any action. If John's second offence merited what was a seriously harsh yellow, how did Tohill at least not pick up the same sanction? So not only are we down to 14 at this stage, but it also seemed like Derry might be playing with 16 in the second period.

Bring it on.

Going off towards the dressing-rooms in Clones, you have to make your way up those old steel stairs together. It gets pushy and one or two low and out of sight boxes are thrown by Derrymen.

They are looking to goad us into a retaliation.

Through gritted teeth, we stand firm but we give Jim Curran no reason to slight us even further.

'See you f***ers back out there!' I tell them.

We talk about our intentions but no one gets too carried away. The message is simple. We have to work likes dogs now without the ball and, in possession, our best runners have to take their men out of it by being as direct as possible. That instruction works a treat and in a quite brilliant second-half performance we deservingly down Derry and once again rule Ulster!

Derry had initially taken the lead when we got going, but with the likes of James McHugh and the brilliant Tommy Ryan, twice, on the mark, we go 0-8 to 0-6 clear by the 47th minute. Then, I made a mess attempting to clear my lines at the back and it gifted Derry possession.

They work it through the middle and while Damien Cassidy's shot comes off the woodwork, Seamus Downey is there, in the square, to prod home. It's an obvious 'square ball' or so we're thinking.

But after some talk at the foot of the post by the referee and his hapless set of umpires, the goal is given. A Bonner free ties matters up at 1-6 to 0-9.

Gavigan tears at McNicholl… it's an almighty coming together, and he is dragged to the ground. It's 45 metres from goal, but Martin clips a brilliant point and we move back in front. I get my hands on the ball and race through.

With Murray at my side, I shift it over just as I'm closed down, and he does the rest. Enda Gormley though hits the target twice for Derry… we're all square once more, 1-8 to 0-11, going into the final 10 minutes.

A man light, this is where we turn a real corner.

Joyce's direct running is causing John McGurk all kinds of trouble and a foul there allows Bonner to again kick us in front. Noel Hegarty drives from the back and travels all the way inside the Derry half before allowing Bonner to take over.

He sources McHugh on the overlap… we're 0-13 to 1-8 clear.

Gormley does kick another Derry point, from a free. But we save our best for last. First, McGilligan is turned over by James... amazing stuff. He leaves Dermot Heaney for dead as he sets off. Shovlin, who had long since put manners on the hooked Tohill, gets involved as does Reid.

At the very end, Martin has the final say, and laugh, on the hatchet men when, riding some dirty attempts to hack him down, he wriggles through and from what looks like an impossible angle, arrows over the last score of the game.

As if to say, 'f**k you!' to the lads that had been looking to half him all afternoon, he wheels away in pure delight. And then it's over... 0-14 to 1-9, we are once again going to get our hands on the Anglo Celt.

And with it, that beautiful and simplistic passage into an All-Ireland semi-final.

The way it was and the way it still should be.

PERHAPS THE GREATEST test imaginable, of just how far we'd come since our stand in the Healy Park dressing-rooms, had been put in front of us. But a man down, those sickening yards we'd put in together meant we never allowed the heads to drop.

We were built much differently now.

Some still describe it... our second-half performance, as one of Donegal's greatest ever showings. That's for others to decide but I know we clicked like never before that day. Down to 14 men we found something as a group, the likes of which we'd never seen before or, truth be told, after.

We simply didn't need to dig as deep in our All-Ireland semi or final. The fact is, and it's a compliment to Derry, rather than a Dublin knock... but Derry were a better side than Dublin at that stage.

We'd been here before... but this time it felt different.

Or maybe it was the realisation that we knew it had to be different. Believe it or not, we all went home to our own beds that night. There was no tear up in Donegal Town, no embarrassing knocks on side doors on the Monday morning looking to get the party started once again.

And the next night, we were back out in Ballybofey to train.

THE FOLLOWING WEEKEND, McEniff and his management team had the luxury of taking in the Connacht final as Mayo easily defeated Roscommon 1-14 to 0-10. We're a better side than Mayo. Brian says it but we, the players, know it.

It hasn't been spoken about just yet, but our Croke Park bogey is something that we really need to sit down and thrash out. It's not a real thing.

It's a coincidence and something that in reality counts for absolutely nothing in this game. We know it's going to be held up by the media and pointed at. But as a group, when we do finally talk about it, it becomes a bit of a joke and by airing it, amongst ourselves, we can see some humour in it.

We start looking at Mayo and what they'll bring. Michael McGeehan, a Letterkenny native and army man, is their trainer. And we know they'll be ferociously fit as a result. Also, Padraig Brogan has been drafted back into their ranks so they will have some real inside knowledge on us.

They have an embarrassment of riches around the middle... TJ Kilgallon, Colm McMenamin, Sean Maher, my old ESB Inter-firms partner Willie Joe Padden and, our former 'guest' Brogan. They can even bring Liam McHale out to that area.

All of those lads are 6' 3" plus. The media centres in on that battle and Brian also goes out of his way to impress on both myself and big Murray that so much of Donegal's hopes rest on our shoulders.

It is, he insists, Mayo's strongest line.

I received a nice boost in the lead in as the BBC named me their Player of the Ulster Championship. So I certainly didn't hold any fear of Mayo, regardless of what pair they'd go with. Observing Brian, there was a change in him over the next few weeks. Some of us had the sour memories of 1983 and most of us had 90's hurt still very fresh in our minds. But Brian's All-Ireland semi-final trauma stretched way beyond that and back to his playing days. He'd also suffered All-Ireland semi-final defeat as player-manager in both 1972 and '74 to Offaly and Galway.

But he didn't look any less assured or determined. He was in a whole new zone. That's the only way I can describe it. The one thing that was much different this time out for Brian and Donegal was that the bookies had us lodged as red hot favourites. Mayo had only just been edged out by Cork in the 1989 final. And with a large chunk of that team still involved, it irked Brian that Donegal were being talked up like we were. But the Derry performance had captured the imagination of the All-Ireland public and it was just something we were going to have to deal with.

There is a reshuffle from Derry. Barry McGowan's patience has finally paid off and he comes into the corner-back position, with 'Raza' the one to make way. Some will have long forgot that Barry, one of Donegal's greatest ever defenders, had previously operated as a half-forward. But having been sprung for the second-half against Derry, the Killybegs man had shown his class and indeed real calling. McEniff simply couldn't deny him his shot any longer.

And our All-Ireland semi-final team, the one looking to make history would line out as follows: Gary Walsh; Barry McGowan, Matt Gallagher, Noel Hegarty; Donal Reid, Martin Gavigan, Martin Shovlin; Anthony Molloy, Brian Murray; Joyce McMullin, Martin McHugh; James McHugh; Declan Bonner, Tony Boyle, Tommy Ryan.

We prepared so diligently and the fact we were so heavily tipped was a non-issue. Physically, we went to an even greater level than the one we were at prior to Derry. And that is saying something.

But our own demons, those genuine and perhaps closet fears of losing another All-Ireland semi-final, were too potent and raw for us to buy into the pre-game talk. In the end, we almost buckled.

Maybe we did bend but Mayo, with their own complicated baggage, just couldn't take advantage. I don't know. But what was for certain was that we let the fear back in and it came very close to costing us a shot at our biggest moment.

In his subsequent *Irish Times* report Paddy Downey would describe our historic win over Mayo as, *'The poorest semi-final ever played'*.

Stage fright had taken a hold of both sides and, in the end, we were the ones that had stumbled over the line. That's the way it was. We'd been the better side but we just wouldn't click and because of that, the match hung in the balance right until the final whistle.

Wide after wide – 16 in total by the end – piled up and had McHale's flicked effort not come back off our crossbar in the 18th minute it might have been a very different story. But we rode our luck and plodded on.

Matters were level at 0-6 each at half-time but I'd made an absolute mess of an opportunity just before the whistle. I skewed horribly wide from a great position but, the truth is, I should have got my head up and seen Tony standing all alone to my immediate left.

Disgusted with that mistake, our half-time words were a blur. But when we did get going again, myself and Murray's midfield superiority really began to show. Mayo did strike early, with points from McHale and Jarlath Jennings initially propelling them two ahead. Tony cut that lead in half.

Brogan got introduced midway through the second period and a few of our lads 'greeted' him as he sauntered in. But he made little or no difference.

Manus, in off the bench, hit three pointed frees, while Bonner also lofted over a placed ball. And near the end, after Barry Cunningham gets dragged down inside the square, Martin chooses to clip an injury-time penalty over the bar… 0-13 to 0-9, ultimately our job was done.

It might have been an excruciating watch but we didn't give a damn.

ALL OF THAT was sort of lost on us as we celebrated.

This was uncharted territory for Donegal football. It was euphoric. We'd broken ground we'd only ever dreamed of. And that Jones' Road hoodoo was off our backs. The result was all that really mattered.

And even when the sharp criticism did finally come, we didn't care. Dublin, even though they were yet to play Clare in their semi-final, had turned up to take the action in. And their presence was very noticeable. And it was spoken about right away in our changing room. Sunglasses, smiles and some shaking of the heads… that cluster of players and management apparently left bang on the final whistle.

Some, we were told, left before it was even over. And the word was they were more amused than amazed with what they'd just taken in. Donegal's contingent in Dublin was plentiful and the word making its way back to McEniff and a lot of our lads was that we were being viewed as some sort of joke.

Jamsie, my close pal and owner of the Portabello, a real GAA talk pub in the city, was able to quote one Dublin player who'd told him they'd easily fancy themselves to beat a combination of both ourselves and Mayo.

The GAA and the capital media would get their spectacle, seven days later, when Dublin put Clare away 3-14 to 2-12. To put the tin hat on it, Hollywood's biggest star at the time Kevin Costner, who was in the country filming a movie, was in attendance. The media hullabaloo that followed almost completely centred in on Dublin's unsinkable date with destiny.

From that point on, we'd be disrespected in so many ways that it became pure fuel. Ran like wild horses since before the Ulster final, we were given so much material to pin to the wall that it empowered us.

No one needed any extra motivation going into the All-Ireland final. But that's exactly what Dublin gave us in bucket loads.

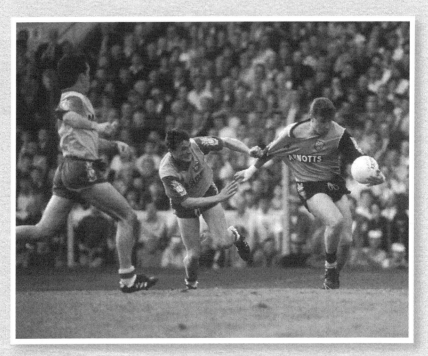

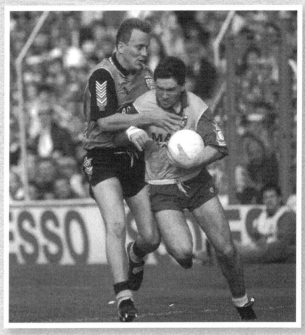

The Dubs really got under our skin, way before the 1992 All-Ireland final. Charlie Redmond's taunts did him no good in the end (above, he feels the close attention of John Joe Doherty) while Keith Barr set himself up for a fall with his bravado, and fall he did when the 'Wee Man' Martin McHugh ran straight through him.

« CHAPTER 12 »

'Had we got to grips with Murphy, I'd have been very interested to see what Dublin's Plan B was or, had they one at all?'

– Clare boss John Maughan, August 31, 1992

I DON'T KNOW what it was, whether it was by design or just how he viewed it at a particular time, but you could never second guess a Brian McEniff starting team. You might get up as far as 13 starters, but it always felt like there were still a few spots up for grabs.

Win, lose or draw, and even coming in off the back of an All-Ireland semi-final victory… even if it wasn't a pretty one, there were still quite a few men in our camp on edge. There were lads on the line that were certain they deserved to start, and there were fellas in the team that maybe felt they might be edged out.

And that was a very potent and powerful thing to take into the next month and a bit.

August 16 right up until September 20… we literally went to war on the training field. With each other. It was ruthless.

At times it came to blows.

Myself and Murray went at it a few times… Reid and Joyce had their moments.

John Joe almost halved Bonner and showed absolutely no remorse for doing so. It was cut throat at the time. But without fail, at the end of each one of those sessions, we were that little bit closer to exactly where we wanted to be.

Clare, fresh off their five-point semi-final loss to Dublin, accepted an invitation to travel up to Donegal to help open the new Naomh Brid pitch in Ballintra. And it was from that moment on that the real paranoia set in. With

Barry McGowan nursing a shoulder injury picked up in the Mayo win, John Joe came in at corner-back.

It was a forced change. Reid was also still sore, so Paul Carr stepped in there. But it was the placing of Manus, our semi-final hero in off the bench, in the full-forward line instead of Tommy Ryan, that got everyone wondering and, I'm sure, especially Manus and Tommy.

Tommy had lit up the championship right up until the Mayo game.

Besides Martin, he was our second highest scorer with a fine 1-10, all from play. Barry Cunningham had put a firm hand up against Mayo also. 'Razda', wronged in the Ulster final by a ridiculous sending off was, as usual, looking the part in training. It might have been a pitch opening, but Clare was a genuine chance to catch the eye so there was a tense energy to matters as we ran out onto the field.

Manus would nail two points, but Tommy came in off the bench and rattled the net almost immediately. John Joe was once again applying himself like a man possessed and a clash between him and his marker Padraic Conway lit the touch paper on the inevitable dust-up just before half-time. At the end of a 3-9 to 1-7 win, tempers had simmered down and hands were universally shaken.

Myself and McEniff hung back and shared some thoughts and words with our opposite numbers John Maughan and Francis McInerney. It was another small but significant moment for us. Both men were adamant we'd be beating Dublin.

And it wasn't just lip service. Maughan, in an unguarded moment, held his hands up and said he'd gotten a few match-ups wrong.

'Get things right on the line and that side there will do Dublin real damage. Vinnie Murphy is a savage, an unbelievable target man. We didn't deal with that.

'They are a supremely confident side. But had we got to grips with Murphy, I'd have been very interested to see what their Plan B was or... had they one at all?

The weather was atrocious so I jogged off to finally grab a shower. By the time I'd towelled off and looked back out the door, Brian was still there, and still deep in conversation with the knowledgeable Maughan.

JACK O'SHEA HAD been holidaying in Donegal and Brian was particularly interested to hear his take on managing the sideshows in the build-up. The Kerry man explained that the Kingdom had five simple guidelines, a creed they followed religiously.

Get the media work you're obliged to do out of the way as soon as possible. And from that point on… don't read the papers, don't talk to the papers and, if something comes on the television, simply get up and leave the room.

Finally, and this is going to be the Donegal players' biggest concern and distraction in the lead-up… but take the responsibility for tickets completely out of their hands. However, make sure the people they want sorted, get sorted.

When we got back down to training on the Tuesday night after Clare, McEniff had his instructions. The national media had their evening, photographers and journalists as well as TV crews were all in attendance. The only instruction really was to say as little as possible about anything that might compromise our objectives or give Dublin some sort of inside knowledge on us. Coincidently, 'Rambo' was due to get married the following weekend to his fiancée Kathleen. They'd been prudent enough when they planned and just in case, avoided the All-Ireland final date.

A draw and a replay had the potential to play havoc with those plans and it was a good yarn for the Dublin writers to latch onto. They ate Martin's 'predicament' right up. But Martin, like the rest of us, was quite confident there'd be no second day out needed at Croke Park.

McEniff knew we weren't reading any papers so we had to go on whatever he told us. And he dropped plenty of bombs in there… wee Dublin nibbles.

Some were true but, he'd later confess, many weren't!

We laughed and we joked at a lot of it, and we got angry and motivated by the ones that did sting. We were in a serious frame of mind at this stage… a week out from the final. Hand on heart, I knew we were going to win.

I can't explain why I felt that way.

But each and every single one of us did. We were in the shape of our lives. We didn't need anything to pin to the dressing-room wall. This was an All-Ireland final but we had so much additional incentive for the simple reason that Dublin were odds on favourites and no one was giving us any hope.

The one thing that was to the back of my mind but coming to the fore quite quickly now was what team McEniff would go with. As captain, I knew it was something that had the potential to wobble us as a unit. The truth is, some men were going to be left heartbroken.

They'd suck it up no doubt, but grown men were going to be left in tears at some stage. It was a distraction now. And the sooner we got it out of the way the better. Finally, on the Tuesday night before the final, McEniff called us in.

Once the perspiration had completely evaporated and the heavy panting slowed down, off Brian went...

'Gary Walsh.

'Barry McGowan, Matt Gallagher,...Noel Hegarty.

'Donal Reid, Martin Gavigan... Martin Shovlin.

'Anthony Molloy... Brian Murray.

'James McHugh, Martin McHugh... Joyce McMullin.

'Declan Bonner, Tony Boyle ... and Manus Boyle.'

I COULDN'T HELP but look at Tommy just as McEniff made his final call.

It was as if someone had literally reached into his soul and ripped the life right out of him. In an instant, his wildest dream was shattered to smithereens.

It was a mix of anger, dejection, genuine shock even... because that's the emotional spin Tommy was now lost in.

Tommy was the star of the Ulster Championship for us. Down to 14 against Derry in the final, he was electric. We never dug so deep on a football pitch and Tommy went through more shovels than most that day.

The absolute roasting he gave Danny Quinn is something Donegal supporters, and some Derry ones even, still talk about to this day.

But what do you do in that situation?

As captain... I felt lost. Because as much as I felt for Tommy, I was also really proud of Manus. He'd been frozen out since the first day against Cavan.

He had taken his medicine for the rest of the campaign, but stepped up to the plate in some style against Mayo when the chance came his way. Manus' showing there, and his clinical ability to kick frees under pressure, was something the management ultimately just couldn't ignore.

Lost in the middle of that big call... the biggest call really, was the fact that the likes of John Joe, 'Razda' and Barry Cunningham had also missed out.

But to all those men's credit, not one of them put their own pride first. It had to have been the instinctive reaction, especially in Tommy's case, to be angry... and to even kick off. And listen... they were shattered.

But the group, the team and the objective still came first.

Tommy sucked it up, took a deep breath and said it was about the squad… the team came first. No one could have really blamed him for packing up his gear and telling Brian where to go.

EMOTIONS WERE RUNNING high, but a cooling off period between then and the Thursday night would hopefully take the edge off all of that.

Thankfully, the dark mood we'd left behind in the dressing-room that evening had lifted when we all walked back through the same door less than 48 hours later.

I'm icing my knee before I go out, but when I do join the stretching and warming up, I see Tommy and Manus together, smiling and leaning on each other for support during those exercises.

All is good.

The weather is baking, the grass cut… and the smell and warmth of all of that is energising. I miss that feeling as much as anything.

We're winding down now really.

The work has been done. And we're three days out from picking up Sam. That was the mindset. It wasn't a hope, we knew it was coming.

We'd been meticulous.

Every single base had been covered. My knee, as wonky as it was, had behaved now for so long. Surely that was the greatest sign of all!

It felt like fate… destiny even.

I TROTTED AROUND the pitch that evening.

Anyone that wanted to win a ball above me, I let.

I wasn't going to jeopardise it all at this stage. The team had been named, no one needed to prove anything or impress anyone. It was a leisurely session and all we really did was kick ball.

Some light contact was involved in some instances, but just shadowing really as lads got their passes and shots away. But I can see right away something is up with Shovlin.

There wasn't any obvious coming together… but he's got some sort of bother with his head or neck. Pound for pound, Martin was the toughest bit of stuff we had.

I ask him what happened?

He says he turned direction and something has popped… or went in his neck. It was a completely innocuous movement and no one was really near him. Dr Austin and some of the management come together and look at the thing more closely.

The next morning in Killybegs, I get talking to James McHugh, a colleague in the ESB, and both he and Martin had travelled back with Shovlin the night before. They said he was in real discomfort. And for a tough nut like Shovlin, that must have meant agony.

He was sent to a physio in Sligo and he was getting injections to numb the pain. But he was now in a real race against time to be included.

Again, I fretted about the impact this was going to have on our chances and the group. Shovlin was crucial to the mix. As well as that, I knew how much this would hurt him if he had to sit the final out.

And all those lads who had their hearts broken the previous Tuesday night well, suddenly, the wheels would begin to turn in their minds, once again, and various reshuffles were no doubt being made in their own heads about how it could be that they were now going to be the one shoehorned back into the mix.

WE DEPARTED FOR Dublin on the Saturday morning, to our base in Finnstown House, on the outskirts of the capital. Some papers had made their way onto the bus, but McEniff didn't seem to mind.

How could he, as they all were forecasting nothing but a comfortable Dublin victory. Our semi-final struggles were playing beautifully into our hands. Their players were doing fashion shoots for Arnotts… and even advertising washing machines! They haven't a clue… they are completely oblivious to what is coming hurtling down the tracks towards them.

Out of nowhere, someone produced a lighter.

A blue cigarette lighter with, *'Dublin: All-Ireland Football Champions 1992'* written down the side of it.

We couldn't believe it.

When we arrived at our base, it was this big old sort of estate or manor. It was perfect. We were away from the hype a city location would bring. There was no video analysis session to sit through back then, so we kind of just wandered out into the majestic looking grounds. We were so relaxed.

To a man, we all knew who we'd be in direct competition with!

Shovlin did depart with Austin soon after, to see some kind of specialist in the city. When he got back the news seemed good, reassuring even. It looked like he was going to make it.

We meet up for dinner and there is just this beautiful calm.

We don't need to talk or really state our intentions all over again. Dublin have done enough of that in the lead-in. McEniff allowed some of us to head into the dogs at Shelbourne Park and the rest of the lads simply hung back and hung out.

Brian wasn't concerned.

He said for the boys that need a distraction, go see the races, but for the ones that were happy enough to sit and relax, then they should do just that.

Interestingly, we'd all been assigned our rooms and the sleeping arrangements matched our lines on the pitch. This approach was new from Brian. All the other lads were grouped in threes, but myself and big Murray had that little bit of extra space.

We were lying on top of our beds laughing at that fact, when Brian suddenly sat up straight and asked, 'What about Gary, does he have his own room all to himself?'

He wasn't concerned, but perhaps momentarily jealous. But I was able to reassure him Paul Callaghan, our second choice stopper, was bunking in with his fellow Ballyshannon man and all was well once again. Eyes were closed and just like that, we both enjoyed a perfect night's sleep.

The next morning, I meet McEniff.

We chat and he gives me a briefing on the day's itinerary. Things like when we'll eat dinner or what they now call a pre-match meal, and what time we will eventually pull out for Croke Park are casually discussed.

As I walk into the dining room, I already know there will be three empty chairs at breakfast. One belongs to Austin, one to Brian and the other… to one of my best friends Martin Shovlin. There are nerves now but not in relation to the games itself.

I'm just concerned about Martin.

They've headed off to a nearby pitch for some sort of fitness test. I grab a coffee, pick up a copy of the *Sunday World* at reception and dig through it, on my own, near a big, bright window. My old Donegal teammate in New York, and former Kerry star, Pat Spillane is their marquee columnist.

And he's picked his 'winners' in our various match-ups with the Dubs.

'Molly will finally meet Sam once again,' reads the headline.

No she f***ing won't, I think to myself. *But Molloy will, for the very first time!*

Spillane pinpoints midfield as Dublin's Achilles heel and backs myself and Brian to get the measure of Paul Clarke and Dave Foran. He can't split the goalkeepers but, after that, backs Dublin to come out on top. Led by Keith Barr, he tips the Dubs half-back line to have far too much power for our 'small and light' trio of Martin, James and Joyce. Our full-forward line of Bonner, Tony and Manus has, he writes, *'been something of an enigma this year. Bonner hasn't been having a good season by his own standards. Tony Boyle won't be afforded much latitude by Gerry Hargan. Manus Boyle's frees against Mayo steadied the team and he deserves his place today. An excellent free-taker, but may face a torrid afternoon against Mick Deegan.*

FROM WHERE I'M perched, my concentration is broken as I see Brian, Austin and Shovlin return and make their way up the steps and in the front door of the hotel.

I can instantly tell the news isn't good.

Martin has that same vacant look Tommy wore just a few nights prior. He gathers himself and explains that when he goes down to put his toe under the ball a searing pain overwhelms his neck and back area.

Austin is upset as well.

But between them, they've made the sensible call… the selfless one really.

I put myself in that position and I wonder could I have done the same? But Martin has put the team first here… and it was a powerful thing to do.

CRUELLY, WE HAVE to quickly move on as a group.

But Martin was right with us, even if it was in a much different kind of way.

The drama isn't over though.

One door had closed but for someone else, one has suddenly just reopened. 'Razda' might get the nod. Or McEniff could well turn to John Joe.

In a group where there was so much harmony and unity, this was the last thing we needed on the morning of the biggest game of our lives.

When the decision is finally made, it is John Joe that gets the last remaining spot. John Joe had spent the early part of 1992 working in Paris on the Euro Disney theme Park. And he only returned after Easter. He missed the entire league and, dogged by a pelvic injury, didn't start a single championship game up until this point.

'Razda', just like Tommy and Shovlin, was obviously gutted all over again but it was a tougher pill to swallow this time out. John probably expected to miss out first time round, but I'd say felt he'd be the one getting the nod that morning.

John is an intense guy, but genuine and honest to the bone.

And he wears a very big heart on his sleeve. As we prepared to pack up and ship out, there was a mood I could just sense. There was real tension now.

Every little detail had been taken care of, but how could you legislate for what we'd all just been put through. Emotions were running so high, the fear was that things might kick off spectacularly... and at the worst possible moment.

LED BY A garda escort, our bus begins to make its way towards Jones' Road.

As we near the venue, the crowd and colour is something else. The previous stress and anxiety... that angry silence even, begins to lift and we all fade into our own zones. We empty out and into the dressing-room.

And the door is closed.

Martin, who had been unusually quiet at our base, now speaks up. There was huge pressure on his shoulders. Quite simply, we needed Martin to perform if we were to win this game. And the whole country knew it.

But I'd little fear or worry about Martin on this day.

He was ready.

'Remember Breffni and the league... well, that proved we have Dublin's measure. They're next door thinking about the same game and the outcome.

'And because of the way it ended that day, they think that no matter how good or bad they play... they'll still beat us.

'Take Murphy's influence out of the equation... and we take Dublin out of this game.'

Martin was right.

But Paddy Cullen was next door telling Dublin the exact same thing.

'Stop McHugh... and you'll stop Donegal.'

BRIAN GOES INTO what was a simple enough gameplan.

But if we applied it like he directed, he believed it wouldn't fail. We were to isolate big Vinnie and do our best to limit the supply of ball going into him.

Whenever Dublin were awarded a free around the middle third, I was tasked with dropping back in front of him. Matt was assigned to staying in behind and trying to break as much ball as he could. Noel and Barry McGowan were backed one-on-one to get the better of both Dessie Farrell and Mick Galvin.

McEniff had bumped into Sean O'Neill, a veteran of Down's glory years in the 60s, in the weeks leading up to the final. 'Make McHugh go down the barrel of the gun, Brian!', O'Neill advised. And that was the last crucial piece of our blueprint.

Martin was to drive at Barr who, like Murphy, was the Dub supporters' other real darling.

Brian's last words before we stood were… 'Make small boys out of that cocky pair and we'll silence the Hill'.

OUT WE TORE through the door, cracking it off the wall behind it.

The muffled roar of the crowd has already met us long before we come out into the bright opening between the old Canal End and Hogan Stand.

But as soon as we do come into sight, we're greeted by a sea of green and gold. It's like a trembling wall of colour and noise, and it's completely wrapped around three-quarters of the stadium. Our supporters haven't let us down.

The place is hopping.

I can feel every inch of my body suddenly start to shake… fight or flight.

It's deafening… that's the only way to describe it.

We go through our warm up before I'm finally ushered towards the middle of the field where referee Tommy Sugrue pulls both myself and Tommy Carr together.

I call tails on the coin toss.

As it hits the ground, just like it had every single other time that season, it lands in our favour. Myself and Brian had already discussed this and we elect to play into the Hill.

'Down the f**king barrel.'

We're ready to go… we've never been more ready.

But there is even more pageantry to get through. We line up to greet the President Mary Robinson... before we're finally led round by the Artane Boys' Band. We take our positions, beside our markers... and we stand for Amhrán na bhFiann.

Finally, Sugrue throws the ball in.

IT BREAKS MY direction right away.

I send it in low to Tony... he's fouled.

McHugh takes the ball but is off cue from a free he'd usually stick over. Barr is immediately in his ear.

'You haven't the f**king balls, lad!'

Dublin go direct in search of Murphy and as I look to get in around him, I commit the foul. Charlie Redmond easily kicks Dublin in front. Tony kicks another poor wide, before Niall Guiden stretches the difference to two.

We need to lay a marker here.

Barr makes a break from defence, and I look to clatter into him. He stands firm but is blown for over-carrying. He smirks as he back-peddles... *'Up the Dubs... UP THE F***ING DUBS!'* he barks, as he stabs the crest on his chest with a finger.

Martin takes the free but his attempt to find James is poor. Murphy climbs brilliantly to fetch but the possession comes to nothing. Matt and 'Rambo' combine well to prevent another long ball finding its obvious target.

'This is more like it, lads.'

We've been labelled a running team with an ugly style.

But Bonner goes against the grain and delivers a free from way out the field into the area. It breaks perfectly for McHugh... James that is. But his superbly flighted hook over the shoulder rebounds back off John O'Leary's crossbar.

Quick as a flash, Martin is onto it and he kicks our first point.

We've finally settled, or so I think. But to my amazement, as Noel Hegarty goes to thwart Farrell near goal, the pair go to ground. Sugrue doesn't need any time to weigh the situation up... he's pointing to the spot.

Despite being well behind the play, Tommy doesn't even see fit to consult his umpires. Redmond places the ball. But there is no doubt he looks nervous.

It's not the Hill he's looking into... there is no sea of blue.

The Canal End is Tír Chonaill territory. He goes through his routine but with no real conviction. Matt offers some words of 'advice' as he eventually strides towards the spot. I'm not one bit surprised to see it come off his right boot... and fly wide of the target.

'THEY'RE RATTLED... THEY'RE RATTLED!!'

DESPITE OUR INTENTIONS to snuff him out, Murphy again rises majestically above Matt before turning and angling over the crossbar.

James grabs our second point to leave it 0-3 to 0-2.

On 15 minutes Murphy is at it again, turning provider for Jack Sheedy. Murray is already having a stormer beside me and I can feel we've already got on top around the middle.

Bonner nails a 35metre free. Dublin are still posturing, they're playing to the crowd. Barr is mouthing.

They still don't realise the momentum is shifting.

Matt breaks successive balls away from Murphy as we collect the resulting scraps. I send a box-punched pass all the way into Tony.

He rounds Gerry Hargan, but squares it across to Manus at just the right moment. Right man... right place, but his smacked shot clips the top of the crossbar and goes over. We're level, but we should be in front.

Sheedy does make it 0-5 to 0-4, but one of the game's decisive moments arrives, probably unnoticeable to some... but it's a game-shifter.

THE 'WEE MAN' picks up on the run, and he has that look in his eye.

Six steps, with the head up... that's what he always reckoned you could get away with. He surveys what's in front of him and almost goes out of his way to find Barr.

He puts the burners on and leaves their defensive talisman a beaten man... beaten in the moment, and beaten for the rest of the contest.

'Who has the balls now, Keith?!'

ON 22 MINUTES BONNER puts us in front for the first time... 0-6 to 0-5.

Tony wins a brilliant free and Manus does the rest. He quickly returns the favour... setting up Tony... and we go three up.

Farrell gives Hegarty the slip on a rare occasion to make it 0-8 to 0-6. Barr goes into the book for a hack at me… his head is gone now, rattled completely.

Manus is at it again soon after, with a superb fetch and kick, as we once again go three up. Charlie and McHugh swap points and we go in at the break… 0-10 to 0-7 in front.

I make sure the lads all funnel in front of me and that we don't get dragged into anything silly. We don't need to stoop to that level… but they do.

McEniff comes scurrying in behind me as I finally duck inside.

'We're right where we want to be.'

Brian gets off a serious amount of instructions as we slow our walk down before we get back to the dressing-room. We both believe that one or two more points and the Dubs could fold. They were that brittle at that moment.

But we couldn't bring that sentiment into the room. We'd both been in this position before… in 1983. We also had three to spare on Galway on that occasion, and we f**ked it up. And that was the point that was emphasised as we regrouped.

But there's no panic in how that message is constructed or even delivered. Bar the pulsing din of the 70,000 people outside that just couldn't be shut out completely… it was a really calm place.

I lay my head back against the concrete wall and, for a moment, almost plugged back into the bedlam going on above. The vibrations of all that weight and noise were travelling down through the old structure.

It's a distraction, so I sit right up to find that little bit of calm once again.

FINALLY, IT'S TIME to go once more.

Mick Galvin posts first for Dublin.

It looked a bad call… wide even, but we get on with it.

Manus nails a free at the other side… we again lead by three. John Joe puts in a super block on Vinnie as he desperately looks for a goal that's not on.

We can see their heads dropping once again.

Barry Cunningham comes in for Murray, who has picked up a knock, and wins a free with his first possession. Manus kicks his fifth point… we go 0-12 to 0-8 ahead. On 45 minutes, Manus posts his third in-a-row… we open up a five-point gap. There is still close to half an hour to go, but this game feels like it's close to being won.

Guiden fires back for Dublin… but it's wiped out by a Bonner free.

Hapless and headless, Dublin are looking for goals.

But they just aren't on!

Redmond is denied by a combination of Gary, John Joe and Noel. Noel had taken Charlie's *'Fat lady sings'* taunt after the league smash and grab... and can't resist a dig.

'The fat lady is clearing her throat, Charlie!'

Good lad, I think.... *Rub it in!*

And it's us that continue to kick on, thanks to Manus... we now lead 0-15 to 0-9.

WE EASE OFF and Dublin rally... three overs are rattled off through Paul Clarke, Murphy and Eamonn Heery, after I carelessly allow myself to get turned over.

Gary comes to the rescue at his near post after Reid is dispossessed on a crowded 14metre line. Manus and Charlie trade points... it's 0-16 to 0-13... four minutes to go.

Barry Cunningham makes another huge contribution when he sails a long ball towards Manus, who rises easily above Deegan. The goal is on, but he takes another point. How the Dublin management at this stage, seven points down the line, still have Deegan on Manus is mind-boggling.

He's been roasted.

Paul Clarke kicks one last point for Dublin... a '45'. We're in added time... three points, just one dying goal... separates the teams.

But it's Bonner on his trusty left that signals it's time for the bonfires to be lit... he angles over the insurance point.

We batter around into men and look to spoil whatever seconds remain.

I'M LOOKING UP at the clock on the Canal End.

I'm looking towards the bench... *Get someone on,* I'm thinking.

For God sakes, get a few of them on.

Razda... Tommy, Mulgrew... give someone the chance to be on the field at the final whistle.

But no one comes in.

I'VE NEVER SPOKEN about this, but that was my train of thought in those last few seconds. I knew the game was won.

I hoped someone else's dream… life really, could be *made*.

Sport is a team game but it's made up of individuals… quickly enough, that concern leaves me as I'm swamped in a blanket of delirious Donegal supporters.

Croke Park ard-maor John Leonard grabs a hold of me… he attempts to usher me towards the steps of the Hogan Stand.

I tell him we're never going to make it through.

He politely tells me he makes it through every year and will likely make it through again next year… with or without me! I find sanctuary on the first few steps. I look up… and I take it all in. A county's eternal yearning for success, to be taken seriously on a football field was finally over. I make that journey on up… the one I'd pictured in my mind a thousand times. Peter Quinn, the president of the GAA and a Fermanagh man, whispers to me it's the outcome he wanted.

Finally, the cup I'd got close to so often, but had no right to touch… the cup I'd seen so many others lift… was mine… ours.

IMMEDIATELY, I REALISE the speech I'd so diligently prepared, the one my good friends Bart Whelan and Pól MacCumhaill helped me pen, is still in the back pocket of Anthony Harkin's tracksuit bottoms.

In that moment of panic, I can't see Harkin anywhere.

I could have caved to the anxiety and just waited for Anthony to appear… script in hand. No one would have probably noticed. But with the eyes of a nation on you, the seconds feel like an eternity. Instead of caving, taking the easy way out, I'm determined to kick back against all that trepidation.

I'm going to have to just speak from the heart here…

And I did.

With one deep breath I did my best to articulate just what our victory meant. What it meant to us as individuals… as a team, as a county… and as a people.

I could quote it here word for word, but at this stage, that would be the easy way out. My point is, I've taken many of those same deep breaths since.

They're the ones that have pulled me back from the brink on so many occasions. And it's only now that I realise I owe so much of my strength to that moment.

Sam Maguire didn't break me… it made me.

Anthony leads Donegal around Croke Park before the 1992 All-Ireland final against Dublin.

The Donegal team before the 1992 All-Ireland final and Anthony lifts the Sam Maguire Cup. Anthony (below) with his mother Nora and Sam!

1992 meets 2012! The McHughs, Martin and Ryan, have a very special 'father and son' moment after Donegal finally reclaimed the Sam Maguire Cup in 2012, and the two great men, Brian and Jim (right) unite after Donegal's second All-Ireland triumph.

In 2017, the men of 1992 got together and revisited Croke Park as the GAA's Jubilee team.

Printed by Amazon Italia Logistica S.r.l.
Torrazza Piemonte (TO), Italy

40397805R00139